THE LAST DUEL IN SPAIN
AND OTHER PLAYS

A series in twenty volumes of hitherto unpublished plays collected with the aid of the Rockefeller Foundation, under the auspices of the Dramatists' Guild of the Authors' League of America, edited with historical and bibliographical notes.

BARRETT H. CLARK

GENERAL EDITOR

Advisory Board

ROBERT HAMILTON BALL, QUEENS COLLEGE

HOYT H. HUDSON, PRINCETON UNIVERSITY

GLENN HUGHES, UNIVERSITY OF WASHINGTON

GARRETT H. LEVERTON, FORMERLY OF NORTHWEST-
ERN UNIVERSITY

E. C. MABIE, UNIVERSITY OF IOWA

ALLARDYCE NICOLL, YALE UNIVERSITY

ARTHUR HOBSON QUINN, UNIVERSITY OF
PENNSYLVANIA

NAPIER WILT, UNIVERSITY OF CHICAGO

A complete list of volumes, with the names of plays contained in each, will be found on pages 266-7 of this volume.

The Last Duel in Spain

& Other Plays

BY JOHN HOWARD PAYNE

EDITED BY CODMAN HISLOP
AND W. R. RICHARDSON

WILDSIDE PRESS

PREFACE

This is the second volume of two volumes of plays by John Howard Payne in the series of America's Lost Plays, the first of which is entitled *Trial without Jury and Other Plays by John Howard Payne.*

CONTENTS

THE LAST DUEL IN SPAIN

THE LAST DUEL IN SPAIN

THE manuscript of *The Last Duel in Spain,* apparently in an unknown hand, is in the Harvard collection.

The Last Duel in Spain, a romantic comedy of "heroic" love intrigue, which was never performed, has been attributed traditionally to Payne. G. Harrison (*The Life and Writings of John Howard Payne,* Philadelphia, 1885, p. 395) lists it as Payne's work, and A. H. Quinn (*A History of the American Drama from the Beginning to the Civil War,* New York, 1923, p. 439) not only ascribes it to Payne but states without qualification that the manuscript is in Payne's hand; whereas actually the writing seems more cursive and legible than Payne's. What positive evidence there is, however, indicates that it is Payne's play. In the first place, the unknown hand may be that of a professional translator, as Payne occasionally employed one. In the second place the play seems to have been designed as a kind of companion piece to *The Spanish Husband* and to have been written during the same period, 1822-1830, for like *The Spanish Husband,* it is drawn indirectly from a play of Calderon, *El Postrer Duelo de España,* but as the scattering of French phrases through the manuscript indicates, it is probably drawn directly from a French prose translation, D'Esménard's *Le Dernier Duel en Espagne,* which is included with *Le Peintre de Son Déshonneur* in the first volume of *Chefs-D'Oeuvre des Théâtres Étrangers* (1822).

For two reasons the play seems extremely old-fashioned for a nineteenth century audience. First, Payne in his close translation failed to shorten the many long, sententious passages, which, as Washington Irving pointed out to him, apropos of *The Spanish Husband,* interfered with the rapid progress of the action demanded by the contemporary theatergoer. Second, the audience could not be expected to be satisfied with a "heroic" play, highly conventionalized in its motives of love and honor and its plot of intrigue and counter-intrigue, unless the central situation possessed some permanent interest. The emphasis in *The Spanish Husband* is placed upon pathetic domestic love, but in *The Last Duel in Spain* upon the solution of a problem that had long since lost its power to attract attention: the abolishment by Charles V of the legally authorized public duel in Spain.

[CHARACTERS

DON PEDRO TORELLAS

DON JEROME DE HANSA

CHARLES V

ADMIRAL OF CASTILE

THE CONSTABLE OF CASTILE

MARQUIS OF BRANDENBOURG

DUKE OF ALBUQUERQUE

COUNT DE BENAVENTE

GINÉS, *servant of Don Pedro*

GONSALVO, *servant of Don Jerome*

BRITO, *servant of Seraphina*

FABIUS, *servant of Seraphina*

FERDINAND, *servant of Count de Benavente*

CHEVALIERS, HERALDS, SOLDIERS, MUSICIANS, SINGERS,
PEASANTS, SERVANTS

DONNA VIOLANTE DE URREA

DONNA SERAPHINA

FLORA, *Donna Violante's maid*

GILETTA, *Donna Seraphina's maid*

THE ACTION TAKES PLACE IN SARAGOSSA AND VALLADOLID]

THE FIRST DAY

Scene 1: *An apartment in the palace at Saragossa. Drums and martial music and shouts at a distance.*

SEVERAL VOICES. Long live the King! Long live Caesar!

OTHER VOICES. Long live Charles!

ALL TOGETHER. Long live Caesar! Long live the King! May the King live forever. [*Enter Don Jerome de Hansa and Don Pedro Torellas, meeting*]

JER. Signor don Pedro, welcome. How glad I am to see you!

PED. And you, my friend, my dear cousin, how happy I am to see you here!

JER. Well, and how have you been?

PED. Why very well at setting out, and in the end received in the best manner by our young king, by all his court. And you, my friend?

JER. I hardly know how to answer you. You breathe joy and happiness. Ought I to recount to you my troubles? No, let us leave that for another time. Relate to me your journey.

PED. My friend, good or ill fortune are in common between you and me; my joy is yours, your cares are mine. Would it not be better to tell me first of these? The recital of my good fortune will then be a consolation.

JER. No, my friend. Let us begin by the good first. 'Tis the best method.

PED. Much might be said upon that subject: there is always an advantage in being able to reckon upon a favorable conclusion. 'Tis like a couch of rest that awaits us who suffer.

JER. You are full of content; and it is better to succor the afflicted by administering the remedy beforehand.

PED. Well, since you insist, I yield. As soon as the invincible Charles the Fifth, the heir of Jane, the descendant of Catholic kings, and daughter of Philip the First of Austria, to whom Spain owes the glorious union of the Lion of Castile with the Eagle of the Caesars; as soon, I say, as the invincible Charles became of age and had taken possession of this kingdom, weighty motives obliged him to return into Flanders. Like a faithful and devoted lover Spain for a whole year lamented an absence which seemed to her ages. Today she hears that her lord returns shining with a new splendor and that the imperial diadem glitters on his august brow; that his illustrious grandsire, Maximilian, has bequeathed to him the sceptre of the Romans. All hearts

intoxicated with joy and hope press to meet their monarch. The cities hasten
to nominate deputies to bear to him the homage of his people; and I who had
not dared aspire to such an honor (howbeit that fortune is pleased at times
to favor the least worthy) obtained the votes of my fellow citizens. As deputy
of Saragossa, I was admitted to the honor of kissing his Majesty's hand. I
have nothing more to ask of Heaven; all my wishes are gratified. Ah, dear
Don Jerome, if like me you had enjoyed the happiness of contemplating this
illustrious monarch! How admirably were majesty and grace mingled! How
at once he inspires both respect and love! My soul is divided between the two
sentiments. I have seen the countenance, have touched the hand of this young
hero, who, scarcely in his eighteenth year, possesses all the experience of a
ripened age. This is not yet all. The nobility of the two Castiles attended his
Majesty. The first grandees looked upon it as a duty to be there in person;
and indeed, what finer ornament for a court than the presence of so many
illustrious knights? I should tell you too, my friend, that all these lords
treated me with great good will. I return thence loaded with honors. But he
who most sought to attach me to him is the Admiral of Castile. Scarcely arrived in town, he came to my house. He has permitted [me] to accompany
him to the fête at court. Three noble dukes were the only ones invited, those
of Alba, of Albuquerque, and of Bejar. But all the gentlemen of his family
or his suite have partaken that honor. I know well that this distinction was
not made to me entirely on my own account. My rank as deputy from the
capital of Aragon partly conduced to it. For the Admiral, already descended
from the blood royal of Castile, before the marriage of our King John the
Second with the daughter of Fabricio Henriquez, of whom Ferdinand the
Catholic was the worthy grandson, delights to see in that alliance a motive of
interest for the Aragonese. That, probably, was the cause of the distinction
I was honored with. But there is always a certain pleasure in the enjoyment
of a particular favor, if it be due even to the merit of a noble, and we often
find our vanity flattered by it. Impelled by gratitude, as soon as the King had
determined to make his entry into Spain by way of Aragon, leaving Navarre
on his right, I felt it my duty to offer the Admiral my house during his stay
in Saragossa, which he has condescended to accept. Judge then if I have not
reason to be satisfied. The important suit concerning the inheritance I lay
claim to, my advancement whether in peace or in war, the honors to which
I may aspire, my existence (and no one can tell what one's destiny may be);
in a word, my every interest may render the support of a patron necessary.
The Admiral will become mine, and I know not where I could have found
a better.

JER. This happiness is general. Without wishing to wound the self-love of anyone, since everyone may think at least he has the same rights as another, I dare say all the gentlemen of Saragossa are as well satisfied as yourself. I, for instance, thought it my duty to make an offer of my house for the service of the court and have received as my guest the Marquis of Brandenbourg, a German nobleman, who enjoys the good graces of the King, and who by his great valor has merited the honor of being commander in chief of the armies of the Empire.

PED. Indeed, the Marquis of Brandenbourg adds to the splendor of illustrious birth and distinguished valor, the most amiable qualities. He is universally esteemed. But let us speak of other matters. Till the King comes out to go to mass, we have all the time before us. Let me know, my friend, the cause of your grief.

JER. Don Pedro, I will not conceal from you that my misfortune is, to have seen a beauty whose portrait I will not attempt to give you, for I must make use of commonplace praises, and then should tell you without exaggeration that the tresses of her golden hair are like rays of the sun; that her fair and polished skin possesses the brightness and the whiteness of the driven snow; her eyes are shining stars, are roses on beds of jasmine; her teeth are orient pearl; her neck an ivory column rounded by the graces; and to conclude, her shape is that of a nymph.

PED. By my faith, I am transported with hearing you. The affair was rather cold at the beginning. There must be love in a story; otherwise it is a body without a soul.

JER. You mock my troubles.

PED. Why, what would you have? I trembled at first for fear of some unfortunate event.

JER. What more unfortunate event could happen, Don Pedro, than to die deceived in one's sweetest hopes? One harsh breath has chased away the ideas in which I had cradled my infant happiness; and the illusion has vanished as the light, shining clouds are driven away and scattered by the stormy winds.

PED. Now that was really very well, my friend: now this an aërial kind of sorrow, and very elegantly expressed. Never has a lover more grace than when he deplores the pangs he suffers. Some kind of folks require a gratified love; a man of wit only requires a motive in his sorrows to complain with a grace. Come, my friend, suffer, love, hope, and believe that love will recompense you for all pain it causes. To know how to suffer is to have every right to its favors.

JER. Your counsel would be more valuable if it did not come too late.

PED. How so?

JER. The cause of my torment—

PED. Say on.

JER. Is the rigor with which I am treated.

PED. Ha!

JER. And then, jealousy—

PED. That's another thing. Of whom are you jealous?

JER. That I know not, but jealous I am.

PED. And not know of whom?

JER. Yes.

PED. Tell me then—

JER. In the commencement of my passion for this fair <one>, I tried the fidelity of a waiting-maid, who before entering into her service, had been acquainted with my valet. This girl informed me that the heart of her mistress was no longer her own; but she could not give me to know my rival, as she has but lately entered the situation. Seeking to know the cause of that disdain of which I am the victim, she one day heard a girl who has been there a long time say to her mistress, "Madam, soon he will be restored to your love; Heaven will favor his arrival. Your request will be favorably received, and he will attain the rights of the property which belongs to him. Then there will be but one wish in the whole family, and your marriage will no longer be deferred." Thus without knowing the name of my rival, there no longer rests any doubt of my misfortune. I have watched day and night without ever losing sight of the dwelling she inhabits and have never yet been able to discover the slightest sign of whom I wish to know; whence I conclude that those words "soon will be restored to your love" means that there has been some particular trouble which has prevented them seeing each other. Your arrival—[*Enter Gonsalvo*]

GON. My lord—

JER. What do you want, blockhead?

GON. It is time to come if you wish to join the procession. The Emperor has already entered the first court of the palace.

JER. I here then suspend my tale. I had just got to the moment when I met you. 'Tis you that should be—But we'll speak of that at a better opportunity. This lady I am speaking of will come presently to present to his Majesty a petition, on the subject of some right she lays claim to as hereditary in her family. I do not wish to have a mortified appearance in her presence. I must be at the court. I cannot stay to say a moment more. Have the kindness to wait for me. I shall return in an instant. [*Exit with Gonsalvo*]

Ped. Ah! It is not thus I act with love. No one knows a syllable, and I am myself my only confidant. O my dear Violante! For all the riches of the world, I would not trust my secret to my best friend, my dearest kinsman. I come back to Saragossa on the wings of the wind, and the delay of minutes seems ages; yet still have I not dared to approach the dwelling she inhabits. I wait till night, the silent patroness of my love, lends me her friendly shade.
[*Enter Ginés*]

Gin. Thanks to Heaven! I find you once more alone and disengaged.

Ped. What do you want?

Gin. I want you to pay my wages and let me go.

Ped. Indeed! What's the matter now, that you wish to quit me so?

Gin. What's the matter? An injustice which you have done me! I only waited till you got home, to go about my business.

Ped. I have done you injustice!

Gin. Yes, and so shocking that it has no example since valets have existed in the form of pages in the service of masters who are not old.

Ped. What is this injustice? I don't comprehend—

Gin. A contraband love affair which has been smuggled in without paying toll or fee to me, your faithful esquire! What a whole year you keep all to yourself; speak it between your teeth and never open your lips to me! Soon as night appears, off go you, and never come back till dawn. If you return pleased, no one knows it but yourself; if sad, why then I pay for your ill-humor. Beat me, with all my heart, but at least say, "Such a one is an aspic, a fury!" Then it's all well and good. But to be beaten and not know the lady who occupies your thoughts! My honor won't consent to it. I can't bear it any longer. If I can meet with a master more communicative, be his temper what it may—

Ped. Why you have drowned your senses in wine.

Gin. No, signor, wine is not got here for nothing. I deny your major; either the lady's name or my wages, and I go. [*Music heard behind*]

Ped. Retire. We shall see about it. This is no time for foolery. The King is coming out.

Gin. See, there is a lady of quality in the way who is advancing toward his Majesty. She is well attended. Among her knights I see one—

Ped. Whom?

Gin. Don Jerome de Hansa, your friend and kinsman.

Ped. Heavens! What do I behold? Violante is doubtless the lady of whom he spoke to me. O grief!

Gin. Here is the King! [*Exeunt*]

SCENE 2: *Court of the Palace.*

VOICES. Make room, gentlemen. [*Enter Charles. At his side, the Admiral of Castile and the Marquis of Brandenbourg; behind him, the Constable of Castile; on the other side, Donna Violante de Urrea in mourning; Don Jerome de Hansa; numerous suite*]

VIO. [*Kneeling at the King's feet*] Sire, I am—

CHAR. Rise, madam.

VIO. [*She sees Don Pedro. Aside*] Another source of trouble! I can scarcely breathe. [*To Charles*] Sire, I am Donna Violante de Urrea, daughter of Don Diego de Urrea, whose services in your army and in your councils obtained for him the confirmation of a recompense merited by his ancestors, the office of hereditary governor of Alarcon. My father is dead and has left but a daughter. I have no other position than the right of naming, with your royal approbation, and that of my elder relatives, a gentleman to fill this post. I supplicate your Majesty for the enjoyment of my claim. The new governor will become my husband; and this is the only dower I can bring him.

CHAR. [*Takes the petition*] I shall not forget it. Constable.

CON. Sire—

CHAR. [*Giving him the petition*] Put me in mind of this presently. Keep that petition apart. [*The knights file off before the emperor who addresses them*] Chevaliers, it is my will that henceforward recompense should accompany merit and not that merit should sue for recompense. [*Exit with suite. Martial music*]

VIO. May Heaven eternally preserve your days!

1ST CHEV. [*As he passes her*] How beautiful!

2ND CHEV. And how she has recovered from her first alarm! Her sense equals her beauty.

MAR. OF BR. The Spanish ladies surpass those of all other countries. What a shape! What grace!

AD. If you say so, Marquis de Brandenbourg, what compliment will you have left for the rest?

MAR. OF BR. The same thing. There is no vanity in doing myself justice. [*Exeunt*]

VIO. Stop, Don Jerome. You should not follow me.

JER. Madam, I know what I should do. I place myself amongst your servants.

VIO. Stop, I say, or I must.

JER. Madam, my accompanying you is not an act of familiarity on my part. 'Tis only discharging a duty.

Vio. I have done, sir. Let us respect the place where we are. [*Aside*] Ah! Don Pedro, if this night should be favorable! Bring it quickly, god of love! [*Exeunt*]

Gin. Now we are alone. Let us return to our accounts. I have served you since—

Ped. Wretch! Don't speak to me of that, when I am bursting with anger and vexation.

Gin. And what is it all about? Just now, you were as calm and affable with me! Signor, who has turned your wits?

Ped. What, you will talk when you see what I suffer! [*Beats him*]

Gin. And I, too, for company.

Ped. Peace, nor anger me farther.

Gin. Calm yourself, signor; since I am not worthy to learn by words what's the matter with you, don't tell it to me with your hands, I beg of you. I don't understand the language; and return to my account. I want to go, or to know who is the fair lady to whom I am indebted for all the contradictions of which I am the victim.

Ped. You shall neither know, nor go. Take care of yourself. [*Enter Don Jerome*]

Jer. Don Pedro?

Ped. [*To Ginés*] Retire.

Gin. There it is again!

Jer. Now, you know who it is that I adore. I told you she was going to present herself before the Emperor.

Ped. Yes.

Jer. What think you of her? Is she not enough to justify my passion? Has she not in her favor, sense, birth, and beauty?

Ped. Oh, certainly. [*Aside*] Let me think first what I shall say.

Jer. Now, my friend, learn what you can do for me. She can have no suspicion of you, since you have never testified any desire of attaching yourself to her. With an appearance of being engaged in some other affair, you must fix yourself in this street. Between us two, it is impossible but in the end we shall make some discovery by those who pass through it with apparent design or cast the slightest glance of meaning toward the Venetians of that balcony.

Ped. I shall be here every hour, I promise you.

Jer. I have yet another design in my head, should this not succeed.

Ped. What is it you intend?

Jer. To keep no longer any measures with her, but to push gallantry to scandal. My rival in his turn must suffer what I have borne myself. This evening I fill the street with musicians; if it is honorable in a gentleman to be silent when he is blest, a coward only can contain himself when his jealousy is provoked. He will be compelled to make himself known. Adieu! The gauntlet's thrown. I am going to follow her carriage. [*Exit*]

GIN. Signor, may I approach?

PED. No! Now—nor never! But is it this poor fellow's fault? Ginés, my good lad, my friend, my faithful companion, do what thou wilt henceforth; but leave me at present to myself.

GIN. What the deuce has calmed this storm?

PED. I know not. Leave me.

GIN. Diocletian never invented a torment equal to that of serving a master who never tells you his affairs; if it were only that one might at least chat over them with a friend. [*Exit*]

PED. Just Heaven! Where am I? My love is such a secret that Violante and one servant only know it. To see each other we have a mysterious passage which leads from her house to mine on the opposite side of the street; and this concealment should last till our several affairs, her claim on the Emperor, or the end of my law suit, give us the means of a favorable union. To confess my love to Don Jerome is to break my oath. I forfeit my word to speak of it to anyone whomever; and not to avow it is coward-like to bear the shame of knowing that another woos her. On the other hand, to be myself the cause of jealousy to Don Jerome, whilst he gives me all his confidence, is to act with duplicity; 'tis treachery quietly to let the time run on, and wait till it become more favorable, is yet a baseness, for at last our marriage comes, and all must be revealed. And then, what infamy! It will be said that I consented to another's love at the very time I thought of making her my wife. Besides that, Don Jerome has said that none but a coward could contain himself when his jealousy was openly provoked. To show myself in this case is to hazard the honor of my mistress, and to commit myself with a friend who will not demand a satisfaction. And not to do so is much the same: She will be openly addressed, and he her declared lover. I shall have the right then to complain of both and yet should lose them both. How to find a mode of justifying a quarrel with Violante? That would leave me at liberty to act as I would with Don Jerome. Let me see how I can contrive it. I'll go and see her this evening. I will dissemble my joy; and the serenade shall serve me for a pretext. I will complain of it, accuse her of inconstancy, and my jealousy shall serve as an excuse to her. She will have to reproach herself as being the cause of it; and after all, should this not succeed, should I lose Violante, I can think of no other means. My brain's distracted. This dragging in different ways, these doubts, these transports of jealousy, this torture of the mind and heart force me to break silence. Let me at least preserve honor. Though the amorous proverb says, "My mistress above all," the proverb lies. Honor has precedence. 'Tis honor above <all!> [*Exit*]

SCENE 3: *Castle of Donna Seraphina. At the back of the stage a confused noise of peasants singing. Giletta and Brito, with a crowd of peasants who sing and dance before Seraphina.*

SER. You have done your best, my friends; nothing can remove my melancholy.

BRIT. Bless me, mistress, I can't think what cause of sadness a handsome, rich, young lady can have. If I were you, I should like 'em always to be singing and dancing before me.

SER. Brito, the cause of my grief is so public, that it would be useless to endeavor to conceal it. I take a pleasure rather in telling it, that everyone may see the injustice of it. That is my sole consolation.

GIL. Madam, if that can console you, ease your heart with us.

SER. Don Pedro Torellas is my cousin; we have both of us a claim to an estate of importance, to which we each think ourselves equally entitled. Our mutual relations wished to make up the dispute between us by joining our right in a union of our hands in marriage. Don Pedro at first appeared pleased with the intended union; and I was not insensible to his attentions. All at once he changed his conduct in the most offensive manner when the affair was finally proposed to him. He had ceased to desire, when I had gladly yielded my consent. This insult has inspired me with an aversion for him. It was enough that I was a woman, had I not been his cousin even, not to have shown me such contempt. My love is changed into hatred, into fury; if I could, I would tear out his life. This is why I have sought a retreat in this castle, why I keep out of his presence, till I find some favorable moment to avenge myself on his honor or his life.

BRIT. Our mistress is right. And I too, one day that I went to town, I saw Don Pedro; and says I to him, "You're a wicked, ungrateful, disloyal knight, and if I had you where nobody was by, I'd take the life of you."

SER. And what said he?

BRIT. He never said a word. To be sure, I spoke to him in such a way that he couldn't hear me.

SER. What stupidity!

GIL. Madam, he only does it to amuse you, to divert you, like the ball which we have prepared to celebrate your arrival.

SER. There is no longer any pleasure for me.

BRIT. We shall sing and dance anyhow, and try to make you share in our joy. [*They sing, dance and go out. Exit Seraphina*]

BRIT. [*Detaining Giletta*] Giletta?

GIL. What do you want?

BRIT. Why, to say the truth, I want you to love me.

GIL. How sensibly he expresses himself. Why, that's quite a new way of declaring love.

BRIT. To love honestly and openly is the true way of loving.

GIL. What folly! Don't you see that everyone has their eyes on us?

BRIT. Do you appoint a properer place then.

GIL. [*Aside*] He shall pay for his familiarity. [*Aloud*] I am going to-morrow morning to the forest; try and hide yourself in the copse in such a way that no one can see you, except myself when I come; and there I can listen to you without intermeddlers.

BRIT. Oh! I'll hide in such a way that the devil himself that always finds his own, would seek me in vain.

GIL. I'll come; but take care.

BRIT. Lord, you have made me so happy.

GIL. Let no one see you. [*Aside*] I swear I'll keep him there all day!

BRIT. I tell you I'll hide well enough. I'll not stir till I see you. [*They go out dancing*]

SCENE 4: *The house of Donna Violante. Enter Donna Violante and Flora.*

VIO. Is everyone gone to bed, Flora?

FLOR. Yes, madam. I have fastened the door of this chamber where we are alone.

VIO. Come, clear away the large picture which conceals the secret entrance. Keep yourself near the door. See if anyone comes to listen to us, for we have curious girls in the house. There is one I have only lately taken into my service, and whom I do not yet know. [*Aside*] Either my heart deceives me, or Don Pedro is already waiting. [*She draws away the picture, and Don Pedro is discovered. Flora goes off*]

PED. Yes, 'tis I; he who waits for happiness is ever impatient.

VIO. At last, my only good, my love, my lord, I have the bliss again to see you.

PED. If you complain of absence, what should I do? [*Aside*] Alas! How dissemble my feelings? [*Aloud*] 'Tis I, who should accuse the slowness of the hours; I, to whom thy presence is life, thy absence, death.

Vio. Let us leave this discussion, of which suffers most from this absence. It does not please me.

Ped. Wherefore?

Vio. If you are in the right, 'tis a proof your love is the more tender of the two; if I, then I love you more than you love me. Poor alternative, in which each must necessarily find something to regret. So, my dear friend, let us be content one with the other, and let it suffice to know that not a single minute flies, without thy image engraved upon the memory, and on the heart of thy faithful and affectionate Violante.

Ped. Here is another question to resolve. Have I not done better on my side, in not seeking to remember, fair Violante?

Vio. How! Pedro?

Ped. Yes; need we endeavor to remember what we never have forgotten?

Vio. Truce with these subtleties and flatteries, my love; let us speak seriously, with perfect frankness, of what really concerns us. How are you?

Ped. As all who come near you, happy. [*Aside*] I should indeed be happy, if other troubles did not oppress me. [*Aloud*] And you, Violante, how are you?

Vio. Doubly happy: first, in having the pleasure of seeing you; and again, because I trust the audience I had of the King, where you saw me, will eventually prove favorable to my wishes. The goodness of his Majesty gives me hopes of obtaining what I solicit, and of offering it to thee. Were you glad when you saw me?

Ped. I think I never suffered more.

Vio. How?

Ped. You know the property I possess is little. I would that I possessed the riches of the world, that you might have nothing to solicit anyone. This thought afflicts, distresses me increasingly. When I saw thee at the King's feet, I felt my heart oppressed. I suffered a thousand torments. I would have given all the world, all, save my honor, not to have seen thee in that situation.

Vio. Ah! If I had thought that could displease you, had the world's empire been in question—

Ped. Do not suppose chimeras. Violante, I mean to say that I was grieved at not possessing fortune; for when I cast over in my mind, when I calculate that—[*Musicians play in the street*]

Mus. [*Singing*] "Cupid was one day in the Cyprian bowers, at the moment when Aurora—"

Ped. That was not what I wished to say.

Vio. What ails you, Don Pedro? Why that angry look?

Ped. Nothing at all. But this is another thing: I was shedding tears, and here people come to sing. 'Tis everywhere the same—some sing, while others weep.

Mus. [*Singing*] "Cupid was one day in the Cyprian bowers, at the moment when Aurora shed pearls on the flowers of the garden—"

Vio. Don Pedro, your angry air—

Ped. Why, truly 'tis very agreeable for me to listen to serenades under your window!

Vio. I am not the only one who lives in the street. There are other ladies—

Ped. There are none like thee.

Mus. [*Singing*] "He wished to choose one for Psyche—"

Vio. Don't pay attention to the music. What does it concern you whether they sing or no?

Ped. The ear willingly listens to sounds which flatter it.

Mus. [*Singing*] "Love wished to choose one for Psyche, the most fragrant, the most beautiful."

Vio. Tell me—

Ped. I'll answer directly. Wait till love has made his choice. [*Aside*] Let me have some pretext for breaking out.

Mus. [*Singing*] "The orange flower, the rose, the pink, the jessamine tempt him each in turn. He fixed his choice upon—"

Vio. Is it possible that music can fix your attention more than my company?

Ped. On the contrary; not to hear it, I would my heart were deaf.

Mus. [*Singing*] "The orange flower, the rose, the pink, the jessamine tempt him each in turn. He fixed his choice upon the *violet,* whose modest air bewitched him. Violet, violet, henceforward take precedence of all other flowers. Love has chosen thee as the most beautiful."

Ped. Violet, violet, love has chosen thee as the most beautiful! [*Aside*] I wished to feign a grief. That which I feel is but too real. [*Aloud*] Why do I wait longer? I go to—[*Is going out*]

Vio. [*Detaining him*] Don Pedro, why this passion?

Ped. Oh, feign not to understand the allusion. You know well it is to you those words are addressed. Yes—*Violet, love has chosen thee as the most beautiful.*

Vio. My dear Don Pedro, may Heaven—

Ped. Seek not to justify yourself. I know that absence is worse than death; some honor at least is paid to the defunct—the absent are forgotten. [*Is going out*]

Vio. [*Detaining him*] Whither do you go?

PED. To see and thank this singer for his officious gallantry.

VIO. Should it even be meant to me, is it in my power to hinder or restrain a mad or silly passion?

PED. No, but if that is your excuse, is it my business to suffer it?

VIO. Listen. [*She forces him to stay*]

PED. Let me go. I am determined to see and know this gallant.

VIO. It is Don Jerome de Hansa, if that be all you wish to know.

PED. You knew it then! Perfidious! And how feigned surprise!

VIO. Every woman who boasts to him she loves of inspiring love in others, merits to be punished for his vanity; in place of flattering the self-love of her lover, she does but provoke contempt.

PED. Oh, that was not the motive.

VIO. What, then?

PED. Oh, 'tis all in accord with the music.

VIO. I have neither authorized his passion nor his serenade.

PED. 'Tis false. Such liberties are never taken, but where they are sure of being favorably listened to. [*Singers continue and repeat the burthen frequently. Don Pedro and Violante speak in dumb show*]

VIO. Don Pedro, my love, you shall not go.

PED. Cease to oppose me. If you shut the secret passage, you will force me to open the door, and it will be more scandalous to have me seen leaving your house at his hour.

VIO. And is it thus you would commit me? Thus you hold your word to keep the secret?

PED. Are you astonished at it? When you betray your faith, ought I to fear to break my word? When love was repaid by love, I promised to be silent; but tormented with just suspicions, 'tis another thing. Let me go—

VIO. Remember—

PED. Remember you—

VIO. That I—

PED. That I—[*Speaking very loud*]

SERV. [*Outside*] Madam, madam, open quick! There are thieves in the house. [*Flora enters*]

FLOR. Heavens! Madam, what a noise you make! The servants are running from all quarters. They think there are thieves in the house. [*They knock at the doors outside. Music continues*]

1ST SERV. Open the door, Flora!

2ND SERV. She can't, perhaps. Break it open.

VIO. I am betwixt two terrible dangers. This, however, is the most pressing. Flora, run, say that I awoke in affright, that I have had a dream which troubled me, and I'll come after you to confirm your explanation. And do you go. I fear lest they should insist on entering to my succor. But remember well that if ever my name escape your lips, no matter to whom it may be, you will never see [me] more while you live.

PED. Your pardon, madam. Devoured by suspicions and jealousy, I cannot condemn myself to silence. 'Tis you who have given birth to those suspicions; it is your fault. [*Aside*] Now I may speak.

VIO. My fault! Mine!

PED. Yes. Is it not you who have given me to hear those charming words, that delightful music?

VIO. No! It is not I. 'Tis the mad passion of another. [*The singers repeat "Violet, violet," etc.*]

THE SECOND DAY

SCENE 1: *In front of Don Pedro's house. Street. Enter Don Pedro. Ginés watching him, behind.*

PED. She has justified my quarrel and has nothing apparently to reproach me with, should I even reveal our secret; 'tis she who appears culpable. I have little to fear from her anger; the anger of a jealous man does him little harm in the eyes of his mistress. Now, let me see. I must find a fair mode, in which, fulfilling at once the duty of a gentleman, a friend, and a lover, I may tell Don Jerome the plain truth: That 'tis I who am the cause of his alarm, and that 'tis he who has given me offense, both unintentionally. Now to do that. But who is behind me? [*Sees Ginés*]

GIN. 'Tis I, who am following you.

PED. You!

GIN. Yes, master, as up to this moment you have not been pleased to make known to me your mistress, nor to settle my account, and that still you keep me in your service, why here I am.

PED. And since when is it you have been so officious, so exact?

GIN. My lord and master, God touches hearts. I ought not to be always accused. As I have many faults to reproach myself with, and as I am about to quit your service, I wish to make reparation and to make up for the omissions I have made in the exercise of my duty. I will neither quit you, nor lose sight of you till you have paid my wages or confided to me the object of your desires.

PED. Do you think, scoundrel, that I don't understand you? You are here on tiptoe to discover if, in my grief, some indiscreet word escape me, and pick it up.

GIN. Why, the devil must have told you so. And since it is a true hell's torment to be always spying and listening without catching the least thing to say, I beseech you, master, take pity on your servant, relieve him from the state of uncertainty, if it were only to spare him the regret of having formed a rash judgment; for if I were to imagine your lady [as to whom I have only conjecture to form] is round as a ball, or as meagre as a skeleton, or as black as charcoal, or as red as the fire, or old, and that's saying everything, for the greatest fault in a woman is to be a living ruin, bearing witness to the power of time—

PED. Truce with buffoonery. Go see if Don Jerome has left his house.

GIN. 'Tis but a little while since I saw him enter the palace.

PED. Go seek him. Tell him I wait for him in the Cathedral Square and that I beg he will come here and speak to me.

GIN. That's an evasion to send me from you.

PED. Yes, perhaps it is.

GIN. In what comedy did one ever see a valet treated thus? [Exit]

PED. Why should I torment myself? Each way has it disagreeable; but I know Don Jerome. He is haughty, passionate; I shall never make him hear reason. However, the lot is cast; the business is commenced. Let me do my duty, and let fate look after the consequences. [Enter Don Jerome, Gonsalvo, and Ginés]

JER. If I had known where you were, Don Pedro, I would have saved you the trouble.

PED. I wish to speak with you. [To Ginés and Gonsalvo] Retire.

GON. Ginés, what's the meaning of all this? What's the matter between our two masters?

GIN. They are our masters.

GON. Come, you shall know what I know of mine.

GIN. I'll do more: I'll let you know what I don't know of mine.

JER. How I am obliged by your kindness! How fortunate I was in opening my heart to you! Do you know this gallant?

PED. As I do myself.

JER. You will tell me his name then.

PED. There are first two things to observe. [Aside] If my moderation could but have any effect! [Aloud] First, if he had ever foreseen that he should be your rival, he would never have so engaged himself as not now to be able to draw back. Secondly, if you knew his name even, it would grieve you.

JER. Why?

PED. Because he is your friend; and since he is admitted and preferred by this lady, and you are not, you ought not to cause him a pain he never had an intention of giving you; for he was favored before you were known.

JER. As to his disposition to renounce his designs to please me, had he previously known mine, I admire his delicacy; but as to my giving up in his favor (be he who he may), as to my renouncing, I say, a pursuit in which I am so heart and soul engaged, it would be a folly to think of it. If he could not foresee the pain he might cause me, I in turn, cannot spare him that which my determination may give him now. So, my dear Don Pedro, as you have been kind enough to find him out, tell me at once his name.

PED. It is one who so far humbles himself, as to beg you would not trouble the smooth heaven of his love; and I, throwing myself at your feet, I ask that favor as your near relative, as your dearest friend. Do it for my sake. Be generous enough to desist from your pursuit. You will oblige a common friend; I shall regard the kindness as a favor done unto myself.

JER. Do me the pleasure to let me know, whether he has you engaged to look after his interests, or you are occupied with mine.

PED. I am occupied with yours, since I seek to spare you the regret of having done an unjust action. See you not that the intention of a mediator may be to serve both parties and avoid an unhappy quarrel?

JER. If such be your intention, Don Pedro, it is he who owes you kindness for your good will. It is he who fears the quarrel. As for me, I fear it not, and I owe you on that account no obligation. [Going]

PED. Listen.

JER. What would you?

PED. To tell—[Aside] should I fear his passion? [Aloud]—what I have said on his part, although I have employed the tone of entreaty and submission, should not allow you to think he is deficient in valor.

JER. What then?

PED. It is that he has consulted prudence alone, the common resource of him who has nothing else at heart.

JER. By my faith, when a man is not in such a case ready, sword in hand, and seeks a mediator, the thing is clear.

PED. Would you wish to find that this is not the case, and that he hesitates only because he is your friend?

JER. Yes.

PED. Well! Know then—

JER. Say on.

PED. This rival is—

JER. Who?

PED. I.

JER. You!

PED. Yes, I! I love Violante. It is I who, I will not say favored by her (a gentleman may have such honor, yet should not boast of it). It is I, who, if not favored by her, have not to complain of her neglect. And if it be necessary to call any other witness to witness of what I say, it is of me that woman spoke at Violante's house, when she said to her mistress that "soon I should be restored to her affection." Now, have you heard me?

JER. Before any reflection—why, when I confided to you my passion, did you not tell me what you now have said? I ask you that.

PED. I thought thereby to have in my power to oblige you.

JER. How, to oblige me?

PED. I hoped to obtain sufficient empire over myself to give place to you. I found the effort was beyond my strength; for after, 'tis difficult to conquer one's self, and I dare not promise, lest I should not have courage to execute. I have answered to the reproach for not having spoken openly in the beginning; but I remember our conversation was interrupted, by I know not what accident, and that I had not time to explain myself to you when I wished it. Now, 'tis for you to judge if, being your rival, this disposition on my part to seek a roundabout way, a mode of conciliation, has been, could have been, as you have termed it, a shameful submission, a base humiliation in favor of a rival, a resource which none employ but those who have heart for no other; finally, if this has been a want of courage concealed under the veil of prudence—

JER. I am sorry for having said it, but I never retract; therefore, Don Pedro, what is said, is said.

PED. And what have you said?

JER. If we were in a less public place, I would tell you.

PED. Well! Say what place you would choose to tell it to me in.

JER. On this side we go straight to the Ebro—

PED. Go on, I follow you.

JER. We can go together.

PED. Come on then. [*Enter the Admiral of Castile*]

AD. Don Pedro!

PED. My lord!

AD. I have a thousand reproaches to make you.

PED. To me, my lord! How have I had the misfortune to deserve them?

AD. You are not a good host. I never see you—since yesterday—

PED. Your reproach is a new favor. I receive it with gratitude. The motive I have had—

AD. That's enough since I have found you. Come with me. Take leave of that gentleman.

PED. [*To Don Jerome, aside*] You perceive—should I decline, it might raise suspicion.

JER. Very well. There is nothing lost. I shall wait for you.

PED. Where?

JER. Near Belflor, a quarter of a league hence, there is a retired spot where I shall expect you and where no one will trouble us.

PED. As soon as I am at liberty, I will be with you. [*Gonsalvo and Ginés enter*]

JER. Gonsalvo?

GON. Here, sir.

JER. Bring my horse to the other side of the bridge. [*Aside*] Don Pedro, to use such duplicity with me! At first reserved, then haughty, because he was embarrassed in his studied explanations. As God lives! I'll teach him what it is to betray my confidence. [*Exit*]

PED. My lord, I am at your command.

GIN. And so am I.

AD. What, Ginés? You too? I have not seen you these several days.

GIN. I have a great many affairs, my lord.

AD. What affairs?

GIN. A certain account to settle, a certain lady—

PED. My lord, he'll tell you a thousand follies. [*To Ginés*] Peace, fool.

AD. No, no, Don Pedro; you know he amuses me. What is this account?

GIN. I dare not tell you too much. I tremble lest my master should have the *active* on his side, and my back have the passive only, and that not in its favor.

PED. My lord, do not let this impertinent blockhead deprive me of the pleasure of knowing how I can pleasure you.

AD. I wish to ramble over this city whose glorious name reminds me of Augustus Caesar. I would visit the temples, the public buildings, know its chief streets. No one can better be my guide than you, one of its most illustrious inhabitants, or procure me the pleasure of admiring those beauties of which I have heard so much mention.

PED. Doubtless, my lord, Saragossa is worthy of your curiosity. [*To Ginés*] Let the carriage come here.

THE LAST DUEL IN SPAIN 23

AD. We can do better: let the carriage follow. Otherwise we shall be infinitely the loser. We shall be deprived of the sight of that multitude of handsome women who are at the balconies. Let us admire at our ease these living stars, these flower gardens suspended in the air, that prodigious variety of colors as vivid as the rainbows of a light shower in the month of May.

PED. My lord, the brightness of the court is reflected from the city. All give themselves up to joy; the front of each house is decorated, and the ladies everywhere crowd the windows.

AD. Come along, let us take advantage of the opportunity.

PED. It seems to me, my lord, that your mind is already preoccupied.

AD. Preoccupied? No; but to say the truth, I feel a very natural desire to find out a female whom I only had a glimpse of for an instant, for the first time today.

PED. And where have you seen this fair one? If you will give me some token, I could perhaps conduct you thereabouts.

AD. At the audience of the Emperor, where she came to petition his Majesty, on some affair I know not what.

PED. [*Aside*] This blow too, pitiless fate! Had I not enough, when my existence hangs at this instant, as it were, but by a thread?

AD. Might you by accident be acquainted with her?

PED. I can hardly tell you, my lord, I was not paying much attention.

GIN. He was very absent. From that day it is that a certain vertigo takes date that from time to time suspends the use of his intellectual faculties. But I, who have not lost my senses, I will tell you the name of this lady. Come, my lord, along with me. She lives at the Coso. She will certainly be at the balcony like the rest. She's handsome, and won't be vexed at being looked at.

AD. Thank you, Ginés; we follow you.

PED. My lord, do you credit this fool? What does he know, the booby, of the story he has been telling you?

GIN. Oh! I know well enough; and if not, you shall see that I'll bring you straight to the house of Donna Violante de Urrea.

AD. That is in truth the name she gave herself.

GIN. I have not told stories then; it is I, I that have got my wits, and my master. . . . Come along. [*Enter the Marquis of Brandenbourg*]

MAR. OF BR. Ah, my lord Admiral, here you are!

AD. I wanted to see the city.

MAR. OF BR. You have not heard the great news?

AD. No.

MAR. OF BR. The King has just learned that the city of Vallodolid is divided into two factions which are on the point of coming to blows. His Majesty sets off instantly for that place.

AD. In that case, let us go into the palace again.

MAR. OF BR. I shall have the honor to accompany you.

AD. 'Tis I who shall have honor in that. Adieu, Don Pedro; and you, Ginés, take this ring for your good wishes. 'Tis a keepsake. [*Admiral and Marquis exeunt*]

GIN. And for life! Lord, what a big one! Master, only look at this diamond!

PED. Wretched, rascally scoundrel!!!

GIN. The fit's coming on again.

PED. And thou hadst the insolence to tell the name of a lady, to point out the street of her abode!

GIN. Well! And how does that affect you, sir? Another gives me a diamond as big as a fist, and you, it's a thump of the fist you give me. Is it your lady that I spoke of?

PED. Wretch! [*Aside*] I'm in a passion—I'm wrong. I am just going to let him know that 'tis because he has guessed—my imprudence won't escape his shrewdness. [*Aloud*] Ginés, my boy, excuse me, let me beg you to make them bring my horse here.

GIN. In Heaven's name, master, if you want to get rid of me, don't let be with this double-edged weapon. At one time you flay me without pity, at another with deceitful kindness you—

PED. Do as I bid you. 'Tis of importance to me.

GIN. Yes, and to me, to keep out of your reach. [*Exit*]

PED. My life hangs but by a thread. I live but—I am over late—Don Jerome is waiting. [*Enter Donna Violante and Flora veiled*]

FLOR. My lord, Don Pedro?

PED. To me?

FLOR. Yes.

PED. Your commands?

FLOR. A lady who wishes to speak to you knew you were here. There she is.

PED. A lady! To me! I wonder at that.

VIO. Wherefore?

PED. Because I am born rather to deserve being hated than sought after by the ladies.

VIO. It would be easy to prove to you the contrary.

PED. How?

Vio. [*Raising her veil*]   Thus. Judge, Don Pedro, if they hate you or run after you.

Ped. Violante! Thus disguised! You in this habit so little befitting your rank, so contrary to all delicacy.

Vio. What! And have not you yourself trampled on all delicacy, and affronted me in the grossest manner? I have no longer any such consideration to restrain me.

Ped. I?

Vio. Yes, you. After your menaces yesterday, I feared lest you should commit some mad folly and have come disguised thus to seek you. The step, I allow, is unpleasant, but yours, Don Pedro! Yesterday evening, the outcries, the noise and grief had distracted me; I knew not what measures to take. I come today to beg that you will listen to me. In better spirits at present, perhaps I may find means to persuade you. The ruinous condition of our fortune, Don Pedro, and the embarrassment attendant upon a birth which has need of being accompanied by other advantages, oppose our union. Of two evils let us choose the least; let us declare everything to our relatives, with frankness and in the customary forms; let us resolve to brave the reproaches of wounded vanity and set down to the account of love the privations for which we ought to be prepared. Provided that I live with you, the most humble asylum would be sufficient for my happiness, and what signify other riches? On the other hand, if our secret must be made public, in place of serving as a pretext for duels and jealous transports, is it not better that it should be known in a manner which neither compromises our honor nor endangers your life? Once my husband, troublesome gallantry has no longer the least excuse; my honor is preserved as clear, as brilliant as the star of day. Let us then take a better stand; a husband's presence has more power than a lover's sword. Thus, my dear Don Pedro, my only good, hear my humble prayer, and believe me innocent of that which has given you so much pain.

Ped. The means are good, doubtless; but why did you not think of them sooner? [*Aside*] But when do we think in time of what is fittest to be done?

Vio. What, signor, to this humble entreaty, to a proposition so just, to a love so delicate, you answer but by sighs or rather answer nothing? Sighs belong but to rejected lovers, and you have not to complain of my affection.

Ped. Violante, Heaven is my witness. [*Aside*] What shall I say to her? I am lost; the remedy comes too late. [*Aloud*] That I am affected deeply by thy love, that I admire thy judgments, that thy counsels are dear to me! To such a degree that—[*Enter Ginés*]

Gin. Signor, the horse is ready.

PED. But—adieu! I have not the power to tell thee. Adieu once more! A thousand times, adieu!

VIO. Can you be offended that I come to seek you?

PED. No. This touch of affection is graven on my heart.

VIO. Do the means I have proposed displease you?

PED. On the contrary, 'tis worthy of your understanding.

VIO. Are you satisfied with my explanations?

PED. Yes, quite satisfied.

VIO. Well! Why leave me then with no answer?

PED. It is impossible for me to tell you.

VIO. Ah! Do not let me imagine, by this mysterious reserve, by this refusal to speak, to agree to my proposal, that your love is but a feint; that you, that you seized the pretext of a reproach to make me, that you might return to the former ties which attached you to your cousin.

PED. I engage to answer all as soon as I return, if ever your eyes behold me alive.

VIO. Is it kind to quit me thus?

PED. An imperious duty renders me unkind and will not suffer me to console you. Law of honor, tyrannic power, cursed be thy author! Thou compellest me to shun the caresses of love and fly to meet the embrace of death. [*Exit*]

VIO. Flora, where am I? What has happened to me?

FLOR. See what one gains by making them advances? They're all the same, the fire of Heaven devour them.

VIO. A woman like me! What an abyss of confusion, grief, distracting uncertainty! A woman like me, I say, and I cannot cease to say it, abandoned in the midst of the street, without his deigning to reply to her! What shame! Without having the slightest regard! What torment! He had not even the courtesy to offer to accompany me! But why yield me to despair? Why afflict myself? I shall know how to—alas! Wretched girl, what dost thou know? How to forget him? Ah! Can I forget him now, I, who from the first day have never been able to banish him from my thoughts! [*Exit*]

GIN. Here at last is the fair unknown. Since the opportunity is so favorable, this time I will know who she is. I must follow her.

FLOR. Where are you going that way, my gentleman?

GIN. Madam, I am going my ways, madam.

FLOR. I would have you turn on that side, unless you wish to find somebody that will make you repent the other.

GIN. I should be very sorry anyone should give themselves the trouble to put me to pain.

FLOR. Do you wish to be unmercifully beaten?

GIN. No, thank you, my master never does anything else. Good-bye!

FLOR. Adieu. [*Exit*]

GIN. Sun, moon, planets, stars, and all the heavenly bodies to whom the unfortunate address their solitary imprecations, when shall I get out of this labyrinth? [*Exit*]

SCENE 2: *Forest. Brito concealed in the underwood, nothing seen but his head.*

BRIT. Ever since the dawn of day, till the setting of the sun, Giletta keeps me here in the open air like clothes on a hedge left out to dry. I shall be ill. I am dying with cold and hunger and thirst. Oh, but a lad that hides himself waiting for his sweetheart makes melancholy calculation! I think I hear a noise. Should it be Giletta? No, faith! Unless by a sudden transmogrification she has not taken the features of a man, 'tis a cavalier that's coming into the wood. What is he seeking? Me, perhaps! I tremble only to think of it. Let me conceal myself all I can. [*Enter Don Jerome*]

JER. Don Pedro stays long. But perhaps 'tis my impatience which makes me think so. Anger finds hours long; and here is the proof: he comes full gallop. His steed is swifter almost than my thoughts. 'Tis clear, the delay does not proceed from him; 'tis my uneasiness which would not give him time to arrive. I will make him a sign with my handkerchief. [*Don Pedro utters an exclamation behind the scene*]

JER. Oh, Heavens! His horse has fallen down; let me fly to his assistance. [*Exit and re-enter with Don Pedro, who can with difficulty support himself*]

PED. I could wish almost this act of generosity on your side were not useless and superfluous, had it even cost me dearer.

JER. What do you mean?

PED. That my fall is nothing. The merit of your action is lost, as I have no need of your assistance.

JER. Yet, if you feel the slightest pain in the world from your fall, as I have waited here in this forest, given up to my thoughts, till you had finished your business, I can as well wait till your strength be perfectly re-established.

PED. It is re-established. Though my arm has suffered, that forms no motive for my accepting the delay you offer me. Besides, he who, knowing that *I* was his competitor, could believe, after repeating, "what was said, was said," that my courtesy was only an excuse for my fears, may think now that the pain of my arm is but a pretense. While I can hold a sword, I fear no danger, and I feel no pain.

JER. I in no way doubt your valor.

BRIT. [*Showing his head from the bushes*] What good souls! To come here to cut one another's throats! Why, this here is the cousin of Madame Seraphina, my mistress.

JER. Now fair honor! [*They fight*]

PED. Unsullied reputation!

BRIT. What's this to me? Let me hold my tongue. I don't want anyone to know I'm here till Giletta comes.

PED. [*Lets fall his sword*] What agony! Heavens! How unfortunate!

JER. You have let fall your sword.

PED. My arm is swelled and I suffer dreadful pain. My sword has escaped me. There remains no longer anything but courage and—[*Carries his left hand to his dagger*]

JER. Be of good cheer! You have time to regain it. Take it again, and let us continue—

PED. To what wretch could this misfortune happen but to me?

BRIT. [*In the bushes*] What nonsense, to let a disarmed man take his sword again! Would it not be better to fall on him at once?

JER. Don Pedro, what are you thinking of? Resume your sword, if not to continue the combat, your strength failing you, let it be to return home; and when you shall be re-established, we will conclude our quarrel.

PED. I am doubly confounded by your greatness of soul and by the fatality which pursues me. Don Jerome, I am twice conquered. In this complication of extraordinary accidents I know not what part I ought to take. If I resume my sword, it can only be to replace it in the scabbard. Can I draw it against him who has just returned it to me? Doubtless, no! Well, let me acquit myself by another sacrifice.

JER. What is it you mean?

PED. I throw myself at your feet. Give me death. Let them say that I have fallen in the fight, and not that I have been disarmed.

JER. So! When 'tis you who have been overcome, you would have the shame to fall on me! How could I be vile enough to assassinate him who begs his death of me?

PED. Honor is beyond life. It is more generous to kill me than to leave me a life I must blush thus to receive. You will render me a greater service to deliver me from it. To die is but a common misfortune; to live dishonored, is a shameful punishment.

BRIT. [*In the bushes*] What silly compliments to get himself killed!

JER. When we are faithful to the sentiments of honor, we always aspire to what is most generous. I do not wish you should lose more than I give you; take your sword, Don Pedro; but as the delicacy of a man like you ought to be fully assured, I declare to you that what has passed between us shall go no farther. The secret shall never escape my lips; I here promise you: I pledge you my hand and word. There. [*Presents his hand*]

PED. I owe you life and honor. Dispose of me, your rights are absolute. I am your slave.

JER. That, Don Pedro, you were never born to be. I do not require so much gratitude.

PED. What then can I do for you?

JER. I ask you nothing. I do not sell my services. Do nothing but what you think worthy of you; but remember that in all cases I adore Violante, and that it is impossible for me to renounce her. [*Exit*]

PED. Unfortunate that I am, has anyone ever witnessed such a contradiction? He gives me life and tears it from me at the same time! After a conduct so noble as that which he has held, after the promise which he has made me, it would be ungrateful, base in me to dispute with him the object of his love. My honor descends on his discretion; but to abandon Violante (I speak not of the difficulty of putting her out of my thoughts), to abandon her, when she comes humbly faithful, suppliant to throw herself, I may say, into my arms! 'Twould be an infamy! There is but one, one only remedy: 'tis to seek a pretext to absent myself, to answer everything by absences. Violante can have but doubts; she will not have the grief to have been positively forsaken or despised. Don Jerome will be entirely delivered from my rivalry, and I shall not have to accuse myself of ingratitude towards one or the other. I think I have hit upon an excuse for the absence; but to give it all the appearance of necessity, I will go see her at her own house. I can get through the secret passage from my house to hers; 'tis but to give the appointed signal.

CONFUSED VOICES. [*At the back of the stage*] The other side! The other side! At the back of the hillock!

PED. They are beating the bushes, they are hunting in the forest. There is nothing wanting but to be recognized here. Come, my cares and pains, dispute between you the power of my soul. The pangs of absence are about to unite themselves to those of jealousy! And how to fulfill duties so opposite to one another? [*Exit*]

VOICES. To the valley! To the plain! To the forest!

BRIT. 'Tis well there is somebody coming. I won't stir from here till Giletta comes to find me.

VOICES. The boar is wounded. He makes to the foot of the ravine. [*Enter Donna Seraphina, couteau de chasse in her hand; Giletta, with a boar spear; a servant*]

SER. I wish to give him the last blow myself. I see the tracks of blood. The dogs point the way. Let us penetrate into the copse.

GIL. I am at your side. My spear may serve in case of need.

SER. See! The branches stir. I see something among the brambles.

GIL. The boar is here without doubt. He's expiring, perhaps, or else stopping to gather strength.

SER. Come, why hesitate? Let us attack! Let him die!

GIL. Stay, stay a little. 'Tis a strange animal, but not a wild boar. [*Brito comes out from the brambles*]

SER. What have you been doing there, Brito?

BRIT. I have seen such extraordinary things, as you will be astonished to hear.

GIL. He's such a coward that he hid himself, that he might not come to the chase.

BRIT. You wicked woman! I came this morning to cut wood. [*Aside*] Who could put it on their shoulders! [*Aloud*] I was obliged to hide myself. I was afraid if they happened to see me, they might kill me.

SER. Who?

BRIT. Only hear what has happened.

SER. I wish to, for I no longer hear the dogs. They have lost the scent.

BRIT. Your cousin, Don Pedro, and another came here to kill each other very politely. After having each distributed to the other several hard blows with the sword with infinite delicacy, with a courtesy that would have done honor to a Cid, at last, as I tell you, at the moment when they were most enraged, behold you—

SER. What?

BRIT. Don Pedro's sword fell out of his hand.

SER. And Don Jerome killed him?

BRIT. A little patience. "Signor, resume your sword." "No, 'tis you who ought to take it." And then there was so many compliments, each insisting on his side, till one picks up the sword and restored it to the other, who answered, "I receive from you honor and life." And then they each went away different ways, as is the case when all such affairs are finished, the conqueror making a great bragging, and the conquered doing the same.

SER. But tell me, did you hear the motive of the dispute?

BRIT. Why, something—some words here—and some words there—it was for I don't <know> what lady, Violante; for he said, as he presented him his sword, "Remember, 'tis understood that I adore Violante, and that I won't renounce her." And the other replied, "I abandon Violante, who came to supplicate me, to weep, to throw herself in my arms! 'Tis an infamy!"

SER. What have I heard? Heavens! 'Tis Violante (Oh, cruel friend!), who is the cause of Don Pedro's refusal! 'Twas to betray me with such perfidy that she received me at her house when I went to the city, and whom, on my side, I treated with so much friendship when she comes to my castle to enjoy the pleasure of the chase. Oh, furies! Under the semblance of the most sincere attachment, to assassinate one's friend! She has not even the pretext of being ignorant of what she was doing, for a thousand times have we spoken together of the union that our parents and friends had judged so suitable to Don Pedro and to me. It was not enough then, that Don Pedro should be disdainful and ungrateful towards me, but Violante must superadd on her part this treachery! If I was indignant at his conduct, when he rejected because it was his pleasure, what must I feel now that he quits me for another? Ah, what said I? Let me rather bless the chance which arms me with the means to avenge myself on both. As God lives! Perfidious cousin, false and ungrateful friend, but ye shall dearly pay me. He shall lose, on his side, honor; and she, her dearest hopes. Quick, Fabius, let them bring up the carriage. [*Goes off with servant*]

BRIT. And now, you wicked hussy, you shall see what it is to leave a man exposed to the sun and wind, covered up with leaves like a pitcher of water to cool in the air.

GIL. Better worth to compare yourself to a leathern bottle which is full of wine, and not to a pitcher only fit for water.

BRIT. I swear by—

GIL. Ah! Don't kill me. I had so many things to do.

BRIT. What were they?

GIL. Why, I had a goose to pluck.

BRIT. Go along, Giletta. I forgive you. The excuse is admirable and leaves me nothing to say. [*Exeunt*]

SCENE 3: *An apartment in the house of Donna Violante. Enter Donna Violante and Flora*]

FLOR. Madam, they say tears are soothing; but then they come from the heart. To weep so much must weaken it.

VIO. Let me weep, Flora. In affliction our weakness has no other resource; 'tis our only vengeance.

FLOR. I do not say your grief may not be just. Yes, not to deign even to answer you, to leave you in the midst of the street and turn his back on you, 'tis shameful; but still reason ought to weigh above all.

VIO. And you never say a word of the cruellest of my pangs?

FLOR. I do not know—

VIO. 'Tis on account of Seraphina—

FLOR. Madam, that is but an imaginary fear, for he has told you himself that he will return and will answer everything. One should not always think the worst; we are ignorant of his motives. Perhaps his explanation may fill you with joy. Be calm; depend upon it, he will be here tonight.

VIO. Ah, Flora! I shall not be so happy! Had he intended to explain himself, must he not have seen the state in which I was? He would not have waited till this evening to see me. The entrance of this apartment is equally open to him day and night.

FLOR. Hush! Listen!

VIO. What?

FLOR. Good news, madam, 'tis the signal. The explanation arrives just in time to dissipate your grief. 'Tis he! Now I hope your tears will cease. All your wishes will be satisfied.

VIO. Go place yourself near the door. I will take on me to remove the picture. [*She draws the picture, and Don Pedro appears*]

PED. Sweet Violante, do not complain; do not doubt my faith nor my tender attachment to you. Listen to me first.

VIO. Ungrateful, mad, imprudent man!

PED. Listen. [*Aside*] I know not what to say to her. To tell her a falsehood for the first time! [*Aloud*] A dreadful affliction rends my heart. You will not be insensible to it; you will excuse me. You know my uncle, Don Alphonso of Barcelona. A courier who has just arrived, they say, has related at the inn, that he has been assassinated in the most barbarous manner. I ran after this courier for the purpose of knowing the truth. This is the reason for which I left you, when they brought me my horse. I had the happiness to get there and to learn from him—

VOICES. Stop! Stop! [*Enter Flora*]

VIO. What noise is this?

FLOR. One, madam, we are accustomed to! 'Tis Donna Seraphina who according to custom has just stopped at the door.

PED. I must then retire. [*Going*]

VIO. Yes, from this room, but not from the house. For you shall not go till I have heard what you have to say to me.

PED. Well. But as Seraphina has no doubt of you and is pleased to trust you with her confidence, speak to her of me; you will find that as you imagine that you have two causes of complaint, you will be doubly satisfied.

VIO. Without doubt. I will speak to her; and I shall do it in such a manner that you may hear. [*Exit Don Pedro. Enter Donna Seraphina*]

Ser. [*Speaking as she enters*] Let the carriage wait. I shall be down in an instant.

Vio. How, my dear friend, so short a time to stay? You begin by giving me bad news. Disagreeable things are always the first which announce themselves at my house.

Ser. Ah, Violante, my dear friend! 'Tis a dreadful affliction which brings me here, an affliction of which I shall die. I am come to implore your aid, to trust to you my life, my honor, my soul.

Vio. You need not say so much. You know you may confide in me with safety. Calm yourself, my dear. Take breath a moment, and let me know what it is you wish me to do.

Ser. I wish only—

Vio. Speak.

Ser. That you would have the goodness to let me speak two words to my cousin, Don Pedro, here. [*Aside*] Shall I be able to conceal my agitation? [*Aloud*] It would be better that I should speak to him in your presence; for you must know that the old dotards among my relations have begun again to plague me on account of him. At first I listened to the proposition with pleasure; but as he hesitated to give his consent, I won't hear tell of it. I abhor him to that degree that, were he a sovereign prince, I would not marry with him. What said I, marry him? To speak of it, aye, to think of it, is injurious to me.

Vio. That's an affair easily managed. [*Aside*] Heaven bless you!

Ser. [*Aside*] How she's rejoiced! [*Aloud*] And as I am not so far mistress of my actions but that I must pay some respect to white hairs, faithful to my resolution, yet not wishing to offend my family, that which I cannot say to my old relations, I have formed the design of saying to himself. Since he has already acted so disdainfully, I wish to beg him to continue it; and thus I shall have nothing to reproach myself with. Your friendship then will suffer me to send for him here? I have no other house in town at my disposal for this interview.

Vio. Make no difficulty with me, my dear; you shall see him here. Why, this is a trifle.

Ser. One thing more.

Vio. Speak it.

Ser. As I have no one with me, let me beg of you, to let me have some one to go in search of him for me. I suppose, distant as he has shown himself, he will have politeness in the room of love. Let them say 'tis I who wish to speak to him.

Vio. Whom shall I send? Flora!

FLOR. Did you speak to me, madam?

VIO. Do you know him?

FLOR. So well that no one in the house could sooner or more easily discover where he is.

VIO. And where did you get these directions, pray?

FLOR. Madam, before I came to you, I lived at the house of a gentleman in the city, who saw him every day in a society close by this house.

VIO. Well, since it's so, go, tell him that Seraphina wishes to speak to him at my house, do you understand?

FLOR. Yes, very well, madam. [*Aside*] He will follow me through the gallery, and I'll conduct him round by this door, as if he had come from the street. [*To Don Pedro at the back of the stage where he is concealed*] Come, follow me. [*Exit with Don Pedro*]

VIO. [*Aside*] Very well! I shall have the pleasure of hearing her tell him to his face she abhors him. I shall be revenged, Don Pedro.

SER. [*Aside*] How happy she is now! Ah! She forgets that pleasure's day is often sorrow's eve.

VIO. So, my dear Seraphina, the vexation which the indifference of your cousin caused you is converted into determined hatred?

SER. [*Aside*] How she loves to hear me repeat it, and I'll not balk her. [*Aloud*] Yes, my dear. What woman scorned would not do as much?

VIO. He is blind to be insensible to your charms.

SER. Ah! Your heart is too good. I knew I might rely on you.

VIO. Most assuredly you may; I deserve all your confidence. [*Don Pedro and Flora enter*]

FLOR. Was I not right, madam? Here is my lord, Don Pedro.

PED. I am quite at a loss, ladies. I know not to whom I owe the happiness of being called here. Is it to charming Violante I am indebted for the permission? Or is it you, fair Seraphina, who have furnished the motive? However, since both one and the other have claims upon my soul, my life, in what can I employ them?

SER. My lord, Don Pedro, let us lay aside compliments and come to the fact which interests us both. You think probably that under favor of a friendship which I abuse, perhaps, I have taken the liberty of sending for you here, to complain of the indifference with which you have regarded your conquest and your having scorned in my person the blood, the rank, the advantage of our family. No, signor, I have not the silly pretension to constitute myself the judge of your conduct; I ask not of the stars an account of their secret influences. You shall see that I have other thoughts; far from addressing my reproaches, 'tis my thanks I give you. But since you have had the glory to refuse me, let me profess that of bearing the injury generously. You have taken the first step, you commenced the breach. Continue it, and spare me the regret of being compelled to the same in my turn. It is too painful for a woman who respects herself to cause vexation to succeed sentiments of another nature. Do not imagine this is a resolution lightly conceived. Listen to my motives: This very day I was spoken to about you. Our relatives wishful of preserving the estates of the family in the right line, ever fear lest they should pass through you or me to some minor branch, and the arms of Torellas be confounded with those of a stranger. But it is not I who have refused to confirm their hopes by our marriage. 'Tis to you then, they will naturally address themselves, to you who first testified the repugnance for this reconcilement of family claims; so I have thought that their present applications may have been induced on your part. Has it chanced to be the case that you have turned your steps back, on account of the rigor of a certain lady for whom you drew your sword today? This perhaps is a rash judgment, and in this case the misfortune is not great; but if I have guessed aright, it is fit you should know that I am not made to serve your love's last shift. Since the dangers to which she exposes you, whose name I leave to others the care of publishing, have made you come to yourself again and change your intentions respecting me, 'tis a stronger reason on my side why I should pay no respect to them; so I repeat, and will never cease to repeat, Don Pedro, I beg you will keep your character and refuse having anything to do with me. I am perfectly consoled for your contempt, and you can stand in need of no consolation, you, who commenced by being insensible for my kindness. If the question should again be brought on the carpet, and I find myself under the necessity of stating in my turn why I will not hear mention of such a thing, no matter what persuasion or violence they may employ, here is my answer: I will never give my hand to a man who in an affair of honor, could not keep his sword; I will never associate my existence with that of a man who owes his life to the mere pity of his adversary. [*Exit*]

PED.   Hear!

VIO.   Wait!

PED.   Ah! Wretch that I am!

VIO.   And that I am!

PED.   What deadly coldness!

VIO.   What shuddering has seized me!

PED.   What sudden terror! Cruel fate!

VIO.   A fatal destiny.

PED.   My heart has ceased to beat.

VIO.   The words expire on my lips.

PED. Disloyal knight! Was it thus shamelessly to falsify it, thou hast given me thy word?

VIO. There is no doubt but it is in the crucible of our rage that generosity is refined. Don Pedro, if the matter which now presses on your mind had not deprived of the faculty of thinking, you might think perhaps that I should give myself up to grief and overwhelm you with reproaches for having betrayed our secret, compromised my honor, and trampled under foot all consideration for me. But think otherwise. My affection gets the better of my anger. I think no longer of the injury done me; I complain neither of your passion nor your fatal imprudence; I admit the cause of jealousy. Would you aught more? I agree to look upon a folly as a proof of love. Let us have but one only thought; let us forget what regards me and think now only of you. Some fatal accident (I judge so from what that cruel woman has just spoken), a fatal accident, I say, has deceived your valor. Your reputation is at stake. 'Tis sufficient that your perfidious adversary, insolently boasts of having given you life and honor, and that a woman publishes it openly. In affairs so delicate a single witness suffices; and although you may except against the testimony of an avowed enemy, still, the public made acquainted with the tale, nothing can prevent scandal which gathers as it flies like the contagion of a pestilence. You know your duty, Don Pedro. Here is mine. All I can do, all that I profess belongs to you. Dispose of it. Do not render yourself unhappy on my account. I shall hide my tears in the cloister's gloom, with no other hope but that of being always faithful to you. Your honor, no matter at what price, must above all be saved. I love you, Don Pedro, I adore you, idolize you. But love, adore, and idolize your honor still more! Adieu, till I see you revenged, or adieu forever! [*Exit*]

PED. Stay! Hear me! She has shut the door after her. Alas! I had not time to tell her, her counsel should be followed to the tittle. Oh! Doubly, she shall not see me till after I am avenged, or she shall never see me more.

THE THIRD DAY

SCENE I: *Before one of the gates of the city, and entrance of the public walk of Saragossa. Enter Don Pedro and Ginés, the latter from the gate, the other from the promenade.*

GIN. It was high time I should find you.

PED. You are come in fine time, if you think I have any to hearken to your foolery.

GIN. What are you going to ill use me again at first, to be sorry for it directly afterwards? Signor, let us reason amicably. What a thing, to leave the city with that woebegone melancholy air, at the moment when all the nobility and the people, attracted by the news of the King's departure, are crowding the avenues of the palace; and you who a little while ago were the first presented to his Majesty, you are not even the last today.

PED. It is precisely because all are content, because the King treats them all with honor, that I shun speaking to anyone, whoever he may be, and that I fly to this solitude. [*Aside*] In truth, since I left Violante's house, I have not dared to look at anyone. I tremble lest they should have known my disgrace. Shame o'erwhelms me; therefore, I seek this solitude to meditate on means of re-establishing myself in the public opinion. Come, let me first see what the whole city will say of me when it shall be told that—

BRIT. [*Singing behind the scene at the back of the stage*] "Two cavaliers fought for life and death. One let his sword fall—"

PED. Wretch that I am, my misery is beyond my bearing. That which I feared to whisper to myself I hear published on every side. The report of my infamy rings through the air.

BRIT. [*Behind the scenes*] Get along, you devil's she-ass. See only how she goes on one side. [*Sings*] "Two cavaliers were fighting together, and one let go his sword."

GIN. Holla, you rapscallion! How he quavers and his chorus with him. Master, cease thinking for a moment of your lady. Hearken to the song this fellow sings as he carries things to the market. It will amuse you.

GIL. [*On the other side of the stage and behind the scenes, sings*] "Two cavaliers fought for life and death; when behold, one of them let go his sword."

GIN. Why, that peasant girl sings the same burthen. The air is lively enough. It won't be long before everyone repeats it.

GIL. [*Sings*] "One of them let go his sword."

GIN. [*To Don Pedro*] What do you say <to> it, sir? The air and the words, how do you like them?

PED. There wanted but this new torment. Behold me become the common talk of the dregs of the people. Nothing is heard but—[*Enter Giletta and Brito from opposite sides singing*]

BRIT. and GIL. "Two cavaliers fought for life and death."

PED. Silence, dolts!

BRIT. Heaven bless us!

GIL. Lord save us!

PED. Or you die by my hand.

GIN. The delirium comes in good time on him. It isn't I who shall suffer for it.

BRIT. and GIL. In what have we offended you, signor? In saying [*Sings*] "One of them let go his sword?"

PED. Your song makes me mad, and you continue it? [*Beats them with his sword*]

BRIT. and GIL. We are lost, dead!

GIN. My friends, 'tis nothing. The fit will soon be over. By and by he'll load with favors after having broken your bones.

PED. Say, you wretched, miserable animals, who taught you those couplets?

BRIT. Lord bless me. Lord save me! I'm a dead man if Giletta says 'twas I who saw him.

GIL. I know nothing of it only that they're singing it everywhere. Brito can tell you. He knows all about it.

BRIT. All I know of it is, that old and young, women and all, everyone sings, "Two cavaliers fought for life and honor, and—"

GIL. That's what I said, "One of them let go his sword."

PED. As God lives! But alas! What will be said of me? That I let the guilty live, and avenged myself on these poor peasants? My friends, go in peace, pursue your way.

GIN. I told you so. As soon as the fit's over, he's an angel.

BRIT. and GIL. Oh! We'll go fast enough.

BRIT. Since that makes you angry, swear never again to say—

GIL. I promise never to say—

BRIT. and GIL. "Two cavaliers fought for life and honor."

PED. Begone, nor urge me farther.

GIN. But, signor, how does it concern you that these rustics should go along singing? [*Giletta and Brito return and say together:*]

BRIT. I swear never ⎱
GIL. I promise never ⎰ to say, all my life, "One of them let go his sword."

PED. The die is cast. I can no longer reflect on means. There are no measures to be kept now. Find him where I may, he dies. [*Exit*]

GIN. Where is he gone with that determined air? Into the city? I'll follow him. [*Exit*]

GIL. What's all this, Brito?

BRIT. Why, it is, it is—

GIL. Speak out.

BRIT. Why, this is Don Pedro, that fought with a cavalier in the wood yesterday and let his sword fall.

GIL. Ah! If I had known that sooner!

BRIT. What would you have done?

GIL. To teach you to chatter, and to get you punished by him, I would have told him—

BRIT. Yes, and I would have told him that I was only hid in the copse on your account; and that you were the cause of the first indiscretion, so that—

GIL. Well, we are both in fault. Hold your tongue and I'll hold mine.

BRIT. There is a little something hurts me in doing so.

GIL. What?

BRIT. The itch of talking of what I ought to hold my tongue about. It would choke me.

GIL. Well, then, let us say softly—[*They sing in a low tone:*] "Two gentlemen fought for life and honor; and one of them, d'ye see, couldn't hold his sword." [*At the back of the stage behind the scene, the clash of swords*]

PED. [*Outside*] As God lives! I'll be revenged!

JER. [*Outside*] Is it thus you repay one for having given you life?

VOICES. [*Outside*] Part them! Part them!

GIL. What's the matter, Brito?

BRIT. I can't tell, but down yonder in the palace square there is a great clash of swords.

GIL. Don't let us go near. Blows and music are best at a distance. [*Exeunt. Enter Don Pedro and Don Jerome, swords in hand and endeavoring to get at each other. A group of persons try to keep them separate. The Admiral comes down on one side, the Marquis of Brandenbourg on the other*]

PED. You die by my hand! Man devoid of truth and honor!

JER. Is it thus you repay my generosity?

SPECTATORS. Stop! Separate them!

GIN. Oh, madness in the first degree! Attacks his friend, his relation.

SPECTATORS. Remember the place where you are!

MAR. OF BR. Don Jerome, what is it you do?

AD. Don Pedro, what can you be thinking about?

PED. Pardon, my lord. I revenge an insult.

AD. An insult! Then I hold you no longer. I am rather on your side. [*Marquis and Admiral carry their hands to their swords without drawing them*]

JER. Pardon me, my lord. I punish an ingrate.

MAR. OF BR. Be it what it may, I am your guest. Reckon upon me. [*The Constable enters with attendants*]

Con. How! Such audacity! Here, under the eyes of the Emperor, who stands there, whom you see before you ready to mount his carriage. I will say no more. He comes this way himself.

Ad. Quick, signor, your sword in its scabbard. Let not the Emperor see you drawn in his presence.

Mar. of Br. Do you withdraw. Not through fear of your adversary, but through respect for the King!

Jer. The King! At that name every gentleman obeys. I withdraw. [*Exit. Enter Charles V and suite*]

Char. Marquis, Admiral, what is all this noise?

Ped. Sire, I will tell your Majesty. No one here should bear the blame, but I, who alone am culpable. Oh, Charles, first of the name amongst our kings, and fifth among the rulers of the empire, 'tis an affair of honor, an affair which has in one instant o'erstepped the distance between honor and infamy, between the highest elevation and the most ignominious debasement. Yesterday I knelt at your feet, loaded with your favor and blest in your goodness; today sees me here burthened with shame and contempt, a sad example of the vicissitudes of fortune, who frequently reserves the greatest fate for him who rises the highest. The man who seeks to wash out his stain in the blood of his enemy by attacking him publicly, ought to render an account of his motives, that the whole world may acknowledge their justice. A day or two ago I fought a duel with a noble cavalier, Don Jerome de Hansa (in such a case the rank should be remembered); before I reached the spot, wishing to prove by my haste to arrive that some accident had detained me, my horse fell. My arm was hurt in the fall; but I did not complain, nor wish that the contest should be delayed on that account; and courage silenced the expression of the great pain I endured. My arm, much weakened, was visibly swelled, and, soon unable to hold my sword, it fell from my hand. Don Jerome desired me to take it up again. I am free to tell it. I do not wish to take away the merit of what he has done, although I complain of the wrong he has done me. Not wishing afterward to turn my sword against so generous an adversary, I besought him to give me death, preferring rather to fall in such an unhappy affair, than to survive my honor. Don Jerome then promised me solemnly, gave me his word that he would keep what had passed inviolably secret. He added it is true certain conditions which indeed I felt most painful; and although he did not formally exact them, I thought it my duty to begin by fulfilling them.

My misfortune thus became less insupportable by the reflection that the only witness of what had passed between us knew also the accidents of which I had been the victim; and relying on the word he had given to keep the most perfect silence, I re-entered the city. Sire, at the first step I made, I find that he has not only broken his promise, but insolently boasted everywhere of his triumph. He has covered me with reproach. He has so wantonly dishonored me, that my shame is the subject of all tongues; and what <wrings> the hot tears of fury from me is that I am the subject of the rhymes sung on each corner of the streets. Two motives equally sacred call on me to justify myself. In the first place, it should be known that a fatal accident was not a cowardice; and that the revenge I seek is just, since my adversary has broken his promise and violated the faith he gave me.

After these reasons, Sire, by virtue of the privileges of Aragon and Castile, recorded in the Green Book, which assures to every noble, proved to be such, the right of avenging his injury sword in hand, I claim that of meeting in the list in open combat him who has offended me. You see me, Sire, at your feet, humbly soliciting as a favor what your justice cannot refuse me. Give your order, Sire; appoint the place of combat, face to face, on foot or on horseback, armed at all points, or undefended, for the choice belongs to him who receives the challenge. I will maintain to the *outrance,* that he has been a disloyal knight, in assassinating with his words, the man to whom he had left life.

CHAR.   The existence of the privilege you claim is not unknown to me, but the exercise of it has been abandoned. Therefore, address yourself to the Constable, whose business it is to answer you.

PED.   Sire, I appeal to your Majesty. My sovereign should render me justice.

CHAR.   In addressing you to my Constable, I do render it to you. By the ancient rights of his office he is not only captain general of my troops, but is the hand of justice, more especially when I am with the army in person; he possesses both military and civil authority. Edicts, capitulations, laws, marches, regulations, all are made by his order. His salary is a proof; he receives as much each month as one day's pay of the whole army. Thus the Constable is the supreme judge of all *rencontres* and deeds of arms on land, as the Admiral is of all at sea. I therefore refer you to your right tribunal, in order that he may do you justice and you maintain your rights, your honors, and your privileges. Address yourself to the Constable. [*Exit Charles*]

VOICES. [*At the farther end of the stage, cry*]   The King's carriage! Room! Room!

PED.   Illustrious and generous Ferdinand de Velasco, to you the Emperor sends me—

CON.   I know it. Say no more. Admiral, Marquis—[*They talk apart*]

PED.   What is it they say among them?

Con. [*To the Marquis and Admiral*] If I am not mistaken, my lords, you appear to me to have here, each your particular friendship; for you, Admiral, induced one of these noblemen to sheath his sword, and you, Marquis, persuaded the other to retire on the approach of his Majesty.

Both. Yes, my lord, 'tis true.

Con. Then, my lords, before this combat to the *outrance* is engaged in, let me beg of you to join me in the endeavor to reconcile them.

Ad. I engage to do so in Don Pedro's name. [*To Don Pedro*] Come near. 'Tis proper that you should hear me. I engage that he shall desist, provided he obtain an honorable satisfaction.

Ped. All that, Don Fabricio Henriquez (I suppress your titles, as here 'tis the noble knight rather than the great lord we have to do with), can counsel me, no doubt I shall find just and honorable.

Mar. of Br. My lord, you know the affairs of your party; they are public. You may speak in his name. As for me, Don Jerome has told me nothing of his. I cannot speak without knowledge of his cause. [*Enter Don Jerome*]

Jer. Having learnt, my lord, what Don Pedro has said in my absence, I come not only to reply to his challenge by accepting it, but to maintain, in the imputing to me the betrayal of a promise, he does me wrong. The secret has never passed my lips.

Mar. of Br. Now I know his sentiment. I may speak in my turn. What greater satisfaction can a gentleman give than by declaring that he has not said that which he has been accused of?

Jer. A moment, my lord. Before I knew that in my absence you had spoken in my favor, I had just declared elsewhere that the secret had never escaped me; but it was for my own satisfaction that I made the acknowledgment, not for that of another. I never give it in answer to a challenge and at the moment I am to fight; so that which I have said as a fact, I have no wish to conceal. I shall retract if it is interpreted in another manner.

Mar. of Br. This satisfaction is the more positive, as it is given without the intention of giving it.

Ad. No, it is not sufficient. It must be given with the formal intention of giving it, and moreover—

Mar. of Br. What?

Ad. Proofs must be added.

Mar. of Br. Proofs! How?

Ad. In bringing here the person to whom it has been told.

Mar. of Br. It is not easy to know who has seen what passed in the midst of a lonely wood—

Ad. Nor to believe without having—

MAR. OF BR.   What other satisfaction can you have than what has just been given ere it was required?

AD.   Yes, Marquis, if that could suffice to do away the reports which are spread abroad in the capitol, doubtless Don Pedro would have nothing more to desire. But the public, ever ready to believe the worst, may imagine, unless positive proofs are given them, that there has been a mutual concession on both sides; that one has appeared to recant, and that the other is content with the appearance, and both be blamed. Therefore, Don Pedro, unless positive testimony be adduced, does not accept the satisfaction.

MAR. OF BR.   Neither do you, Don Jerome. Have you such evidence at your disposal, now produce it. It would be out of all reason to take on the word of another what is not received upon your own.

CON.   I have chosen good sponsors; neither can recede.

JER.   I persist in repelling an odious imputation and accept the combat.

MAR. OF BR.   Keep to that, Don Jerome.

PED.   And I, that it may not be deferred, will admit of no sort of composition.

AD.   And do you, Don Pedro, hold to that?

MAR. OF BR.   That is to wish absolutely that there should be no reconciliation.

AD.   'Tis you that wish there should be no understanding.

MAR. OF BR.   But that which is just.

AD.   Nor I, but what is positive.

CON.   Gentlemen, this is in one way or another to render the duel inevitable. After all, what is it you decide upon?

PED.   To admit no satisfaction.

JER.   And I to give none.

CON.   Then, there is no longer any remedy.

ALL THE FOUR.   None.

CON.   Chevaliers, the field is granted to you. 'Tis to me it belongs to guarantee its surety. I appoint the Square of the Palace at Valladolid. The King has seen the commencement of this quarrel; it will terminate in the presence of his Majesty. I have done my duty; 'tis for you, cavaliers, to fix the day.

PED.   The earliest. Let us shorten the time; the day after the Emperor's arrival at Valladolid.

CON.   And you, the arms. [To Don Jerome]

JER.   The sword: 'tis the weapon of a soldier. And that no one should be so uncourteous as to suspect a motive for my choice, let us also take the battleaxe; to manage that requires equal strength and agility.

CON.   Well, gentlemen, adieu. I shall expect you at the rendezvous.

MAR. OF BR. Don Jerome, to the field of honor. I promise you to be by your side.

AD. To the combat, Don Pedro. The field is accepted, body to body; although in public duels the sponsors must not draw their swords, and are only there to share equally the ground and sun, I do more than if I fought for you: I will be your sponsor.

MAR. OF BR. [*To Don Jerome*] And I yours.

ALL. Adieu! We shall soon see each other again. [*They go out*]

GIN. Can two such madmen be found elsewhere on the earth? It costs them more care, more ceremony, more preparation to know how to cut each other's throats than it costs many people of wit to know how to live. And me! Poor me! What will become of me? An orphan both of master and mistress! Of master, since mine is gone without a word to me and placed himself by the side of the Admiral in his carriage; of mistress, because I never have known any. [*Enter Flora and Violante, veiled*]

FLOR. You are then determined.

VIO. I can wait to hear uncertain news and vague reports at home. Under favor of this veil I can learn what passes. We may seem as if we wished to buy something in the shops, at the jeweller's for instance. There we shall know all.

FLOR. Stay, I see Ginés. He'll not fail to chatter. Gentleman!

GIN. To me?

FLOR. To you.

GIN. I am no gentleman.

FLOR. But you wear a diamond ring.

GIN. But the cut of my habit, you see, contradicts it.

FLOR. Let us not talk of that; women, you know, are curious. Can you tell me, what is this affair about some Don Pedro Torellas?

GIN. I am his valet. I can tell you even without knowing. There was a Moorish queen who was wandering among the mountains enchanted, where the Moorish king had left her. My master saw her one Saint John's Day, combing her flaxen hair, like the rays of the sun, when—

FLOR. Leave the nonsense and speak seriously. Tell us the truth.

GIN. Well, then, I believe that, in love with some fanciful being that nobody knows, and that in a transport of jealousy, like a couple of fools, they are going to Valladolid to cut each other's throats—he and Don Jerome de Hansa—you see—an affair of knight errantry. I was right to tell you of the enchanted queen. It's all of a piece.

VIO. They go to Valladolid?

GIN. Yes.

Vio. Why?

Gin. Because it's the farthest off, and because, folks say, it should be a public satisfaction memorable in ages to come. It's all about a sword and a secret that one let escape his hand and the other his mouth. Don Pedro is gone in such a hurry, so uncharitably, that he never even said to his squire, "There are the keys." Adieu—I have nothing left but to seek out a master, whose sword, as old as himself, may be rusty, yet quick.

Vio. Listen; since your master, occupied solely by the consideration of his honor, has neglected his personal affairs, I can place you with some one who will conduct you to Valladolid, where you will arrive as soon as your master. You may continue to serve him and may tell him you did not wish to leave him.

Gin. That would be too fortunate. Who is this new master?

Vio. 'Tis a mistress.

Gin. So much the better!

Vio. Go at once to the house of Donna Violante de Urrea, who is about to set off for Valladolid, where business of importance calls her, and who is in need of some servants to accompany her.

Gin. I am off there this instant. But who shall I say sent me?

Flor. Donna Briande de Ribadeo.

Gin. Good-bye, ladies. Here's luck! [*Aside*] If I get into Donna Violante's service, I shall lose nothing by the Admiral. [*Exit*]

Flor. Madam, what have you just said?

Vio. What I mean to do. Is not the Emperor's decree signed at the bottom of my petition, by which I am authorized to propose the person who is to fill the post of governor of Alarcon in the council of Aragon? Does not this council sit at Castile? This is a plausible motive to justify my journey to the court. Ladies of the highest rank go themselves to solicit on their own affairs without any remark being made. And since I am determined to set out, can I do better than address myself to Don Pedro's valet to take me to him? He will be a witness of my tears.

Flor. And what then?

Vio. I shall see with my own eyes. I would rather know all my misfortune than be condemned to the torture of suspense and uncertainty. If he live, I live with him. If he die, I wish not to survive him. Doubt is more dreadful than reality. Yes, I must go. Let us prepare everything for the journey. Ah! Don Pedro, I as well as you may complain of the secret betrayed. But if it be at the risk of thy life, which is mine, still would I rather never behold thee again, till thou had'st avenged thy honor, which is dearer to me than all. [*Exeunt*]

SCENE 2: *House of Donna Seraphina. Enter Donna Seraphina, Brito, and Giletta.*

GIL.   I'll tell the story.

BRIT.   I can tell it better than you.

SER.   Tell me the fact, and don't dispute about it.

BRIT.   I was following my neddy—no—jenny—and singing as I was going along—

GIL.   I was singing as I followed my neddy—

BRIT.   When all at once your cousin in a rage—

GIL.   When all at once, in a rage, came your cousin—

BRIT.   And coming to us, said—

GIL.   And cried, as he came up to us—

BRIT.   Oh! It was dreadful to see him—

GIL.   His looks were terrible—

BRIT.   "Where did you get that song?"

GIL.   "That song! Where did you get it?"

BRIT.   After having thumped us both, quite out of his senses—

GIL.   He thumped us both; and like a madman—

BRIT.   Back he goes into the town and falls foul of someone or another.

GIL.   He attacks somebody whose name I don't know.

BRIT.   At the clashing of swords came two gentlemen—

GIL.   At this noise two gentlemen came—

BRIT.   "Was that right?" says one. "That's wrong," says the other—

GIL.   "That's wrong," says one. "Was that right?" says the other.

BRIT.   The thing was to have been kept secret—

GIL.   The matter was to be a secret—

BRIT.   He brought forward some law—

GIL.   Which the Emperor himself acknowledged—

BRIT.   So that the whole affair is to be settled at Valladolid.

GIL.   So that at Valladolid everything is to be determined.

BRIT.   By the death of one or the other.

GIL.   Or by the death of them both.

SER.   Oh! The plague of silence confound you both!

BRIT.   Amen!

GIL.   So be it!

SER.   What patience have I had to listen to them! What one tells badly, the other disfigures, makes worse. But alas! Confused as their tale appears, I have but too well understood it. This news fills me with confusion. Don Pedro, doubtless ignorant that this rustic has seen, from the place where he was concealed, all that passed in the contest, thinks his adversary has himself published it through vanity; and to obtain reparation, has, as a knight, defied him to single combat in the lists. Oh! That I could have suppressed my anger! He was right that said, "Oh tongue! Thou art more cruel, more untameable, more dangerous than the most savage beast." For this reason did nature place it under a double lock. Vain precaution! Nothing can restrain it. A breath is sufficient to deceive its guards.

How shall I act that the truth may be known, and the duel not take place? That Don Pedro may know his rival is incapable of such baseness? What! Do I hesitate? The viper that has given the poison, should it not afford the remedy? My imprudent, angry words have done the evil, and they shall repair it. [*To Brito and Giletta*] Come, both of you, come with me.

BOTH. Madam, where are you going to take us?

SER. Where both of you will declare the truth. Heaven grant my fears be not confirmed, and we arrive too late! Ah, woman's anger, what evil hast thou not done in the world! [*Exeunt*]

SCENE 3: *Palace of the Governor of Castile at Valladolid. Enter Count de Benavente and servants.*

COUNT. They write me word that his impatience to revisit Castile has caused the Emperor to take post horses, and that he quitted his carriage as he left the capitol of Aragon. From that, I expect him here tomorrow at the latest. Let everything be ready to receive him. I go to meet his Majesty. [*Servant enters*]

SERV. My lord, I am glad to have found you.

COUNT. What is the matter, Ferdinand?

SERV. While all the people are rushing to the gate of the fields to see the King enter and congratulate him on his arrival, his Majesty with only two noblemen in his suite, has slipped in secretly by the park gate. He is now in the palace.

COUNT. I am glad I am here then. I would not that another should have the honor to kiss his hand before me. [*Charles, Marquis of Brandebourg, and Admiral enter*] Sire, how is it we so soon have the pleasure to behold you?

CHAR. Count de Benavente, I am glad to see you. Embrace me.

COUNT. Sire, this favor enchains all my faculties to your service.

CHAR. Well! How's all here?

COUNT. The factions of Salamanca have agitated the whole of Castile. I am grieved that calm was not re-established before the news of our troubles had reached your Majesty. You would not have had it on your mind during your journey; but order at present is re-established. Sire, pardon the means I have used. To keep Salamanca in order I caused myself to be made the corregidor of it, and I have caused justice to be respected. Finally, partly by rigor and partly by clemency, I have had the happiness to appease the tumult. You will find peace now throughout the province. The chiefs who were the heads of the party have taken flight, and happy for them, for had they waited my coming, they would have lost their own.

CHAR. You have no need of pardon, Count. On the contrary, I owe you thanks; and Salamanca may boast in its turn of having a Count de Benavente among its corregidors.

COUNT. We are only, Sire, feeble rays of the sun. Deign to enter, and repose yourself after your journey.

CHAR. I wish to accustom myself to the profession of a soldier. I do not fear fatigue. [*Exit*]

COUNT. What an age! And what courage! Never will his enemies dare to resist him.

AD. Count, your hand.

COUNT. Admiral, you are welcome.

AD. At your service. I have a thousand things to tell you. But bye and bye. I must not leave the Emperor alone. [*Exit. Enter Marquis of Brandenbourg*]

MAR. OF BR. My lord Count?

COUNT. Your commands? Your pardon, if not knowing you—

MAR. OF BR. This will instruct you. [*Gives letter*]

COUNT. [*Reads*] "The Marquis of Brandenbourg, my relative, accompanies Charles into Spain. You know that the Pimentels are under obligation to Germany, which has so often been the theater of their glorious exploits. As a stranger, the Marquis cannot be versed in the etiquette of Spain. I recommend him to you as to the best of all models. God preserve you. Maximilian." The Emperor prescribes me a duty; your rank alone would suffice, my lord. I am at your service. Dispose of me.

MAR. OF BR. My lord, you shall judge whether I reckon upon your kindness. I begin by claiming it.

COUNT. In what can I have the pleasure of serving you?

MAR. OF BR. I have need of you. Two Aragonese noblemen, for motives which personally concern them, are coming hither. Tomorrow they have to settle an affair of honor. The rendezvous is appointed at this city, all according to the ancient privileges which gentlemen, known to be such, have inherited from the valor of their ancestors. Being by accident lodged with one of them, I am engaged in their quarrel, and cannot do otherwise than act as sponsor for him. The Admiral is sponsor for his adversary. What can balance the influence of so great a lord? I do not wish that he whom I uphold should enter the lists with less splendor than his rival; therefore, I venture to ask of you, Count, to honor me and the cavalier whose cause I espouse, with your support.

COUNT. Marquis, I and mine are all at your disposal. Although the Admiral be the sponsor of one cavalier, since he wishes to do honor to one of the combatants, I may fully as well render the same service to the other, and especially as it will be agreeable to you.

MAR. OF BR. 'Tis a high honor done to him and me. [*Noise of drums*] What is this noise?

COUNT. It is, I imagine, the publication of the ban. Doubtless, the commencement of the ceremonies of this barbarous duel. Oh! When will Spain be delivered from it? [*Enter Admiral*]

AD. Marquis, the King expects you.

COUNT. Adieu, Marquis. [*Exit*]

MAR. OF BR. Farewell, Count. [*Exit. Enter Don Pedro*]

PED. My lord, I have come here with your suite. We set out after you had taken post horses with the King. Not to be wanting in any of the requisite formalities, I come to ask you what is there I should do? There are trumpets and drums echoing on all sides. They are publishing the first ban of the duel.

AD. This ceremony has been so long out of use, that I know not whether we may err by omission, or by unnecessary formality. What says the ban? Do you know?

PED. I was too much interested to forget the slightest detail. I know the whole. The ban orders that no one shall enter or go out of the circle drawn around the square of the palace; that no one should go to examine the ground or the barrier, doubtless in order to prevent surprise, or trick, which would render the equality of the combat void. The Constable has directed everything as supreme judge of the field. There is a throne for the King, where his Majesty will sit, with a golden wand in his hand. The Constable sits below the King. On the two opposite sides of the square they have erected two tents with entrances without and within the square, by which the combatants enter alone with their sponsors.

AD. Does the ban say anything concerning the sponsors or combatants?

PED. Nothing hitherto.

AD. Since there is nothing for us to do, let us not trouble ourselves about the duty of others. My advice is that you should go to your home and not go out at all. It is disagreeable to be pointed at, and everyone saying, "There is one of them." [*Enter Ginés*]

GIN. Thanks to Heaven, I only looked for one, and I have found two.

Ad. Ginés? Welcome.

Ped. I set out in such a hurry, or rather in such a rage, that I had completely forgotten him and everything else; but his attachment for me has made him follow me—

Gin. You are wrong there, signor; it is not on your account I am here. I hadn't even a thought of remaining in your service, if you won't settle my account, or let me know the lady in question. I have got another mistress. This mistress is nothing to you—but something to the Admiral. I'll give you a little explanation on the subject. Donna Violante, that perfect beauty, that your excellency wanted so much to see at Saragossa, is here. I am in her service. She follows the court, where she has particular business.

Ped. [*Aside*] O fatal charms! Violante here!

Ad. What said you?

Gin. That if you choose to go to the inn where she has alighted waiting till she finds a suitable lodging, you may see her, my lord; aye, and speak to her too. I'll furnish you with an opportunity by having the door open.

Ad. Let us go then!

Ped. Infamous panderer, I'll tear thy soul out. [*To Ginés apart*]

Gin. Why, what interest have you in the matter?

Ad. Don Pedro, do what my friendship counsels you. Adieu!

Ped. My lord, I—when—if—

Ad. You change color and are agitated. What ails you, Don Pedro?

Gin. These are fits which go as they come. You had better get out of the way, my lord, he is apt to be wild.

Ad. But what is the matter?

Ped. I know not how to tell you, that the cause of all my grief, all my misfortunes, all my dangers—I have not strength to say more—is—my lord, you have on one occasion already been my support, the sustainer of my honor. Here is another opportunity: You know how to keep a secret. Let that suffice.

Ad. That suffices without doubt. You could not have told me in a fuller manner that this cause is—Violante. [*Aside*] Farewell, vain hope, dead when just conceived.

Gin. Shan't we go, my lord?

Ad. On my honor, if ever you speak to me again of that lady, if you ever have the insolence to name her before me—[*Lays hold of Ginés*]

Gin. Oh! Lord! My master's disorder's catching.

Ad. I will chastize thee in the most exemplary manner. The name of women of her quality ought never to pass lips so impure as thine, but with the expression of the most profound respect. [*Pushes Ginés from him. Exit*]

GIN. Heaven save us! He's really in earnest. This is from bad to worse. My master, when he was angry, at least it was soon over, and then he tried to make up with good words; but this one gives you blows first and hard language afterwards. [*Enter Gonsalvo*]

GON. Who the devil ever saw the like?

GIN. What's the matter, Gonsalvo? What is it to us, valets, if our masters cut each other's throats. The law of duels does not concern us. Tell me honestly why you are crossing yourself so devoutly?

GON. Considering the piece of work made about, it's no such light matter to get one's self killed. Scarcely has the King arrived, than the lists, the barrier, and the preparations occupy everyone's attention. 'Faith! I believe there's nothing wanting. All is ready.

GIN. You got here sooner than me, who travelled with women. Tell us some particulars.

GON. What I know is, that the Admiral acts as the sponsor of your master; that he is accompanied besides by the Dukes of Bejar, Albuquerque, and Alba. My master has for sponsors the Marquis of Brandenbourg, and being a stranger, he does not want for lords who join his party, such as the Counts of Benavente, Maxera, and Aguilar. The other nobles of Castile range themselves around these illustrious chiefs, as inferior planets around their ruling stars. [*Drums and warlike instruments*] Why should I tell you more? These drums, this music speak more loudly than I do. But as in such an affair a valet is necessary to bear a scutcheon, farewell, Ginés. [*Exit*]

SCENE 4: *The lists. Warlike music. Charles V on his throne, a golden wand in his hand. At his feet the Constable, in an arm chair, a table before him with a missal on it, and at the ends of the table on each side, breastplate, battleaxe, and sword. Lower down than the King and the Constable, four heralds at arms, with their surcoats embroidered with the arms of Castile and Leon.*

At the two opposite extremities of the barrier are seen two tents. The sponsors and their suite enter each from the tents. Ginés bears the coat of arms and shield of Don Pedro. Gonsalvo that of Hansa, before Don Jerome. The valets without cloaks, hats ornamented with plumes, etc.

CON. Sire! Noble image of the God of War, your Majesty presides here over this tribunal of arms. Permit the lists to be opened unto the two champions. The motives of their quarrel are known to you.

CHAR. Let all the formalities be fulfilled.

Con. Make the first, the second, and the third appeal, and let them enter to the sound of warlike instruments. [*Warlike music. The cavaliers enter from opposite sides with their suite and go around the field*]

Ped. Sire, I come—

Jer. Sire, I bend before your august feet—

Ped. In the name of my good right.

Jer. In the name of my honor.

Con. Cavaliers, your knee on the ground, one hand on the pommel of your sword, and the other on the holy evangelists, swear to speak the truth in all that shall be by me required of you. [*He opens the missal. They each kneel in the attitude prescribed by the Constable*]

Both. I swear it.

Con. As you speak truth, so help you God! You, Don Pedro de Torellas, you swear that it is not the spirit of revenge which has made you demand the duel, through hate, or rancor, but only the just desire of defending your honor?

Ped. I swear it.

Con. You, Don Jerome de Hansa, you swear that you enter the lists because you have been called hither, only to maintain your honor and not by a refusal to risk the imputation of cowardice, and that moreover you do not come in hatred or the spirit of revenge.

Jer. I swear it.

Con. Listen then now, to what remains for me to say to you: You swear to fight with equal arms, without stratagem, openly and loyally, and without advantage on either side.

Both. I swear to do so.

Con. I believe it. Knights, go, arm yourselves. Behold, your armor, swords, and battleaxes, of equal weight and temper. Let one of the cavaliers who attend you take the charge of them together with an esquire.

Mar. of Br. My lord Count, that honor is yours. [*To Count de Benavente*]

Ad. My lord Duke and my cousin, it is yours. [*To Duke of Albuquerque*]

Con. Let the trumpets sound while the knights are in their tents. [*Martial music. The knights enter their tents, each with his sponsor and suite. The Count de Benavente and Duke of Albuquerque advance towards the table of the Constable to take away the arms by the respective squires of their knights*] My lord Duke of Albuquerque, what is it you demand?

Duke. The arms of Don Pedro de Torellas.

Con. Take them, and stay a moment. [*To the Count de Benavente*] My lord Count, what is it you require?

COUNT. The arms of Don Jerome de Hansa.

CON. Take them. [*The Count and Duke cause the arms to be taken*] Now exchange the arms you have taken, and bear them to your respective knights, of whom you also are the sponsors. Let them arm themselves before you, and with no other arms than these. And watch that there be no other defense under the armor which may give the slightest advantage to either.

DUKE and COUNT. Depend upon our loyalty. [*They make the exchange. The heralds at arms place themselves at the angles in front of the throne and of the Constable's table. The drums and music lower down in front*]

CON. Let the four heralds at arms proclaim silence. Let the first herald publish the ban aloud. Hearken, hearken all!

1ST HER. On the part of the King and his Constable: It is forbidden to everyone without distinction, under pain of death, to pass the boundaries of the field. It is equally forbidden, and under like penalty, while the combat lasts, to raise the voice in praise or blame of either champion, no matter what happens; not even to make a sign by hands or eyes in any manner whatever; in fine, to use any gesture, word or motion whatever meant to excite the ardor of the one combatant or weaken the confidence of the other.

FOUR HERALDS TOGETHER. Hearken! Hearken all! Thus ordains the King and the Constable. [*Drums beat the charge. Don Pedro, armed cap-a-pie, advances from his tent accompanied by his sponsors and other cavaliers. The Grand Constable advances for the purpose of recognizing him*]

CON. Who is the knight armed cap-a-pie who presents himself? Cavalier, who are you?

AD. He who demands the entrance is Don Pedro de Torellas.

CON. If he does not raise his visor, I cannot know him.

AD. [*Raising Don Pedro's visor*] Now do you know him?

CON. Yes. Let him enter; but let him not pass that line, and let no one enter with him. Stay. I am called to the other side. [*Drums beat the charge. Don Jerome enters from the other tent, armed cap-a-pie, with his sponsors and other cavaliers. The Constable advances towards him*]

CON. Sir knight, who enter here armed cap-a-pie, your name?

MAR. OF BR. It is Don Jerome de Hansa.

CON. If I see not his face, I cannot testify it.

MAR. OF BR. [*Raising the visor of Don Jerome*] Now do you recognize it?

CON. Let him enter, and let his suite proceed no farther. Knights, the field is open. Swear anew that you combat for honor only and not for private vengeance. Let them sound the Ave Maria. [*Everyone kneels. Nine strokes of the drum—three and three. Roll. Everyone rises, and the Grand Constable resumes his seat*] Knights, lower your visors; embrace your sponsors. To the combat, knights!

ALL WITHIN THE FIELD.   On, Knights, and God protect the right! [*Trumpets sound the charge. The combat commences at first with the battleaxes; then they take the sword; at last they join body to body. The King throws down his golden wand upon the field of battle. The sponsors spring forward to separate them. The two champions will not give way but seek to renew the combat. The Constable takes up the golden wand; the King rises from his throne and appears displeased with their obstinacy*]

CON.   They have grappled each other body to body. The King has cast down upon the field of combat his golden wand. The fight should cease that very instant. Sponsors, separate them.

CHAR. [*Descending from his throne*]   What is this? I have thrown down the golden rod. I have taken upon myself the cause of both; I declare them both true knights; and is their fury such they still proceed? Arrest them instantly.

AD.   Ah, Sire!

MAR. OF BR.   Ah, Sire!

CHAR.   Enough! Enough! Be thankful for such sponsors. I consent to pardon you. Let them take off their helmets. Give each other the hand in pledge of friendship. You here proved your valor both. I wish that valor should be useful to me on more glorious occasions.

PED.   Sire, since you do me the honor—

JER.   Sire, as you deign to honor me—

PED.   To reserve me for other enterprises—

JER.   With your confidence in other dangers—

PED.   I have nothing more to desire.

JER.   My wishes all are gratified.

AD.   Sire, since your Majesty deigns to employ them both in your service, let my title of sponsor be of some service to Don Pedro. I beg of you to grant him the government of Alarcon.

CHAR.   'Tis granted to a lady, the daughter of the late governor.

AD.   Your Majesty may give it to Don Pedro and yet not take it from the lady. [*To Ginés*] Run and tell Violante to come hither and throw herself at the King's feet. The favor which she asked is granted, and Don Pedro is admitted unto it. [*To Don Pedro*] I only pronounced her name to place her in your arms. [*Exit Ginés*]

PED.   'Tis worthy of yourself.

Mar. of Br. Sire, I have the same right of sponsor to stand up for. I beseech your Majesty to grant a favor also to Don Jerome.

Char. What favor?

Mar. of Br. To hear another lady who spoke to me this morning to endeavor to prevent the combat. It was too late. I was compelled to refuse. But I wish your Majesty should hear her, that there may not rest the shadow of a doubt of the fidelity of Don Jerome to his word. Gonsalvo, run and call her. [*Exit Gonsalvo. Enter Violante, Flora, and Ginés*]

Vio. Sire, a woman perhaps ought not to show herself in such a place; but pardon somewhat to the excess of my joy. I come to kiss your royal hand and see Don Pedro re-established in his honor and alive. [*Donna Seraphina, Brito, Giletta, and Gonsalvo enter*]

Ser. Sire, I too have my motives. I throw myself at your Majesty's feet to declare publicly that Don Jerome has nothing to reproach himself with. This peasant is he who saw the whole in the wood where he was concealed.

Brit. That's very fine; but Giletta was the cause—

Gil. Good-bye to my good name! In the presence of the King himself to make me pass for a——, if I don't get married.

Brit. Well, give me your hand then.

Gil. There then, take it.

Jer. [*To Seraphina*] How shall I acquit the obligation I have to you, Seraphina? You have done away the doubts that hung over my good name and given me back true honor. I shall be too happy if the offer of my heart may prove agreeable to you and obtain for me your hand.

Ser. Violante, you see there is one who loves me. I am revenged. [*Aside*] Let me make a virtue of necessity. [*Aloud*] 'Tis I who am at the summit of my wishes. [*To Don Pedro*] And do you give your hand to Violante.

Both. What happiness.

Gin. Oh! The unknown is my mistress after all. She was my master's mistress before she was mine then.

Flor. He's such a simpleton that he couldn't find it out till this moment.

Gin. My simplicity goes farther yet.

Flor. Pshaw! Impossible!

Gin. Yes; since others marry, I should like to marry too.

Flor. Simple indeed; but I have no objection.

Char. Constable?

Con. Sire!

Char. Write immediately to Pope Pius III, who at present fills the Holy Chair, that I beg him to have condemned by the Council of Trent, now assembled, this barbarous custom which idolatry has left us. I wish the abolition of these duels should commence with my reign, and that this should be the last.

ALL THE ACTORS TOGETHER. And we beseech all your majesties to pardon the faults we have committed.

END OF LAST DUEL IN SPAIN

WOMAN'S REVENGE

WOMAN'S REVENGE

T HE autograph manuscript of *Woman's Revenge,* dated 1832, is in the Harvard collection. Extant also in the British Museum (L.C. 2/25/32) is the copy, in an unknown hand, submitted to the licenser for acting; this, however is incomplete, as it contains only the dialogue, which is at times illegible. In the following text, the dialogue from the licenser's copy is reproduced as far as possible; and legible readings, when necessary, and the stage directions are taken from the Harvard manuscript.

The play, a one-act burletta, was performed on February 27, 1832, at the Olympic and revived about thirty times during the year. In *The Examiner* for March 4 it is reviewed with approval: "Vestris does not allow the interest of her *Olympic* to flag for want of novelty. *Woman's Revenge* was produced on Monday, with complete success; . . . it is well imagined, well written, and, for the most part, well played."

Neither of the extant manuscripts reveals any traces of French influence; if the play is from a French source Payne has Anglicized it completely. Although several French and English plays have somewhat similar titles, such as Sédaine's comic opera *Les Femmes Vengées, ou Les Feintes Infidélités,* acted 1775, or Cuvelier's pastoral pantomime, *La Damoisel et La Bergerette, ou La Femme Vindicative,* 1799, or Bullock's satire of rogue life *A Woman's Revenge; or, A Match in Newgate,* 1715, the similarity goes no farther.

The strength of the play lies in the vigor with which the wealthy spinster Miss Flashington is sketched, and its weakness in the sentimental treatment of a stock theme, the rescue from financial distress, which is used by many of Payne's contemporaries, among them John Buckstone in *Luke the Labourer; or, The Lost Son,* performed 1826, or Thomas Môrton in *Education,* 1813. Its morality, as *The Examiner* points out, is extremely dubious: "The author should have avoided the foolish and unprincipled commonplace, of calling creditors scoundrels, merely because they insist on being paid what is due to them. The balance of scoundrelism is usually on the other side."

DRAMATIS PERSONAE

Major Sir Thomas Dillon

Frank Merton

Fag

Farmer Gregory

John, *a valet*

Dobbins

Sophia Dillon

Miss Flashington

Mrs. Simper

[THE ACTION TAKES PLACE IN ENGLAND]

ACT I.

SCENE I: *An elegant apartment in the country mansion of Miss Flashington. R[ight] h[and], a work table. Enter Fag cautiously, on tiptoe.*

FAG. [[*Alone*]] Hist! Mr. Merton, hist! Not here? Yet he seemed all anxiety for me to come to him forthwith. Ah, nothing can be done in this village without Fag, that's clear. I do everybody's business and get nobody's respect. [*Miss Flashington heard outside*]

MISS F. [*Outside, vehemently*] Well, sister, and what if I am?

FAG. That must be young Merton's Aunt Flashington. She always, they say, comes, like a witch, in a whirlwind. Vanish, Fag! She doesn't know thee, honest utility; and it may be as well for Master Merton just now that she should not. Vanish, my boy, vanish! [*Exit Fag, l[eft] h[and].*] *Enter Miss Flashington, very rapidly, followed by Mrs. Simper, very slowly. R[ight] h[and]*]

MISS F. And what if I am, I say? Why don't you answer me? That provoking serenity of yours would be enough to worry me into a fever, if I had no other cause. Why don't you talk? Oh, how I hate your sneaking, silent ones who can't even be scolded into a speech. They drive me mad.

MRS. S. But, my dear, Frank Merton is my nephew as well as yours, and you see I don't fly into a passion about his follies.

MISS F. Passion? Ha! Ha! You in a passion! You haven't the value of a passion in you.

MRS. S. If he annoys you, cast him off. He is entirely dependent on you.

MISS F. There's a woman for an aunt! Cast him off, I cast off Frank Merton! Oh, how that's you all over, Wilhelmina Simper. You would not quarrel with the poor fellow, but you'd cast him off.

MRS. S. If you don't, dear, he'll be your ruin.

MISS F. He'll be no such thing. Good lad! With such a heart! But he shan't bring me to beggary. If the rascal thinks I'll forgive him, he'll find himself woefully mistaken. I've sacrificed enough for him already.

MRS. S. Aye, you have indeed! Even matrimony itself.

MISS F. Not I. I never yet found a man worthy to be my husband.

MRS. S. You did not think so, my dear, when Sir Thomas Dillon—

MISS F. Mrs. Simper, have I not forbidden you ever to mention that person's name in my hearing?

Mrs. S. Don't be offended, sister. Though you were disappointed there, everybody knows that to devote yourself to the bringing up of that scapegrace, Frank, you have refused as many offers—

Miss F. As *you* have accepted, sister. You've outlived three husbands and are fishing for a fourth. You've monopolized the matrimony of the family— umph, he is here. [*Enter Frank Merton*]

Mer. Ah, my dearest aunt—

Miss F. None of that. Take off that insinuating, hypocritical face of yours. It won't do, sir. How very like he is to poor sister Laura, isn't he? And how very like you are, sir, to that father of yours, who robbed you of all your fortune and left you a resourceless orphan, when you ought to have been rich enough to have supported us all in splendor.

Mer. With a friend like you, excellent aunt, I could never feel the improvidence of my father.

Miss F. Didn't I tell you I'd have no canting, young impostor! Your father was worth a hundred of you.

Mrs. S. Do you think, my dear, that your father would have squandered in three months an allowance to support a prince for a year?

Miss F. Aye, what have you done with that last three thousand pounds? I know what you'll say: you'll pretend you've spent it in—in—in the Lord knows what! But it is no such thing: you're a gambler, sir.

Mer. Upon my soul, no!

Miss F. Not a gambler! Have you the effrontery [*With a sort of chuckle of delight which she in vain strives to hide*] to say you—you—you're not a gambler?

Mrs. S. Sister, you don't give him time to say anything.

Miss F. Not give him time! After all I've done to prove my affection for you, to pretend that I make a charge against you and do not give you time to answer it. I say no more. Talk all day if you like. Henceforward, you'll find me only a listener, a patient, all-enduring listener. Go on, go on, you shall have time, aye, if you will [*Violently*], eternity! Go on—

Mer. You are aware, dear aunt, how very fond I am of hunting—

Miss F. You don't mean to pretend you've spent three thousand guineas in hunting! Do you think I've forgotten that I fitted you out with horses and hounds and a provision for keeping them like a gentleman as you are, not eighteen months ago—

Mer. Perhaps, aunt, you may remember the day when I followed the hounds some six and twenty miles from this—

Miss F. And did not return till the evening following! I do remember it, Frank. It was a year ago yesterday. And I'm sorry I do; for what I remember of my misery when I was waiting your return that long, long night, convinces me that I am more attached to you than it is in your composition, you unfeeling varlet, to deserve.

Mrs. S. But let the lad speak, dear—

Miss F. Speak! Of course I will. Who prevents his speaking? Well, you were hunting a year ago—come, out with it. But let me take my work and sit down first; for a story beginning from a year ago can be no trifle in the telling. [*Enter John*] What do you want, hey? I'm busy. Don't come to disturb me, sir, when you see I'm busy.

John. Beg pardon, ma'am, but Farmer Dobbins is below and says if you could only let him speak to you a moment—

Miss F. Nothing *but* vexation. Why can't people come at proper times?

Mrs. S. Bid Dobbins wait, John. Bid him wait.

Miss F. Bid him do no such thing, John. The time of a farmer with a family like his is precious. 'Tis only the rich that have leisure and they are robbers when they force the poor to wait.

Mrs. S. Bid him come up. Mayhap he brings his rent. I grant ye, they who come to pay money should never be kept waiting.

Miss F. Nor those who come to ask it, sister. Show him up. [*Exit John*]

Mer. Shall I run to him? [*Going*]

Miss F. Come, come, Mr. Fly, none of your tricks. You think to get off, do you? Sit you down there. Sir, your time shall come presently. [*Enter Dobbins*] Well, Dobbins, how is it with you? How are all the little ones? Why, you seem feeble, Dobbins. Have you been ill?

Dob. Quoite at death's door, ma'am, an it be all the zame to you, my lady. Hard time on't all winter with east winds and the rheumatize. And then it be no troifle of a tramp from farm here, ma'am, considering my shanks be none of the stoutest just now.

Miss F. Why, you haven't come all the way on foot in your state of health? Don't be standing scraping there, man. Here. [*Placing a chair*] Sit down on this chair. Rest yourself and take your time and then tell me what brought you on this worse than fool's errand.

Dob. Crave pardon, ma'am, but I be only come for to pay your reverence my rent.

Miss F. Couldn't you have sent your wife? But she's a grand lady, I suppose. Staying comfortable at home, while her poor husband is packed off to walk a dozen miles with one leg in the grave!

Dob. Please your ladyship, no such thing. My Margery be as hard a working dame as any in all the parish. She be abed of her sisteenth, ma'am, and that be why she couldn't come.

Miss F. Bless my soul, what will the country come to! One couple to bring sixteen into the world, when such multitudes are starving! You ought to be ashamed of yourselves.

Dob. Whoile we pays our way, and does our best ma'am, we doant zee why we're to be ashamed neither. To be sure, your ladyship may think as how you've a roight to find fault because we're a year behind in our rent, but then your ladyship never ax'd for it, and so we let it run on; but at last woife says to I, "Dobbins, her ladyship's a queer 'un, they say, and flies into rare rages, and there be no knowing when she may turn and pounce on us like a she-tigress; zo run, Dobbins, for now it's four quarters we owe her, run and pay her, and then we can snap our fingers at her ladyship and all her tantrums!"

Miss F. Is this to be endured! [*To Mrs. Simper*] And you, Mrs. Demure Face, and you Master Double Face [*To Merton*], if you want to laugh, laugh out, and don't bite your lips and mince and look this way and that way and every way but straight at me. But [*To the farmer*] come, sir, I've had enough of your insolence, now give me a little of your money. Hand it out. You've made a fortune this year, no doubt, or I never should have a farthing of it.

Dob. A fortin? Noa, my lady, we've made no fortin, but we've lost a barn by fire and three cows by the murrain. Had the rot among the sheep and all the corn beat down in the treat rains. Ah, if it had not been that moy woife's uncle, the parish clerk, died, Heav'n bless him! and left her thirty-eight pound, seven shillings, two pence three farden, we never should ha' been able to make up the rent. But when we got it! Aw, woife was in such joy! "Run with it, Dobbins, and pay the rent," says she, "that it," says my woife. The troifle that wus short, you zee, I borry, and here it all is, ma'am. Count it. It be right to a farden, *I* know, and glad I be to pay it and get rid of your ladyship, for now I owes your ladyship nothing. I'ze nothing to be afeared on, ho! ho! nothing, not I.

Miss F. But I'll be even with you. Hand me my desk, Frank. [*To the farmer*] Stop where you are. [*Writes and hands the paper to Dobbins*] There, sir, there's your receipt. No parleying. Pocket and go about your business.

Dob. Stop a bit. Since moy eyes be getting bad with the rest of me, let's try the old spectacles. So, 'tis so. Four years' rent! Ha! Ha! What? No, four years' rent! No, my lady, I'ze only brought you this year's. Alter the receipt, ma'am, an you please, and take the money and let me go.

Miss F. Do you think I don't know what I'm about, man? Put your receipt in your money bag and your money bag in your pocket this instant, and look ye, if ever you have the effrontery to bring me the miserable legacies of your wife's parish clerk relations, or to think of paying rent, till your barn is built up, your farming stock made good, and some of your sixteen brats able to do a little more than squall for a modicum of milk, I'll turn you all, without a moment's notice, adrift. [*He is about falling on his knees*] No antics, here, sir. John! [*Enter John*] The pony chaise this instant, and drive this booby to his farm. [*Exit John*]

DOB. Ah, my lady, you be loike a great artichoke, my lady, rum rhind, but rare eating. Heaven bless your ladyship and all your worshipful ladyship's honorable company. Lord, lord, how woife's heart will caper! [*Exit*]

MISS F. Will nobody stop that fellow's mouth? John, I say! [*Re-enter John*] John, while the chaise is preparing, give that clown a lunch! [*Exit John*] And John! [*Re-enters*] Put a dozen of the best port in the box for his wife. [*Exit John*] And John! [*Re-enters*] Drive him home gently: don't let his crazy bones be jolted. [*Exit John. Turning to Merton*] And now, you disgrace to all your family, you thought to escape in the confusion, did you? Draw near, sir, draw near, and let me drag the truth from you, if possible, respecting your enormities.

MER. You will scarcely think them such when you know all.

MISS F. Indeed! You think to smooth me down with your fine speeches, hey! It won't do.

MER. I only think of telling you a plain tale.

MISS F. Why don't you, then? Haven't I been waiting here this hour and not a word of anything but rigmarole can I get from you yet.

MRS. S. Don't be abashed. You were telling us, when overtaken by night and rough weather, on a hunting party—

MER. Aye, lightning flashed, the darkness was deepening. I was parted from my companions, and both my horse and myself were sinking with fatigue, when, looking about for some inn, I found myself opposite the mansion house of the Dillons.

MISS F. [*Starting*] The Dillons!

MER. What, aunt, and you know the Dillons?

MISS F. Y—y—yes—yes—once, once.

MRS. S. We saw a good deal of the present owner of that mansion when we were all younger: a civil gentleman enough, only somewhat the worse for the pride of his family in the noble blood. About eighteen years ago he paid his court to one of us.

MISS F. [*Aside, with a contemptuous shrug*] One of us? [*Aloud*] Go on with your story.

MER. The rain beginning to pour down in torrents; I thought I could not do better than seek shelter there. I knocked at the mansion and found it uninhabited.

Miss F.   What! Dillon dead?

Mrs. S.   Patience, sister, let him tell it in his own way.

Mer.   I traversed a courtyard in ruins, passed a pavilion once beautiful, but now degraded into a cattle shed, and at length saw a light in the window of a farmhouse, where I was received with the most endearing hospitality.

Miss F.   But Dillon, what had become of Dillon?

Mer.   I asked the cause of the desolation I saw around me. I found that the owner of the estate, involved in ruin by the extravagances of a fashionable wife—

Miss F.   Ah, ha! She ruined him, did she?

Mrs. S.   I always knew she would.

Miss F.   I don't believe a word of it. She was always a spendthrift, and I dare say the fault was his own. But right or wrong, the poor woman always got blamed, and you ought to be ashamed of yourself to take part against your sex. Well, why don't you get on? What of Dillon?

Mer.   His wife being dead—

Miss F.   Dead!

Mrs. S.   His wife dead? He's quite young enough to marry again.

Mer.   He resumed his post in the army and went abroad, for the double purpose of nursing his property and avoiding his creditors, but the scoundrels took advantage of his absence, and all would have been lost but for his agent, the very farmer beneath whose roof I was sheltered. The worthy fellow with the money he had saved as former steward of the family, kept the cormorants at bay and entered into arrangements to preserve the estate to his benefactor, by paying off the various claims by installments.

Miss F.   A worthy deed, a very worthy deed. The man's an honor to human nature.

Mer.   I thought so too, and when I heard how oppressed he was to keep pace with these engagements and that, in spite of all he had done, the estate was still liable to instant forfeiture, I think, aunt, you will do me the justice to be persuaded that I could not listen without something more than pity.

Miss F.   Right, right, but what has all this to do with the three thousand pounds you squandered? I call you to account for your extravagance, your wanton, unjustifiable extravagance, and here you come to me with a long story about a broken-down gentleman and a sentimental clodhopper. What became of the three thousand pounds, I say?

Mrs. S.   Be gentle with him, sister. Proceed deliberately, coolly—

Miss F.   Coolly! You whose pulses would be outrun by a superannuated tortoise, may talk of coolness! Coolness! What became of the three thousand pounds?

MER. The farmer, unable to meet his stipulations, allowed me to supply him with the means.

MISS F. And this is what you have done with your three thousand pounds?

MRS. S. I hope you will give him no more thousands to throw away thus.

MISS F. To save Dillon, for Dillon's sake, my nephew has left himself penniless and parted with the money he received from me!

MER. I have stated nothing but the truth.

MISS F. Our early life was passed in that vicinity. We lived next door to the Dillons. Every spot on that estate bears some remembrance of the sweet dreams of childhood. Sister, get your bonnet and shawl. The carriage was ordered for a drive. It shall drive you to the honest farmer's.

MER. How—*you!* You go to Farmer Gregory's?

MISS F. Why not I as well as anybody else? Come, sister, come.

MER. But suffer me to go before and announce you.

MISS F. You seem rather disturbed, sir, at the idea of my going. Why are you disturbed? I will go now, if it be only to find out the reason.

MER. Do, aunt, do.

MISS F. And you shall go with me, sister!

MRS. S. Give me time to put up my spectacles, dear.

MISS F. What an everlasting dawdle you are, "dear." [*Snatching the spectacles*] Give me the spectacles and come along, "dear." [*Catches her under the arm and hurries her out. Fag peeps in on the opposite side*]

FAG. Is the coast clear?

MER. Fag, fly to Gregory's—

FAG. Fly to the nest of my little Annette? On the light wings of love—

MER. Keep your love for your lady love and take heed of what I say. My aunt knows what I have done for Gregory; but I have not dared to tell her of Sophia.

FAG. Shrewd enough. She'd think the petticoat had more weight with you than the pity—

MER. A stronger reason yet: Sophia is the daughter of a woman for whom Dillon jilted my aunt. Contrive in the best way you can to make Gregory keep Sophia out of my aunt's view.

FAG. How should your aunt see her?

MER. Didn't I tell you she had taken a queer freak in her head to drive post-haste to the farm?

FAG. No?

MER. She has. Look she don't get there before you. [*Miss Flashington calls, outside*]

Miss F. [*Outside, calling*] Merton, I say! Frank Merton!

Mer. Her voice! Away! Remember about Sophia.

Fag. Her voice? Her thunder! What must her presence be, if that's her voice? [*They run out on opposite sides*]

Scene 2: *A beautifully rural spot. In the distance, the family mansion of Major Sir Thomas Dillon. In the foreground, a vine-covered farmhouse, enclosed by a quickset hedge. Opposite to it, some dilapidated buildings. Enter Sophia Dillon, looking out at the back.*

Soph. [*Alone*] I may strain my eyes out, not a glimpse of him is to be seen! This is the third long day! And then papa's unexpected arrival in the meantime! My uneasiness about Merton has prevented my giving my whole heart to rejoicing for papa's return, and I dare not tell him or anyone else the cause. I am sadly afraid papa will be angry when he knows. [*Sings*]

1.

When thou are away, the world's brightest charms
          Look, oh, how drear!
But there's a magic its frown that disarms
          When thou art near.

2.

When thou <art> away, even summer's beams
          All cold appear!
But the coldest winter sweet summer seems
          Beside thee, dear! [*Enter Farmer Gregory from the farmhouse*]

Greg. What's the matter, miss? I hope you're not ill. I never saw you so sad and thoughtful before. Now a sigh, then a quiet little tear, and then up you are on tiptoe and peeping out, first on one side, then on the other. One would say you were looking for somebody.

Soph. Whom should I look for? Whom have we to expect, now dear papa is come back to us? We never see anybody but, now and then, Fag.

Greg. You forget Mr. Merton; and really, I begin to fear he has forgotten us, though I never longed for anyone's appearance more heartily than I do for his this very moment.

Soph. I'm sure, if he don't like to come, he's welcome to stay where he is.

Greg. [*Looking out*] Hey! What? Who's that I see?

Soph. Where? Where?

GREG. Crossing yon field. Now he gets over the stile. Confusion! That is not he.

SOPH. Fag! I'm sure nobody wanted Fag. I'll go away. But soft. He can give us intelligence perhaps of—I'll not go away—[*Enter Fag, left hand*]

FAG. Ah, Farmer, how goes it among ye, hey? Beg pardon, miss. Hope you're well, miss; and your charming daughter, Annette, Farmer, hope she's well, too. Hope you're all well.

GREG. Annette is gone to be bridesmaid at the next village. She's away for the week. But pray, have you seen Mr. Merton lately, Fag? It is half a week since he was here, and that's a long time for him to stop away.

FAG. Mr. Gregory, it is from him I come, minister plenipotentiary upon a special embassy.

SOPH. Then he's not coming at all?

FAG. I didn't say that, miss; but what I have to say, I am bound to say—

SOPH. Well?

FAG. In private to Farmer Gregory. Shocked to seem rude, but affairs of state require to be managed with diplomatic caution.

SOPH. Oh, if Mr. Merton has secrets, I'm sure I—I—have no wish—to be—inquisitive, not I. Good morning, sir. [*Exit Sophia*]

FAG. Off in a huff. Natural enough, hey, Farmer, hey?

GREG. She is only concerned, as I am, at Mr. Merton's unusually long absence. The last installment was to be paid today, and unless he aids me—

FAG. The dickens it was! He can't then.

GREG. How?

FAG. Now I dare say it was about that he wanted me when he first sent this morning. But make your mind easy. He can't help you just yet. His purse is under quarantine.

GREG. Merciful powers! Sir Thomas will have returned then, only to behold his ruin!

FAG. Sir Thomas? The old 'un ain't come back?

GREG. Most unexpectedly, the day before yesterday.

FAG. Whew! What the devil's to be done now?

GREG. I don't understand you.

FAG. Keep him close, Gregory, keep the old 'un close.

GREG. Close! What do you mean by close?

FAG. Merton's two aunts are to be here presently. Don't let the old 'un see 'em. But, above all, don't let them see or hear about his daughter.

GREG. Why not?

FAG. One of 'em, Gregory, is a devil in petticoats. But she's desperate rich.

GREG. Why should I keep my patron, or my patron's daughter out of sight because rich folks are in the way? Zounds, sir, if the King himself was to come, neither Miss Sophia nor her father should be kept back. They're fit company for the best in the land and all the fitter for having known what it is to want and be forsaken.

FAG. You don't hear me, Farmer. You won't understand me, man. There may be reasons why Mr. Merton's aunt should not, just yet, know the affair between him and the young lady.

GREG. What affair? Speak out, what affair?

FAG. Now, Gregory, you can't be such a noodle as to think Mr. Merton has been doing all he has for your sake only, when there were two such eyes to lure him on as those of Miss Sophia?

GREG. He advanced me money before he knew there was such a being as Miss Sophia.

FAG. Yes, but he advanced you more after he knew. [*Sings*]

> If you would by signs discover
> In his own despite the lover,
> See a man from all eyes shrinking,
> Give up sleeping, eating, drinking;
> Nay, where sense is needed, tricks
> Madder than a lunatic's.
> If, to show his wit, he strive,
> Seem the veriest ass alive,
> His job's done: the fool's a lover.

GREG. A love affair! A love affair! Good Heavens, what will Sir Thomas say?

FAG. What can he say if he don't know?

GREG. Mr. Fag, I may be a simple man, but I am an honest man; and I must tell you, Mr. Fag, I don't like this roundabout dealing.

FAG. Nobody wants you to be roundabout. If there's any maneuvering to be done, leave it to me. I'm not so nice about groping through crooked paths when they lead to flowers and sunshine. Mr. Merton will be a glorious match for Miss Dillon. Answer me one thing, Gregory: would such a match come so very inopportunely just now, Gregory, hey, my old boy?

GREG. Umph.

FAG. And if you are the cause of preventing it by prematurely meddling, you'll do your master more harm than all his misfortunes.

GREG. How?

FAG. And I'll tell you a secret, Gregory. One of Mr. Merton's aunts is Sir Thomas Dillon's bitterest foe.

GREG. His foe? His foe? That's indeed to be considered.

FAG. Hark! Carriages! There come Merton and his aunts! This way with me, Gregory—

GREG. But I must attend to the company first—

FAG. Attend only to me, and you'll bless your stars that you have found such a counsellor. Oh, never mind the carriages. Come along, I say. [*Exeunt*]

SCENE 3: *The farmhouse of Gregory. Enter Miss Flashington, Mrs. Simper, and Frank Merton.*

MISS F. Was there ever such a place as this? Knock, knock, knock, and then one head pops out and disappears; then, another. They scamper before me like mice in a granary at the coming of a cat. Oh, oh, so we've somebody at last, have we? Who's this? [*Enter Gregory, followed by Fag, who slinks to the back*]

MER. This, aunt, is the worthy farmer of whom I told you. Farmer Gregory, allow me to introduce my aunts.

GREG. Proud to see anybody belonging to you, Mr. Merton. You've kept away a long time this time.

FAG. [*Running down and twitching him, unobserved*] Mum!

MISS F. So you and this chap are tolerably well together, it seems. He gives me a good account of you, Farmer.

GREG. Not better, ma'am, than I can give of him. He's been a rare friend to me and mine.

MISS F. So I found. He would have concealed it from me, but he failed. Farmer, was it considerate, was it right, sir, to take money from a young man like that without first ascertaining how he came by it? I see you're annoyed, but you deserve it all; you've both of you done a good deed, but you've done it in a very bad way.

GREG. [*Confused*] I'm sure, madam, I—Mr. Merton arranged with the creditors without my knowledge. He enabled me to keep the arrangement without my asking.

MISS F. I must have some private talk with you, Farmer.

GREG. Ma'am—

MISS F. Merton, you're not wanted here. Go and see the horses unharnessed. Farmer, we'll dine with you.

GREG. The best the farm affords, ma'am, is at your command. [*Apart*] My stars, if in this mood she should come across Sir Thomas—

Miss F. Didn't I tell you, Merton, to order the horses into the farmer's stables?

Greg. The stables of Sir Thomas, madam. There's nothing here of mine.

Miss F. [*Struggling against strong emotion*] Farmer, you've the spirit of a nobleman.

Greg. I've the spirit of an honest man. I hope every nobleman can say as much. [*During these last speeches Merton has watched his opportunity and whispered to Fag, who replies to him*]

Fag. [*Apart to Merton*] I'll contrive to get him away, sir. Don't be alarmed. I'll not lose sight of him. [*Exit Merton*]

Mrs. S. Farmer, wasn't that wife of Sir Thomas a sad plague to him?

Greg. It is not me place to judge my benefactors.

Miss F. You are right, Farmer.

Greg. If my lady had faults, Sir Thomas finds ample atonement for them in—[*Fag runs down, out of breath, as if just entering*]

Fag. Farmer, run, run! The grey mare is down and kicking. The cart shaft's over her, and the men tugging at her to no purpose. If you don't make haste, she'll be ruined.

Greg. The scoundrels! Why don't they cut the shaft and harness?

· Fag. So I told 'em, but they wouldn't mind me. They didn't dare cut anything without your orders.

Greg. The dolts! Hey! Giles! Peter! Sam! Cut the shaft! Keep your knee upon her head! Cut the harness! [*Runs out*]

Fag. Aye, cut, Farmer [*Aside*], and don't come again [*Aloud*], for I'll look after the ladies. [*Stands bowing*]

Miss F. And pray, obsequious sir, who may you be, making as many bows there as a willow in a high wind? Do you belong to the house, sir?

Fag. Not exactly, madam, though the house could not get on very well without me.

Miss F. Indeed. In what relation do you stand to it?

Fag. A—a—a—sort of a—patron, ma'am. That's all, only a—patron.

Mrs. S. [*Eyeing him from head to foot*] Patron!

Miss F. Pray be more explicit, sir. I do not understand what you can mean by patron.

Fag. No questions, pray. Be satisfied, ladies, that I take the liveliest interest in you. As for myself, I—I—am—mystery.

Mrs. S. He's a madman. [*Sophia heard outside*]

Soph. [*Outside*] Mr. Fag!

FAG. [*Aside*] Confusion! Here's Miss Sophia coming, and I've not had a chance yet of cautioning her. [*Hurrying towards the side, as Sophia Dillon runs in*]

SOPH. Mr. Fag, have you seen Mr. Merton? Is it true he's here?

FAG. [*Low to her*] Hush! Don't you see those ladies?

SOPH. [*Surprised*] Ha! [*Curtseying very low*]

MISS F. A pretty girl. Who is she?

FAG. This—oh, this, ma'am—you want to know who this young lady is? This young lady, ma'am, is—is the daughter of Farmer Gregory, ma'am. [*Aside to her*] Don't deny it.

MISS F. The farmer's daughter? She spoke of Frank Merton. Does she know Frank Merton?

FAG. Coming here so often as he did, ma'am, it could scarcely be expected, you know, ma'am—

MISS F. Umph.

FAG. [*Low to Sophia*] They are his aunts.

MISS F. Frank never told me Gregory had a daughter. Strange, too, for she's indeed a lovely girl; but that dress of hers seems rather above what one would look for in a farmer's daughter—

FAG. Best clothes, ma'am—Sunday suit, ma'am. Put on in honor of your visit, ma'am.

MISS F. In honor of a visit nobody expected! Your tongue runs fast, sir. Why don't the girl answer for herself?

SOPH. Madam, I—

FAG. She's timid, ma'am, very timid, and that seventy-four-gun look of yours, ma'am, quite overpowers her.

MISS F. Mr. Mystery, if the girl talks too little, you talk an infinite deal too much. Go about your business. I wish to be left with this young woman.

FAG. Business, ma'am? La, I've no business. I pass my life in the business of other people, ma'am. I'm factotum general, a walking refuge for the destitute. [*Whispering to Sophia*] Mind what you say. She's your father's deadly foe.

MISS F. You are prompting her with answers, sir. Leave us this instant.

FAG. Sorry, ma'am, you should value my company less than I do yours. Should you want me, I'm within call. [*Exit*]

MISS F. I should be sorry to be so destitute as to want such a refuge. And, sister, pray do you take a turn around the farm, and, I say, sister [*Aside*], buy something of the farmer and pay well for it, that he may be put to no loss by our visit: hay, oats, anything, but see you pay him well. [*Exit Mrs. Simper*] And now, miss—

SOPH. [*Aside and agitated*]　She makes me tremble. My father's deadliest foe. Fag told her I was the farmer's daughter.

MISS F. [*Eyeing her*]　You shrink away from me, young woman. What is that for? I suppose they've told you I was a tornado.

SOPH.　I have been told much good of you, madam.

MISS F. [*Vehemently*]　Good! Who in the world ever told you any good of me?

SOPH. [*Faltering*]　Madam?

MISS F. [*With increased vehemence*]　Who ever told you any good of me, I ask. No answer. Is it such mighty harm to have spoken well of me that you are ashamed to own who did it?

SOPH.　It was your nephew, madam.

MISS F.　A pretty fellow to go about puffing his aunt in this way, as if she needed his trumpeting. And pray, miss, how came you to know my nephew?

SOPH.　Through mere chance, madam. His generosity to my father—

MISS F.　You're in love with him. No evasion; I see it plainly. Have you told him you're in love with him?

SOPH.　Madam—

MISS F.　Has he ever said he was in love with you?

SOPH. [*Casting down her eyes*]　Yes, ma'am.

MISS F.　And you suffered it?

SOPH.　Yes, ma'am.

MISS F.　You might just as well have sworn you adored him.

SOPH.　Good Heavens!

MISS F.　Young woman, the conduct of Frank Merton to your father can only have been prompted by wild, desperate passion. Men are not given to doing good for its own sake, miss. *That* you should have known, and now see what misery you have brought upon yourself, without fortune, thrown by fate into a sphere of life unequal in the world's eye to his—

SOPH.　I own, madam, I am without fortune.

MISS F.　And pray who marries, nowadays, for anything else?

SOPH.　I never thought at all upon that subject.

MISS F.　What! Are you not aware that after such attentions as you have allowed from my nephew, if he does not marry you, every old maid in the parish will have her joke upon you, and every coxcomb his sneer?

SOPH. [*Terrified*]　Merciful Providence!

MISS F.　Come, come, cheer up. I'm sure you're a good girl, and the malice of those who delight in a friendless woman's sorrows is now and then defeated. Cheer up, my child. I know all I wished now; but I need to be left alone a moment. I am fluttered and not well.

SOPH. [*Much moved*] Madam, pray allow—

MISS F. No, I shall be better by myself.

SOPH. And so shall I, too, for I am very, very wretched. [*Exit Sophia*]

MISS F. [*Looking after her*] Just such was I, as youthful, as inexperienced, when I listened to the vows of Dillon! I loved him with the same deep, the same heedless, love. No, it was not love: it was idolatry! But [*Triumphantly*] never did he, no, never did living creature know the boundlessness of my faith in his professions, the intensity of my anguish at his desertion. Well, well, if I could not be happy myself, I should bless the fate which enables me to be the cause of happiness to others. And why should not an honest farmer's daughter be a fitting match for Merton? Why should she not be a better match than one of better standing? Her attachment will be more exclusive, and if thwarted, the disappointment more withering. A rich girl might wean herself by a change of scenes and faces; but a poor girl forsaken cannot get away from the sad spot where every step reminds her of the happier past, but is chained to pore upon the aching dream of what she was once lured to hope, till her heart breaks. The man's a scoundrel, be he high or low, who can deliberately cause such wretchedness. Should not I be as great a scoundrel, could I be accessory to causing it? Dillon's family conspired to prevent our union, because, forsooth, my father was a merchant, his a baronet. The selfsame cause! Shall I be swayed by the prejudices which have made Dillon a beggar, me an abrupt, uncouth creature whom all avoid and tremble at? No! Frank shall marry the poor girl, or, hang him, I'll make him too poor himself to marry anybody. [*Mrs. Simper runs in*] Well, what brings you here in such a hurry?

MRS. S. Oh, sister, sister, such an occurrence! Oh, I've almost a mind to faint away.

MISS F. Faint indeed! I never saw so much life in you before.

MRS. S. You would never have believed your eyes.

MISS F. What about?

MRS. S. I just this moment met—

MISS F. Whom?

MRS. S. Oh, it took such an effect upon me.

MISS F. I shall be in a rage presently.

MRS. S. Only think. He's here! I saw him!

MISS F. Whom?

MRS. S. Saw him with my own eyes!

MISS F. [*Violently and stamping*] Whom? Whom? Whom?

MRS. S. Dillon! [*Miss Flashington starts, stands a moment as if petrified, then trembles violently*] Sister, sister, speak—what ails you?

Miss F.   The carriage! Hence immediately!

Mrs. S.   Dear sister, be composed.

Miss F.   It is all a trick, a planned thing. I've been ensnared hither to be made a laughing stock—

Mrs. S.   My word on it, sister, no! Had you witnessed Dillon's surprise when he heard you were here, you never would have forgotten it. He seemed enraptured, implored to see you, but I took care to let him know you have a spirit of your own and that you hate him now, as heartily as you ever loved him.

Miss F.   [*Eagerly*]   Hate him! No, no, I hate no one, sister. It is the beauty to quell the power of hating. But I cannot meet the destroyer of my peace, the man who in a moment changed the whole scenery of life from a paradise to a desert. I do not hate him, sister, but I cannot meet him.

Mrs. S.   I only wish you could hear his explanation of his conduct, his remorse at the consequences. 'Twas while you were travelling in Italy that his friends dazzled him with the accomplishments of a beautiful coquette and lured him to a match which has bitterly punished his infidelity. He was not twenty at the time, sister, and much may be excused in the heedless age of twenty. Really, his eloquence and ardor awakened feelings in me which I have not had for a long time, sister. But when he spoke of your soft and gentle manners, I could not for the soul of me keep from laughing.

Miss F.   You're in love.

Mrs. S.   He wasn't in my mood, though, for when I told him that your manners had changed entirely from the moment you heard of his marriage, he burst into a passion of tears.

Miss F.   [*Endeavoring to suppress her emotion*]   He's a fool—and—[*Bursting into tears*] I'm a greater fool than either of you to let you all impose upon me thus and trifle with my feelings. Merton must have known this. I'll not forgive him. The farmer with his quiet hypocrisy—he, too, must—but I'll foil them all. Go get your things and order up the carriage. I'll quit the house. Be off! [*Exit Mrs. Simper*] I'll—[*Going, meets Merton, followed, unobserved, by Fag, who remains at the back*] So, sir! You are come, are you? Come to practise upon your "excellent aunt," from whom you would not hide anything for the world, with a long, vainglorious pretense of disinterested liberality to cloak a vile scheme of libertinism. I know it all, sir.

Mer.   Aunt!

Miss F.   Don't "aunt" me; you've been making love to the farmer's daughter, sir.

Mer.   No, as I live!

FAG. [*Apart*] Plague on my addled pate, never once to have thought of telling what I had done. [*Makes signs, which Merton does not see*]

MISS F. Don't deny it. Don't dare to deny it—why, you reprobate! She told me so herself.

MER. Then she deceived you, aunt. She's a young flirt, who thinks every man that looks at her means a declaration.

FAG. [*Apart*] Not very ceremonious about my little Annette though.

MISS F. She's no flirt, sir. She's a sincere, good girl, and it is my will that you marry her at once.

FAG. [*Apart*] Marry my Annette!

MER. But, aunt, I cannot. To be plain, I love another.

MISS F. Another! Another! And pray, sir, how many ladies may you have in your catalogue of villainy?

FAG. [*Approaches and whispers*] Say you love her and leave the rest to me. 'Tis a scheme of mine.

MISS F. [*Perceiving him*] What are you doing here, pray?

FAG. "Roaming, that's all [*Humming the tune*], I've been roaming. I've been roaming."

MISS F. You impudent varlet, you're in league with my nephew.

FAG. I own, I have the honor to be your nephew's friend.

MISS F. An honor for him to be proud of, certainly, but you are no friend of mine. Go pack!

MER. [*Apart to him*] Go! Don't you see you only incense her? Go, go!

FAG. [*Apart*] Let 'em do as they like, in spite of themselves. I'll bring 'em all round to the right point yet. They'll see me again when they least expect it. [*Exit Fag, l[eft] h[and]*]

MISS F. And this fellow, I suppose, is your go-between in your honorable speculations upon the credulity of poor country girls! Oh, Frank Merton, Frank Merton, that I should have warmed in my bosom a viper to poison even the innocent wild flower which leans its head to smile upon him.

MER. But only let me speak, aunt, and upon my honor—

MISS F. Honor! *Your* honor! The honor of a seducer. Here's a fellow making love to two girls at a time and refusing to marry either, and yet prating about his honor. Forsooth!

MER. I'll marry instantly if you'll consent to my marrying Miss Dillon.

MISS F. [*Astonished*] What? How? Has Dillon then a daughter?

MER. An angel.

MISS F. Dillon a daughter!

MER. See her, aunt, and I'll be sworn you will not hesitate.

Miss F. I see Dillon's daughter! Never! I? So then the depravity of the parent is to be repeated in his child. He brings her back with him accomplished and vicious as the stock from whence she sprang to entice you with all the arts of heartless coquetry from the humble but honest heart which sees but one being in the world, and that one, you! He brings her like a spoiler to turn the beautiful devotedness of the young heart's earliest all-absorbing passion to misanthropy, to desolation, to despair! [*Enter Fag*] That everlasting ape again! You miserable caricature of a despicable sex! You cringing disturber of peace and purveyor to profligacy!

Fag. Beg pardon, ma'am, but no time now to listen to compliments; something must be done now, or there's an end of the Dillons.

Miss F. What?

Fag. Don't you know, ma'am? Oh, then I'll tell you. Better know it from me than the bailiffs.

Miss F. The bailiffs! To the point, to the point.

Fag. Sir Thomas is ruined!

Miss F. Ruined? Frank Merton, did you not tell me you had saved the estate with that three thousand pounds?

Mer. Not exactly, aunt. I told you I paid that sum upon account, but a last payment remained, which, which—

Miss F. Well, sir—

Mer. I fear to tell you of—

Miss F. Fear? How dare you fear to tell anything to me?

Fag. Which last payment, madam, was to be met today, but upon its failure the former payments being forfeited, out march Sir Thomas Dillon and his tribe, and in march the law's staff-officers. Farmer Gregory has in vain sought for an extension of time. The agent of the creditors is inexorable, and a score of representatives of the sheriff are now waiting for the hour of forfeiture to pounce upon their prey.

Miss F. Waiting, now waiting?

Fag. [*Aside, to Merton*] I've hit the mark! 'Twill do.

Miss F. Frank Merton, you know this man well?

Mer. I know him to be honest, though eccentric.

Miss F. Enough. I must speak with him. Wait for me at the carriage. [*Exit Merton, l[eft] h[and].*] Eyeing Fag from head to foot] Mr. Fag—

Fag. Madam—

Miss F. I'm something of a physiognomist. It strikes me you're a rogue.

Fag. Indeed, I have been considered so by strangers, but never by those who knew me.

Miss F. How came you acquainted with my nephew?

FAG. I wrote in a lawyer's office, to whom he came about the embarrassments of this estate.

MISS F. Are you a lawyer's clerk, then?

FAG. Oh, no, madam. Now and then I help an acquaintance when there's a great deal to do. The fact is, I can turn my hand to anything.

MISS F. How do you live?

FAG. Upon the misfortunes and annoyances of those whom I esteem; I'm like one of Mother Carey's chickens, always at hand with foul weather. My friends are given to getting into scrapes, and my life passes in trying to get them out. Though I scorn to be paid for my services, I can never starve; for I always pick up a snack here and there, where I go to be useful, and the King himself is not a more welcome guest, for I'm never asked where they can possibly do without me.

MISS F. Umph! There's good at the bottom of this. Now, what would you say to me, should I put you in the way of something regular and respectable?

FAG. In mercy's name, don't dream of such a thing. I've been often highly patronized, but no good ever came of it. I never yet got anything regular that was not forthwith seized with a spirit of retrenchment, and I speedily found myself the first to be omitted as a superfluity. Number 1 in Schedule A—

MISS F. Execute a commission with which I will entrust you, and I will forthwith give you one hundred guineas.

FAG. Is there such a sum?

MISS F. But I must not appear in the business, and it must be managed secretly and instantly.

FAG. Speak and it is done.

MISS F. [Sings]   Silently, silently,
        Manage this affair for me.

FAG. [Sings]   Silently, silently,
        I'll contrive it all for thee.

MISS F. [Sings]   Be discreet, don't let a word
        By a living soul be heard.

FAG. [Sings]   I'll take heed that not a word
        By a living soul is heard.

[Together sing]   Favors to be kind must be
        Ever granted silently.

MISS F. Pay the balance necessary to redeem this estate. [Takes a pocketbook and writes] Draw the receipt in this name, and place the papers yourself in the hands of the person for whom you make the purchase.

FAG. [*Reading*] Ah, madam, I can't stand this. Excuse my pocket hand-kerchief!

MISS F. Time enough for your tears. They'll keep till you've more leisure. Hasten and remember the result if you do the business silently and well.

FAG. If I should fail, madam, in anything for another, it would be as great a wonder, madam, as—as if I should succeed in anything for myself. [*Exit Fag. Sophia runs in*]

SOPH. Oh, madam!

MISS F. What do you want with me? You tremble, girl.

SOPH. I came, madam, to say—

MISS F. Oh, you may spare yourself the trouble. I know it all. You love my nephew, and he's jilting you for another.

SOPH. No, madam, he has just repeated his protestations of the reverse.

MISS F. Then how came he to tell me a different story?

SOPH. Ah, madam, when you shall be apprized—but no—I am incapable of deception. I will not abuse your confidence in me and the unequalled goodness of your heart. You have been told that I am the daughter of Farmer Gregory, whom you respect. I am not his daughter, but my father is a man you hate. I am the daughter of Sir Thomas Dillon, madam.

MISS F. You!

SOPH. I have been brought up at Farmer Gregory's, and as you cannot look upon me so kindly since you have discovered I am not his daughter, I come to ask one boon from you, and then, madam, I shall no longer be an intruder.

MISS F. You need not name it. I know very well what it is without your naming it.

SOPH. It is that you will forgive my father. He has wronged you, but your resentment added to his other misfortunes will drive him to despair. Oh, madam, on my knees I supplicate you, forgive my father.

MISS F. [*Greatly moved, apart*] The daughter of my successful rival, the daughter of my successful rival, kneeling to supplicate her false father's pardon!

SOPH. Am I to assure my father of your forgiveness?

MISS F. Up, up, young lady, up, or you'll break my heart. [*Raising her and bursting into tears*]

SOPH. Say I may fly and bring my father to you. [*Going*]

MISS F. Stop! Young lady, there can be no meeting between me and Sir Thomas Dillon. I have yet enough of woman's pride left in me to feel dis-turbed even at the idea of his presence. The wrong is done now, and I have no wish to revive its memory; but your good sense will teach you that the anguish of years is not to be forgotten in a day; so tell Sir Thomas Dillon, miss, that if he really remembers me with respect, he will show that respect by sparing me the inconvenience of again refusing an interview which never should, which never *shall* be granted. [*Exit Miss Flashington*]

SOPH. My poor, poor father. This will break his heart. He comes! What *can* I say to him? [*Sings*]

> The pang of all severest
> Is the deep, withering one that's borne
> In being torn
> From those we love the dearest.
>
> Since griefs bear consolation,
> There's none for this, no none! It breaks
> The heart and makes
> The world a desolation! [*Enter Sir Thomas Dillon*]

DIL. In tears, love? Have you then failed to accomplish my most anxious wish? Does she deny your prayer? [*Farmer Gregory runs in*]

GREG. Oh, sir! Oh, dear master! Can it be possible! Have all my exertions, all my sacrifices come to this at last?

DIL. What is the matter, Gregory?

GREG. Your estate is lost, sir.

DIL. Lost?

GREG. You know the time for redeeming it expired this day. A purchaser has appeared, and it is gone.

DIL. Gone! Gone! Irrevocably? And my child a beggar! I am inured to wretchedness, and but for thee, dear girl, I could have borne it without being thus unmanned. But when I look on you and know that I have nothing, nothing left—

SOPH. Cheer, oh, cheer thee, father, you have still a daughter left who can make the education you have given her more than meet all our wants; and be certain, father, we must, oh, we must be happier with a little and no cares than with much and many anxieties. [*Merton rushes in*]

MER. Speak, Farmer—is the estate lost? Am I—it was no error! Now I see it all! Look up, Sophia. Sir Thomas, do not droop. What though the estate be lost, you shall still find a friend in me. Then, as your son-in-law, at once confirm my claim to take you from this misery—

DIL. Mr. Merton, I am sorry, but events have changed my position, and I cannot suffer my daughter to be the pensioner on any man's liberality.

MER. By whose means? Whose is this vile chicanery? Where is the wretch who has possessed himself of what it was my place and my fondest hope to have preserved? Where is he? [*Enter Fag*]

FAG. Here! At your service, Mr. Merton. *I* am the purchaser of the Dillon estate.

ALL. You!

GREG. I always thought you a knave. So you've been prowling about here for months entirely to spy out the nakedness of the land and take advantage of our miseries! I—I—I—oh, that I could—keep out of my way, sir, or what my tongue can't say, my cudgel will.

FAG. Mr. Merton! Save me! Hear me!

MER. Scoundrel, stand back! Dare call for my protection?

FAG. Only let me speak—

MER. When, thus, pretending to promote my purpose—

FAG. A word will clear—

MER. You've been the base tool of a subtle foe.

FAG. Sir Thomas—

DIL. Slave!

FAG. Young lady—

SOPH. Shame on you, shame!

FAG. Some one *shall* hear me.

GREG. Out with you!

FAG. Help!

MER. Hence!

FAG. Help! Help, I say! Will none help modest worth? [*Miss Flashington rushes in, followed by Mrs. Simper*]

MISS F. What's all this racket? [*Sees Dillon and starts, greatly agitated*] Dillon here! [*Low and wildly*] Take me hence.

FAG. Not till I've been heard. Pray don't go till I've been heard, or they'll murder me.

MISS F. Murder! What means all this?

FAG. It only means, ma'am, that because I am the bearer of papers which give a certain young lady possession of her paternal fortune, I am to have my brains beaten out, that's all.

ALL. [*Excepting Fag and Miss Flashington*] How?

FAG. It is true enough that I am the purchaser of the estate, but only as the agent of Miss Sophia Dillon; and although none of you seem very proud of such a representative, if you will take the trouble to glance at those writings, you will find I have not failed in my duty, though rewarded as usual with a cuff on one side and a cudgel on the other.

SOPH. The estate purchased in my name!

GREG. Saved! Saved after all! Can't be—let me look—it is—it is—ha! ha! ha! I shall go mad with joy!

DIL. This noble act can emanate but from one source.

FAG. True, and see how ill you've treated me, notwithstanding all my bounty. Aren't you all ashamed of yourselves?

MER. Dear aunt, receive our benedictions!

SOPH. My guardian angel!

DIL. My preserver!

GREG. Dang it, ma'am but you're a trump!

MISS F. What do you all mean?

DIL. [*Pointing to Fag*] This person, who belongs, as it would seem, to you—

MISS F. To me! The knave belong to me!

FAG. Belong? I belong to nobody. I do not even belong to myself.

DIL. Confess it was from Miss Flashington you received the means of presenting my daughter with those papers—

FAG. Confess! Not to the Pope himself upon compulsion. I am an independent man and not to be commanded: a man of fortune, with a hundred guineas in my purse. [*Holding it up and clinking it*] There, Farmer! What do you think of that? Annette has been bridesmaid long enough. Send for her home, and let her be a bride.

GREG. You shan't be forgotten, Fag. I've done you wrong, and take my word for it, you shan't be forgotten. But as to marrying my Annette—

MISS F. If the girl likes him, let them marry. They shall have a little cottage of mine to live in; and if he can ever contrive to be anything but a vagabond, I'll see what more can be done when the rogue is civilized. And, now, Sir Thomas Dillon—

DIL. Oh, Charlotte, you have indeed humbled me to the dust. The hope which embellished my earlier days has long sustained me upon the rugged path through life. Say, is not the time come when I may make atonement for the past and find that hope fulfilled?

SOPH. You would not deny to make us all happy. No, I am sure you would not.

MISS F. Happy you shall be, if I can find a way to make you so.

SOPH. I can tell you one: give me a mother.

MISS F. If Sir Thomas really wishes to be friends with me, he'll allow me to give you what will answer your purpose much better.

DIL. Name it.

MISS F. A husband.

Dil. Merton, henceforth regard me as a father. You have taken my Sophia from me. Must my life pass in loneliness?

Mrs. S. That pathetic tone goes to my very heart. I have been the pride of three husbands. Sir Thomas, I am a widow.

Miss F. Remain one, then, if you'd not put the other sex out of humor with matrimony. Every stage of life has its appropriate enjoyments, and it is only by confusing these that we are spoiled for the world and the world for us. The wintry hour must seek its pleasures in the warm hearth and the bonny cheer of December, and not make a great baby of itself by crying for the rose and the nightingale of May. In looking after the young folks, Sir Thomas, we shall be more profitably employed than in caricaturing matrimony ourselves. If our years of romance have been wasted, we'll try to make up for it by lengthening theirs; and take my word for it, we shall find that they never can be unhappy who devote themselves to the happiness of those about them. To light the smile upon the cheeks of others has been my only comfort through a life whose fortunes have brought few smiles upon my own; and if you really think that, though I may have failed in the power, I never have been wanting in the desire to please.

Finale:

For old acquaintance sake, my long tried friends,
Let my example in your memory live,
To make you feel, if *this* attempt offends,
The right revenge is woman's: to forgive!

All. But if we sometimes for forgiveness sue,
We never wish you to *forget* us, too!

CURTAIN

THE ITALIAN BRIDE

THE ITALIAN BRIDE

THE manuscript of *The Italian Bride,* in Payne's hand, is in the Luquer collection.

This tragedy, a so-called "dramatic romance," was completed sometime before Payne's return to America in 1832, for in a letter dated September 13, 1836, Payne mentions a copy of it that he had "left in England." (For this reason A. H. Quinn's conjecture in *A History of the American Drama from the Beginning to the Civil War,* New York, 1923, p. 437, that the play was written after the year 1832, seems incorrect.) Although Payne did his best to find a producer he was never successful. On February 5, 1833, just before Kemble's arrival on a tour, Payne wrote from Boston to Colonel S. P. Morris in New York asking him to sound Kemble out about the play; Morris did so, but Kemble, after demanding a more legible manuscript, with which Payne supplied him, rejected it. In 1836 Payne, having received the draft that had been left in England, made "some alterations" in it and sent it to Wallack. Which one of the versions has been preserved in the only manuscript that has survived, it is impossible to say.

Payne probably based the tragedy on some undiscovered French source, for the original text of his extant manuscript is a tragedy of love intrigue set in Paris; by means of extensive revision of this text, however, he Americanizes it completely, altering the scene to Baltimore, changing the characters' names, and adding a few details. Plays that might be expected to furnish a clue in the search for a French source, such as Milman's *Fazio; or, The Italian Wife,* acted in 1816 in London, or Knowles's *The Wife: A Tale of Mantua,* 1833, or a tragedy by S. G. Levy with the same title as Payne's, produced in 1857 in New York, are of no help, for they resemble Payne's only vaguely.

The portrayal of Baltimore society with its varied interests in politics and business, literature, travel, and balls is noteworthy as an experiment. Kemble, however, was justified in turning the play down, for the far-fetched heroics are wholly unsuited to the domestic characters.

CHARACTERS

Mr. Morton

Edward Somers

Mr. Hartley

General Drummond

Galeazzo

Francis

Mr. Harrington

Mr. Montgomery

Mr. Thompson

Mr. Wilson

Clergyman

Belmunda

Estelle Morton

Lucy Colvin

[Mrs. Belmour

Mrs. Harrington

Guests]

SCENE: BALTIMORE AND ABOUT TWENTY MILES DISTANT FROM IT.

ACT I.

SCENE: *Apartment in the mansion of Mr. Morton at Baltimore. Estelle Morton is sitting, with her head reclined on a harp, which, in the earlier part of the scene, she now and then carelessly touches. Near her stands Edward Somers. Lucy Colvin is at work at a little side table.*

EST. And about what year was this that you were at Venice?

EDW. The close of 1829.

LU. Do you think the Queen of the Adriatic merits the high fame which the poets give her?

EST. Or the interest so lately flung around her by the magic pen of our countryman Fenimore Cooper, whose genius has proved to distant lands which so long fancied ours almost barbarous, that we can send forth works upon which even refined Europe dwells with ecstasy?

EDW. No other city in the world could detain Byron three years.

EST. Is Byron remembered there?

EDW. Estelle, cities whose monuments are crumbling soon forget men. Aye, there yet may be Venetians who remember having seen a haughty, pale-browed stranger, whom they heard called Byron; and they remember him, not as the gifted bard who has enhanced their city's fame in the immortal verses of *Childe Harold,* not as a sort of rebel angel wandering over earth upon whose lofty front the hand of Heaven had written: "Genius and Misanthropy;" but because, to a spot where their race is almost unknown, he brought splendid chargers which bore him on the gallop across the humid square of St. Mark's when the promenader could scarce keep his footing upon its shiny pavement; but because they saw him, at the Lido, leap with those coursers the tombs of the Jewish cemetery, where, unless upon compulsion, no Christian step dare, after night-fall, venture.

EST. Ah, this disenchants me with Venice, Edward.

EDW. It ought only to disenchant you with its inhabitants. I have seldom found a people's character to harmonize with the scenery in which they dwell. You should see Venice, dear Estelle, from the height of the obelisk of St. Mark's—Venice, standing with her feet in the waves like the Venus of the ocean; glittering at night with beacon lights blazing in front of her thousand black gondolas, as they dart across each other, like shooting stars. You should see Venice from the Lido, when in the morning, wrapped in mist, each breeze from the Adriatic bears away some fragment of her veil, disclosing now a church, now a bridge and now a palace. Indeed, she may be compared (forgive the simile, Estelle) to some coquette, who, to make the most of her charms, will only let them break on the gazer one by one, each new perfection lovelier than the last.

Lu. You talk more like a poet than a traveller, Mr. Somers.

Est. Once married, Edward, we'll go to Venice together—you'll promise, won't you, dear Edward?

Edw. Yes, my Estelle, and Venice will then look more beautiful than ever, for then you will look with me from the obelisk of St. Mark; you will stand by me at the Lido; and if in you, Estelle, I do not forget Venice, Venice will have charms she never had before for me, for I shall then behold her—not with the eyes of sadness.

Est. And from Venice we will go—

Edw. To Naples.

Lu. Ah, your father, Miss Estelle, will be able to tell us all about Naples when he comes back.

Est. No. Edward shall tell us about it. Come. I long to hear of Naples.

Edw. I must not deprive your father of the traveller's greatest pleasure.

Lu. Rather say, Sir Poet, that your recollections of Naples are not such as you would confide to a lady who only awaits her father's return to be made your wife.

Edw. And wherefore not, Lucy?

Est. [*To Edward*] What does she mean?

Edw. I know what she means, but she is mistaken, as you shall soon be convinced she is. Estelle, as ere long we shall be wedded, it is fitting I should have no concealments from you, love. Your heart is calm, Estelle; no stormy feeling ever ruffled it; but I am not so happy. I bring a heart less pure; a wild attachment lost me for two years in a tempest of passion. My excuse is in one word—then, I had never seen Estelle.

Est. There was a time, when such a declaration would only have raised my curiosity. Now, it does more, I own—but I am not so absurd as to continue jealous of the past, when I have no cause to doubt that all the future may be mine. So tell me all, Edward—tell, tell me all.

Edw. Lucy, I thank you for having opened the subject, even if your raillery had other ends in view than it has gained; even if you did not mean to spare me, as you have, the embarrassing part of a confession, which, as a timid lover I retarded, but as a man of honor it was my purpose to have made (though you seem to have thought otherwise, good Lucy)—yes, to have made this very hour—but knew not how to begin.

Lu. Well, now you've found the way, do begin. Quick—

Est. And as you still seem to be at a loss how, let me show you. First of all, then, her name—

Edw. Over that I have no right, Estelle. That is the only portion of the story that I may not mention.

Est. I honor your delicacy; but you can tell me how you came to know her—how much you loved her—and how long—if she loved you—and if she was beautiful—and what her age was? Tell me all about it!

Edw. And you'll forgive it all? Even to her being beautiful? Can you, Estelle?

Est. Edward—

Edw. Well?

Est. Look at me.

Edw. With all my soul.

Est. You are forgiven.

Edw. You are an angel.

Est. No compliments—my story—come!

Edw. I had been about a week in Naples; my dwelling was at the foot of Vesuvius, in one of those delightful villas which border the gulf of Ischia. One night I was startled from my sleep by a sharp, sudden shiver. I flew to the window—a blood-red brightness glared into the apartment and lit up all the sky—a hoarse hurricane howled—a shower of fire was falling. I at once perceived that I was about to view one of those awful eruptions of which I had so often read and longed to be a witness. Scarcely had I time to hurry on my dress and fling my mantle over me—for the stairs trembled and crackled at each step—I darted into the street. Oh, it was terrible to behold the whole population of a mighty city and its countless neighboring villages outpouring in wild confusion upon the heaving earth, between long rows of edifices whose towering walls swung to and fro above their heads like tall trees bowing in the tempest. Before me hurried two unprotected females, heedless, hopeless. I caught them. I observed a path conducting to the sea. I took it and led them with me. A fisherman had just put off to seek the safety of the opposite shore. I plunged into the wave—detained his boat—forced my companions into it—and sheltering them with a canvas from the falling flakes, the boatman spread his sail, and our bark cut the waves like a belated sea-bird.

Lu. Why, this is like a romance, Edward.

Est. Don't interrupt him.

Edw. From the moment the two females whom chance had thrown under my protection were in safety, the desire of gathering all the wonders of the scene shut out every other thought. Propped against the mast of our little bark, I stood and gazed. Oh, Estelle, let me not even attempt to picture what I saw! Fancy a column of broad flame shooting two hundred feet in air and tumbling, then, in flakes—streams of burning lava leaping in cascades—a sea of fire rolling wildly into the sea of water, first driving it before her, then herself recoiling, alternately repelling and repelled—two elements struggling like gladiators for the mastery—nature in the last convulsion seeming to implore for mercy—in a sky of blood, disheveled shadows, like the damned of Dante, hurrying in throngs some one way, some another, along the palpitating shore. Fancy all this, and you will still have but a feeble idea of a night of Naples from the gulf of Ischia, during an eruption of Vesuvius.

Est.   And what became of *you?*

Edw.   I stood immovable, with folded arms, eyes fixed, and bosom heaving, when, in the tossing of the bark, I felt an arm involuntarily grasping for support, at mine, and heard a voice exclaim, "Is it not, indeed, a stupendous scene? Sublime beyond conception? More than the awestruck mind could long endure, and not go mad?" The sweet tones thrilled me—I turned—

Est.   Was this the object of your love?

Edw.   You have given me your pardon in advance, and I will tell you all. The piercing eye of black, the flowing ringlets dancing in the breeze, the Neapolitan complexion lighted by the fantastic hues of the volcano's blaze; they made me feel as if that voice had come from a guardian angel, commissioned to see the work of wrath accomplished and to shield me from its fury. Never had I seen aught so splendidly beautiful before. The romantic way in which we became acquainted, and the service I had rendered her mother and herself, established a ready intimacy between us, which her father, on his return from a long absence, broke with a single word. She was a rich banker's daughter—I without fortune—he aimed at a splendid alliance which should increase the wealth of his daughter—I had nothing even for myself. Calling one day at my accustomed hour, I learned that she was gone. A letter from her apprised me that she had acted in obedience to her father, and begged me to return to America, without seeking to discover what had become of her, or ever naming or thinking of her, more. I obeyed her and returned. You were then at school, Estelle.

Est.   Oh yes, and I remember to have heard of some great feud between our families at that time about party politics—

Edw.   True. My father was a native of England, where he had left a brother, who was attached to the British Army and fell fighting against us at the battle of New Orleans. The British origin of my father drew bitter sarcasms against him during an election struggle from party papers and from certain hotheaded political opponents, among whom your own father was conspicuous; but mine nobly vindicated his loyalty to his adopted country by arming in her cause; and after he was slain—was slain—

Est. Pardon—pardon, dear Edward—pardon my thus thoughtlessly disturbing you with that dreadful recollection—

Edw. Slain in the same field which caused his brother's death, a sort of generous remorse came over your father, and he sought me, and courted every opportunity of serving me, and often, after he had taken me into his employ, would exclaim, with a smile, how happy it would make him to have a son-in-law like me—

Est. Of which hint you were ungallant enough to take no heed—

Edw. Because till he went on business to Italy and left me the management of his affairs at Baltimore, I had not seen you, Estelle. But when you and I became acquainted, love, how eager was I to remind him of what he had said and how grateful when he confirmed it by his consent. Since then, the memory of my earlier passion has hourly faded, till at length it only comes back to me like some strange dream. I still think of it, of course, but I think of it merely as a touching episode inseparable from the history of that tremendous night when I saw Naples convulsed, the sea upheaving, and Vesuvius in flames.

Est. And when you and I go to Naples, and witness an eruption of Vesuvius from the center of the Gulf of Ischia, you shall turn as you did before and look—not on the dark Italian—but the blue eyes and rosy cheeks of America. Perhaps they, too, may derive a beauty in your mind from the fantastic glare of the volcano. Then as you turn to gaze on me, you'll smile, and oh, Edward, I shan't think, then, upon the girl of Naples, I shall forget your story in your smile. [*Enter Francis*]

Fr. A letter, madam. [*Hands it, bows, and exit*]

Est. Oh, from my father! How my heart beats! [*Estelle eagerly breaks open the letter and reads it hastily and with agitation*]

Edw. Well? Are not we also to be made happier? Do you mean to keep the good news entirely to yourself?

Est. [*Handing the letter to Lucy*] There—Lucy'll read it for you—I am too much flurried—

Lu. [*Reading*] "Dearest girl, this will scarcely reach you, before I am with you myself; but lest anything should retard my coming an hour or two, let me beg Edward to have all in readiness for your marriage ceremony on my arrival, when I shall surprise you, I trust, agreeably. But be sure to remember the instructions in my last. Let our best friends be invited to meet me on my arrival. There are reasons for the request which, when you know them, will give you great delight."

Edw. How kind! How very kind!

Est. But how sudden—

Lu. That was always his way and always will be—

Edw. You know his passion for quick action and agreeable surprises is proverbial—

Est. Run, Lucy! Bid the housekeeper make all ready. Say that my father's coming on the instant! Oh, I could shout to the servants, to the people passing in the street, to my dear turtle doves, to all the world—"My father's coming! Look up! Rejoice! My dear, dear father's coming!" [*Exit Lucy. Estelle looking out, exclaims*] Ha! Here he is—My father! Here's my father! [*Morton enters in his hat and mantle. Estelle springs into his arms*]

Edw. My excellent friend!

Mor. Aye, Edward, a man of business, you see—true to the minute. 'Faith, the Italian sky has made me young again.

Est. How well you are looking.

Mor. Am I?—Ah, I feel as if I was. Oh, people never would be old, if they knew how to live. Well? The wedding?

Edw. We waited but for you.

Mor. Then wait no longer. Life ought not to be wasted in waiting. [*Enter Lucy*] Ha! Lucy? I'll answer for it, now, this busy little Lucy has been looking after the household affairs? Making ready for our guests.

Lu. Making ready to welcome our dear, dear friend.

Mor. Thanks—thanks—and you shall welcome one friend you never yet have dreamed of, any of you.

Lu. Sir, What? Hey?

Mor. How many have you ordered dinner for?

Lu. Nineteen.

Mor. One too few. There's to be twenty. You've omitted one.

Est. How can that be? Look—here's the list.

Edw. There are but nineteen here.

Mor. I tell you there must be twenty.

Lu. Well, then—we'll see where the twentieth can be put. First <Mr. Morton> at one end—Miss Estelle opposite—

Mor. Stop. Estelle will yield her place to the stranger. That settles it at once.

Est. Excellent.

Mor. On with your robes and have your wedding over, for the dinner must not be allowed to cool.

Est. Oh, papa!

Mor. Come, come. They who pause to think, never get married. Bustle, bustle—and Edward! Run and order the horses to the family carriage. It must be got ready to send off for our stranger guest. Dispatch—dispatch. [*Exit Edward. Enter Francis*]

Fr. A foreign servant asks to see you, sir.

Mor. Let him come up. [*Exit Francis*] And now, my love—prepare! Dry up your tears, and don't begin wedlock like a chapter of miseries, with a handkerchief at your eyes. [*Embraces Estelle, and she goes out. Galeazzo appears at the back. Turning, Morton sees him*] Galeazzo!

Gal. The signora Belmunda would be informed at what hour she is expected.

Mor. Instantly. The carriage is already ordered.

Gal. I haste to tell the signora.

Mor. You can return with it and attend her back.

Gal. Be it as you will.

Mor. Was her toilette over when you left?

Gal. Entirely.

Mor. And does she look beautiful?

Gal. [*Receding*] As the madonna of Ischia!

Mor. Stop, Galeazzo. A word with you about yourself. You are now the only being in America who knows the treasure I possess. You have been her faithful servant; while you live, you shall be mine.

Gal. Signor, when on the shore of Pozzuoli I forsook the bark which my father had bequeathed to me with liberty, and entered three years ago into the service of the signora Belmunda di Monte, I was content to take my place about her, next to her favorite dog. But it was for her I did it, not for her wages. To her I will be a slave till death—to others, I am—Galeazzo.

Mor. Do not mistake me, friend. I have no wish to interfere with the understanding between you on that point, which ceased to appear strange, when Belmunda told me your bark had saved her from the earthquake. The preserver of Belmunda never can receive aught but respect and gratitude from me.

Gal. Signor, I know it and thank you.

Mor. Soft—we must break off—take heed—no one here yet knows a word. [*Enter Edward in his bridegroom dress*]

Edw. My benefactor, the carriage is at the door.

Mor. [*To Galeazzo, who bows and is retiring*] You hear? [*To Edward*] Thanks, thanks, dear Edward. [*Galeazzo starts round at the name, and as he turns, he and Edward face each other, while Morton is looking the other way*]

GAL. Edward Somers! [*Morton turns and Galeazzo bows and exit. Estelle and Lucy enter at one of the side doors, in the dresses of bride and bridesmaid*]

MOR. Sweet girl, may all your days to come be as pure and beautiful as your looks are now.

EST. Dear papa, I thought the ceremony was to pass here in the house.

MOR. So it is, love.

EST. And yet I see your carriage at the door.

MOR. Ask Lucy the cause. I'll answer for it she has not allowed it to be there without finding out the reason why.

LU. I guessed the moment I heard. It is to be sent for the unknown.

EST. And who can this mysterious stranger be?

MOR. Ah! You would sooner give up your chance of a husband today than not know, little curiosity! True, hey? Don't be impatient. You'll know in good time. Look, if this mystery has not even thrown Edward into a brown study!

<EDW.> [*Starting from his reverie*] Me? Me?

EST. You don't know him, papa. He's not in the least curious. I don't believe he ever thought about it at all. Look at me, Edward. How do you like my new dress?

EDW. What? What?

LU. How can you expect a man who's going to be married can have his senses about him?

EST. Lord, how churlish and taciturn you are! I make myself as handsome as I can, and only to please you—and when I ask you how you like me, you stare and answer. What is it you mean? [*Enter Francis*]

FR. General Drummond. [*Bows and exit. Enter General Drummond*]

MOR. Ah, my old comrade! Well, are you married yet? Not still a bachelor, I hope?

DRUM. Yes, Morton, and what's worse, always like to be. Why, do you know, Morton, I am eight years older than you are? I am this day sixty-two years, three months and two days old.

MOR. Take a young wife, General. Nobody would believe you over forty.

DRUM. Whether they did or not, Morton, I should be none the less sixty-two years, three months and two days old. [*Enter Francis*]

FR. Mr. Hartley. [*Bows and exit. Enter Mr. Hartley*]

MOR. Our friend and patron, welcome! You have not forgotten this young man, I find, and I thank you for it, Hartley—thank you—thank you—

HART. How could so worthy a young man be forgotten? Faith, I expect to see him one of the first diplomatic characters in our country, and it will not be long, I trust, ere he has an opportunity of beginning his career most nobly. [*Enter Francis*]

FR. Mr. Thompson, Mrs. Belmour, Mr. and Mrs. Harrington. [*Bows and exit. The various guests enter and are welcomed*]

EDW. [*Apart, starting*] I hear the carriage. [*Francis enters and whispers to Morton, who starts, and Francis retires*]

MOR. [*Apart*] Now she comes—and with her, comes my trial! I did not think I should have felt thus strangely. I scarcely dare to look upon my daughter! Oh, should she fancy I shall love her less! [*Approaching her*] Estelle.

EST. Dear papa, what ails you? Your hand trembles, papa—

LU. [*At the other side of the stage, to Edward*] How pale you look, Edward. Are you ill?

EDW. Ill? Oh, no—I, ill? No, no—not ill—

MOR. My Estelle, if she to whom I am about to introduce you, should not prove all to you that I have thought she would, blame not your father, who has fondly fancied what was his happiness, must add to yours. [*Enter Galeazzo*]

GAL. The signora Morton! [*All start. Belmunda appears*]

EDW. [*Aside*] 'Tis she! [*Morton approaches and leads her to his daughter*]

MOR. Friends, I present you my Italian bride. [*To Belmunda*] Signora, this is the daughter that I told you of. You might be taken by the world for her sister.

BEL. But she, I hope, will find in me a mother. [*Kisses Estelle, who, thunderstruck, dares not lift her eyes*]

MOR. Now for the ceremony. You must know the bridegroom, love. I never told you anything about him that you might be the more agreeably surprised. I've long destined this for a day of unexpected pleasures and his acquaintance will not prove the least. Where is he? This way, young man. Don't be abashed. [*Leading Edward to her*] My son-in-law, Edward Somers!

BEL. [*Starting, aside*] Edward! [*Enter <Francis>*]

FR. The drawing room is prepared, and the clergyman has just come.

<MOR.> Away, then! Gentlemen, each lead your lady. <Edward>, be your new mother's escort. Mrs. Harrington, you and I will make a duo of it, with your leave. Strike, music! Now—away! [*Morton takes Mrs. Harrington; General Drummond offers his arm to Estelle; Mr. Hartley takes <Lucy>. Edward and Belmunda hesitate a moment as their eyes meet.*

Morton turns and exclaims] Well, what's the matter now? [*Edward offers his arm, which Belmunda accepts, and they go out first. The rest follow*]

GAL. [*Looks after them, and, when all are gone, exclaims*] Santa Maria! Oh, my brain is whirling! [*Rushes out*]

ACT II.

SCENE: *Another apartment in the mansion of <Mr. Morton>. Enter Galeazzo, alone.*

GAL. [*Alone*] The bridal is past; the bride is a bride's mother now; a new day dawns; but there's one here whose tired eyes the dawn finds open, as each dawn finds mine! Ha! <Morton> comes! Does his young wife's ill rest alarm the old man? [*Seeing a bunch of flowers upon the floor*] Soft— her bouquet fallen—another moment and some base step had crushed it. Here! [*Kisses it*] Sweet remembrancer! Here rest, safe from sacrilege! [*Enter Morton*]

MOR. Galeazzo, have you seen the signora?

GAL. She walks among yon trees.

MOR. Alone?

GAL. Behold her. [*Enter Belmunda. Exit Galeazzo*]

MOR. How's this, love? No mantle—no shawl—no bonnet—and when the air's so chilly, too.

BEL. [*Giving her hand*] Feel there.

MOR. This hand is burning.

BEL. [*With a melancholy smile*] Aye.

MOR. Look up.

BEL. Well.

MOR. The morning dew trembles in your ringlets.

BEL. My brow needs its coolness.

MOR. Your eyes are heavy—your cheeks are pale—

BEL. This climate of yours kills me. It is the air of America which withers the rose upon my cheek.

MOR. Then you shall seek a climate more congenial. My daughter is gone from me to a husband's arms, and I have nothing now to live for, but you and your felicity. You married me for your father's sake. I must teach you to love me for my own. The distracted condition of your father's affairs requires the immediate attention of a man skilled in business, which he is not, nor is anyone about him. Our union has extricated him from bankruptcy, but I should poorly merit the inestimable prize I've won from him in you, did I withhold any effort to make the father of such a wife as permanently happy and independent as she would wish to see him. If you at any time feared you were to sacrifice all you prized on earth to filial duty—

BEL. No more! No more!

MOR. Nay, sob not thus—you shall feel your error.

BEL. I do! I do!

MOR. For my life shall be devoted to convincing you that your fears were groundless. And were I to restore you to the clime where your heart was joyous and your fancy revelling in wild, glorious dreams, perhaps you might forget the selfishness of the robbery which took you for a little moment to skies oftener clouded, and where your warm heart cannot feel at home.

BEL. Oh, you are the best, the most generous of created beings! Yes—you are right—you are right—I ought upon the instant to quit America. Morton, did Estelle love Edward?

MOR. Not violently, perhaps, but—

BEL. Why did she marry him, then?

MOR. Oh, she loved him as—as you said once that you loved me. When I questioned her in the outset of the intimacy, she told me she liked Edward a little more than Lucy and a little less than her father.

BEL. And you call that love to marry for?

MOR. Come to your boudoir and repose—come—you need rest.

BEL. No, no—I am better now. [Apart] "A little more than <Lucy> and a little less than her father." [Aloud] Oh, I am much better now.

MOR. I see how it is. The very thought of Naples has revived you. Oh, if the expectation of return acts thus like magic on you, what wonders may we not hope from the reality?

BEL. You must not make yourself an exile from your own land for me. What! Resign country—family—friends—I don't deserve it from you. No, <Morton>—no, no—I shall conquer this distaste for America—and if I should not? What matter whether I live or die, Morton?

MOR. Die? Talk not thus, Belmunda, but at once decide for our departure. And when, arrived at our destination, we pass together through the beautiful spot of your birth, if there escape from me a sigh when my thoughts turn back to America, there, from the rock of Capri or the promontory of Muniscola, you will exclaim as you point to the fair city smiling from its throne upon its beautiful bay, "There! there is Naples! Naples, banished from which I should have died. Naples, which I never hoped to see again, but which I now look upon with rapture, and this I owe to the gratitude of my husband!" You will say this to me, won't you? And at the exulting tone of your voice, the delighted flashing of your eye, I shall forget that you were

ever sad—I shall forget—oh, I shall forget even my beloved native land in
one fond kiss—and wild with joy, reply, "Ah, Belmunda! Whatever I may
give up for you, you have deserved from me more than a millionfold in the
bestowal of your love!"

BEL. No more, I supplicate, no more. Leave me—leave me alone—I would
meditate—I would weep.

MOR. Tears but of joy, then, since tomorrow we begin our dispositions
for returning with a <ll> possible speed to Naples. It was indispensable that
I sh<ould> be here to marry off my daughter and settle her and Edward
<on an> estate some twenty miles up the country which I have destined
for them. Thither I must accompany them; but this little journey would be
useless fatigue for you; so you can r<emain> here meanwhile and rest.
Tomorrow, you will see <me> again. [*Rings. Francis appears*] Prepare the
cabriolet. [*<Francis> bows and retires*]

BEL. Why not the barouche? Does Ed<ward> remain here?

MOR. I have a world of things to say to Est<elle and this> is my only
chance to get her by herself for any time. <These> young lovers—

BEL. [*Aside, shuddering*] Lovers!

MOR. Are so hard to be kept asunder e<specially> while their honey-
moon lasts. Therefore Edward mus<t precede> us on horseback by himself. I shall return upon his <horse>. But, mark me! Estelle must not be
told of my in<tention to> cross the ocean so soon. It would turn her bridal
<joy into> sadness. You are looking very weary, love. Really, you have
<need> of this interval to recruit your strength. But the future is arranged
to your liking; surely you can afford me one little sm<ile.> Smile, smile,
Belmunda—I need your <help> to sustain me under the thought of thus
doubly <dealing> with my darling child. [*Kisses her and exit*]

BEL. [*Alone*] "She loves him a little more than she loves Lucy and a little
less than she loves her father!" Ha! Can the cold Estelle efface the memory
of Belmunda? "Return to Naples!" Aye. It is fitting. There is no other way.
But to depart just as I have beheld him again, and found the slumbering fire
blaze up with ten-fold fierceness at his unlooked-for presence? "A little more
than Lucy and a little less than her father!" My heart beats more freely since
he told me that! Soft—Galeazzo!—[*Galeazzo appears at the door*]

GAL. Signora—

BEL. What would you?

GAL. A letter. [*Handing one from his bosom*]

BEL. Whence?

GAL. From him.

BEL. Ha!

GAL. He is almost mad.

BEL. From what cause?

GAL. The signora Belmunda.

BEL. Did he name me to you?

GAL. On what theme but you should he converse with me?

BEL. Rash youth!

GAL. Rather say, wretched—wretched—wretched—

BEL. What should make him so?

GAL. Love.

BEL. [*Faltering*] Does he—

GAL. He loves as when at Naples.

BEL. Ha!

GAL. He does not speak of it, but he loves you still; still as from the moment when he led you and your mother to my barge amid the earthquake—

BEL. True—true—it had escaped my memory for the moment that you had been with us ever since that hour—that dreadful hour—

GAL. Would that I, too, could dwell on it so lightly!

BEL. He expects, doubtless—

GAL. A reply.

BEL. Can you guard a secret?

GAL. For three years there has been one buried here which no mortal has yet even guessed at.

BEL. Tell him I will convey my answer to him in person.

GAL. [*Starts*] In person? He shall be told. [*Bows and exit. When Galeazzo goes out, Belmunda opens the letter in haste and agitation and reads in a hurried and confused and startled manner*]

BEL. "Implore you to unriddle the mystery of your marriage and of your presence here—glad that you, as I have done, gave no intimation of ever having seen me before—Mr. Morton—best of men, but sensitive, quick-tempered and wrong-headed—better for him and all, to remain entirely unapprised—" [*Seeing Estelle approaching*] Ha! His wife! [*Hurries the letter into her bosom and repeats, emphatically and in a tone of anguish*] His wife! [*Enter Estelle*]

EST. [*Aside, looking at her*] How strange it is! She seems to have the same unaccountable repugnance to meeting me, that I have in accosting her!

BEL. [*Aside*] "A little more than Lucy and a little less than her father!" [*Aloud*] Madam—

EST. "Madam?" Oh, if you call me madam, I never shall be able to call you mother.

BEL. You need not, if you do not like.

EST. But papa looks so hurt when I do not.

BEL. It costs you an effort, then, to call me mother?

EST. You are so young that it would seem much more natural to call you sister; and I am sure we should be like sisters, if we were better acquainted; and were there no other reason for wishing to prevent your returning so soon to Naples, the hope of that would be enough without the rest.

BEL. Who told you we were going? Your father said he should not pain you with the intelligence suddenly.

EST. Edward told me.

BEL. Edward!

EST. And I promised I would do my best to prevail upon my father not to go.

BEL. Edward desired you to prevent our departure?

EST. And if the most eager desire can give me eloquence, I *will* prevent it.

BEL. Poor child!

EST. And you will add your prayer to mine—yes, yes, I know you will! You will not let my dear, dear father leave me. With two women against him—oh, with two—it would be hard indeed if a man should not give way against such odds.

BEL. I fear we should appeal in vain. There are reasons for the departure which cannot be set aside.

EST. Oh, my lady—

BEL. But as you cannot bear to quit your father, one way can be found— one way by which his views may be brought to meet yours.

EST. Oh, name it! Name it quickly!

BEL. The journey can be made without depriving you of your father.

EST. How?

BEL. You can come with us.

EST. And Edward?

BEL. Oh, Edward cannot quit America without sacrificing his prospects, you know. What would become of the appointment he expects? It would be madness for him to quit America.

EST. But, dear mama, I could not think of going without Edward.

BEL. How?

EST. No, not one step will I stir without Edward.

BEL. Reflect. You must either part with your father or your husband.

EST. I remain, then, with my husband.

BEL. Your husband, whom you love only a little more than Lucy, and a little less than your father?

EST. True—before we were married.

BEL. Since you were married, then—

EST. Mark. [*Mysteriously*] You need not tell papa, for it might hurt his feelings, as I do not think he would understand me as you can, who are a woman. Though I did not care so much about Edward in the beginning—for I had never seen him when my father first thought of making him my husband—and, indeed, knowing that, before I knew him, gave me almost a dislike—still, after a while, all of a sudden a wonderful change came over me. I could think, I could dream of no one but him. I cannot tell you how glad it made me when I found that change was love.

BEL. Girl! But your father—your father—then you no longer love your father—

EST. Not so, not so. I do not love him less than I did, but I love Edward more.

BEL. [*Apart*] Torture! [*Aloud*] And Edward?

EST. [*Sighing*] Oh, as for Edward—

BEL. [*Exultingly*] What of Edward?

EST. I dare say he loves me well enough, though he seems, ever since you came, so absent, so gloomy, so full of strange starts; and, now and then, I've caught tears standing in his eyes—but I've found out the reason.

BEL. You?

EST. Yes. When I think of the past, when I recall the indifference I had for him so long, I almost wonder that he should ever have brought himself to care about me at all. Oh, if I could bring back those days of coldness which I doubt he now remembers deeply! But I will make him forget them in my redoubled efforts to deserve his devotedness in the days to come. The future is in my power, and I will make it atone for the failures of the past. Oh, mama, how I long to have you here to aid me in securing the affections of Edward, and to exult with me in my success. No, no—you must not go. Join your supplications with mine, dear mama, that I may not lose my father, in remaining, as my heart prompts me, with my husband.

BEL. [*Apart*] She loves him! Wretched creature that I am, she loves him! And I, in the confusion of despair, for a moment madly dreamed of decoying her away from him! Oh, despicable fool! Yet to leave them together—together!

EST. Hark! Some one comes! Oh, if it should be my father! No—look, mama, look! 'Tis dear Edward. See, how pale he is—how grief-worn! [*Enter Edward. The moment he appears Estelle runs to him. Belmunda recedes and hastily writes with pencil, looking off at them momently as she writes; then folding the paper, thrusts it into her bosom*] Husband! Darling husband!

EDW.   Have you seen him?

EST.   Not yet, love.

EDW.   Where is he, then?

EST.   Gone to give some directions to the servants. Why look so strangely at me, Edward? Come, come. You shan't be sad. One kiss to your wife, and she will run and fetch him. [*He kisses her*]

BEL.   [*Aside, seeing them in each other's arms*]   Have mercy, fiends!

EST.   But lo! He comes, he comes! [*Enter Morton*] Father—dear father —surely you will not think of quitting us so soon. Promise that you will not—

MOR.   [*Confused, pointing to Belmunda*]   I have already promised—

EST.   To her—to her—I know. But she is all kindness and would not make us wretched. Speak, Edward, add your supplications to mine, that our home may not again be made desolate.

EDW.   [*Significantly and emphatically*]   Lady, one word from you, and we are happy. [*She is silent*]

EST.   Oh, that vast Atlantic and the still more distant Mediterranean— with them dividing us, it will seem as though we were separated by the gulf between time and eternity.

MOR.   But our separation will end sooner than the one which is just over, and when we come back, dear [*Jocosely*], you will have had so much of Edward's company, that you will then be all the better situated to get a respite from it awhile and devote yourself to your father—

EST.   Never can my devotedness change either towards him [*Taking Edward's hand*] or you. [*Embracing Morton*]

BEL.   [*Aside*]   She loves Edward!

<EDW.> [*Low to Belmunda*]   Not a syllable in answer? [*Enter Galeazzo*]

GAL.   [*Comes down*]   The cabriolet of Mr. Morton and the horse of Mr. Somers are at the door.

MOR.   Come, come, my daughter. Bid your mother adieu—

EST.   It must be so, then! It must be so, and I must lose my father! Farewell, lady, farewell! You might have promised not to take from me one I love so dearly.

EDW.   [*Low to Belmunda*]   Lady, not one word—

BEL.   [*Low, giving him the letter*]   There—go—go—go. [*Rushes into the apartment*]

Edw. [*Low, but exultingly*]   No, she has not forgotten!

Mor. [*Apart*]   She dreads my daughter's agitation may sway her from her voyage and has escaped to shun it. [*Aloud*] Galeazzo, I need not bid you see that your lady lacks no attention. And *certes you'll* not be in the opposition to my approaching return with her to your native Italy, since you are to make one of the party, Galeazzo. Come, my children.

Est.   Edward!

Edw. [*As if startled from a dream*]   Aye—aye—away—it grows late—away. [*Exeunt all but Galeazzo*]

Gal. [*Alone*]   Away! Oh, how musical to my ear sounds that word "away"! Away for Italy—away for Naples! Naples which I shall behold once more—behold with the signora Belmunda, freed from the presence of that Edward Somers whom I detest! Edward Somers, whom I shall leave behind, more wretched than myself, for he will no longer view my noble mistress—while I feast my eyes upon her hourly! Aye, I shall be happier than Edward Somers! Young American, how would you exult to exchange your lofty and your affluent station for that of the poor and lowly fisherman of Naples now! Oh, gulf of Ischia, whose waves rocked my infancy in the fishing bark of my father! Oh, pure and beautiful sky of my native land, of you shall I now once more dream, for this night I shall sleep: no agonizing intruder will disturb my this night's visions. This night I shall sleep. Belmunda passes this night alone—alone! Breathe, Galeazzo, breathe! Galeazzo, revel! Be for a moment happy! [*Starting*] Ha! What sound was that? A hurried step—Edward! Edward returned and by himself! What brings him back thus suddenly? He will not stay—no, no—he cannot mean to stay. [*Enter Francis with two lights*] Ho! Whither, friend?

Fr.   To the apartment of Mr. Somers.

Gal.   Is he come back?

Fr.   His horse stumbled and was lamed. [*Enters the chamber. The stage is in darkness*]

Gal. [*Alone, sinking on a chair*]   A curse on him! A curse! a curse! [*Enter Edward, not observing Galeazzo*]

Edw. [*Low, the letter open in his hand*]   Precious remembrancer of love's first dream! [*Kisses it*] Nobly has fortune seconded my purpose! [*Recalling phrases in the letter*] She has studiously, till now, avoided an unwitnessed interview. She cannot bear to part without one word in explanation of the apparently inconsistent and ungrateful conduct forced upon her by events and by her friends at Naples. For this, her last adieu, I must contrive to linger a brief while and come when unobserved to her boudoir. Aye —the fall of the horse accounts for the return—the waiting for another excuses the delay. And yet I know not why, but my heart sinks within me at this interview. Courage! Courage, Edward Somers! Now for the momentary meeting, then to meet no more! [*Turning towards the door of Belmunda, faces Galeazzo, starts and crumples the paper confusedly into his bosom*] Galeazzo!

GAL. Signor—

EDW. What brings you here, Galeazzo? What brings you here?

GAL. [*Having involuntarily and unconsciously drawn his stiletto*] I wait to know if my mistress has anything to command tonight.

EDW. [*Striving to see what he has in his hand*] And in the interim you are—

GAL. Playing with my stiletto, that's all.

EDW. Aye—the favorite weapon of your country, is it not?

GAL. And one whose blow is mortal.

EDW. [*After a moment's pause*] The signora—

GAL. Oh, she is here, signor.

EDW. [*Looks at him a moment, then pauses*] 'Tis well—you may retire. [*Galeazzo bows. Edward hesitates an instant, then turns suddenly and enters his own room. Francis comes out. He passes Galeazzo, but at the wing turns and speaks*]

FR. Are you coming, Galeazzo?

GAL. Presently.

FR. Goodnight.

GAL. Goodnight. [*Exit Francis. Galeazzo, alone*] What! Pray for a good night to Galeazzo, while the torturing demon of his life is there. [*Pointing to Edward's room*] Farewell, wild hope of happy dreams, farewell! Oh, never shall I sleep again in peace, no, never! He is in yonder chamber and alone. Oh, Galeazzo, where's the Italian, who, in thy place—this good stiletto in his grasp—but it may all be accident—she cannot know it—she—hush! Did I not hear—umph! Steps approach this door—this door—they falter—ha! Have I perplexed your dark clandestine rambles? [*Cowers down towards the door of Edward's apartment*] Now they stir again—the footfall grows more distinct—now more—ha! The door opens! 'Tis he! [*Recoiling*] Whither goes he? [*Edward, pale and trembling, appears upon the threshold of his door, pressing his hand to his bosom, as if to still the beatings of his heart. He glides cautiously, gazes around to watch if anyone is within view, listens, crosses the stage, places his hand upon the knob of Belmunda's door, pauses a moment to wipe his brow, then enters. Galeazzo follows him in the darkness, still paler and more trembling, ready to throw the stiletto, which, when he perceives the door of Belmunda ajar, he flings with a wild laugh*] Ha! Ha! Ha! [*Rushes out*]

ACT III.

SCENE: *A more richly decorated apartment than the last. Three doors at the back, opening into another magnificent suite of rooms, with chandeliers and splendid furniture. Enter Edward, meeting Mr. Hartley.*

EDW. Mr. Hartley, this is most kind. I called at your house because I was anxious to see you about what you were suggesting—you remember? The mission to Guatemala—how attentive of you, to return my call so promptly. Has the nomination gone in? If it has, I would accept it on the instant—aye, and gratefully.

HART. Then I think you may make your mind easy; for two days ago I received a letter from Washington assuring me that it has not only been sent to the Senate, but a favorable report has been made upon it by the Committee on Foreign Relations, and it was to have been brought up yesterday finally in Executive Session. No doubt today's mail is in. I will hurry home and bring you the result at once—

EDW. Oh, no—don't give yourself that trouble. Leave it till night. We are to see you at our party tonight?

HART. Of course you are. Do you think I would be absent from the anniversary of your wife's eighteenth birthday? I, who knew her before she knew herself. By the bye, is it not almost time for your father-in-law to return? Why, it is at least six weeks, is it not, since he went to New Orleans?

<EDW.> Full. He finds great difficulty in settling the dispute about the plantation which was left to him there just as he was preparing to embark for Italy. I should not wonder if it detained him at least six weeks longer.

<HART.> The signora your mother was looking amazingly well last Thursday at the ball. Is her intended return to Naples entirely given up?

EDW. Since the sudden illness which prevented her departing the day after my wedding, I have heard no more of it.

HART. Oh, she's getting more reconciled to America, now she knows it better. People are generally homesick when they first come to a country new to them; but I dare say you will manage among you to make her forget Italy altogether in time. She's a charming creature! I should not much like to have such a mother-in-law always near my husband, were I your wife, Edward. Apropos—I forgot to ask—is Estelle better?

EDW. I hope she will be shortly. [*Sighing*]

Hart. I hope so too. I never saw a girl so changed in so short a time.

Edw. Do you think there is really a hope of the mission we spoke of? Will it take me thither speedily? Speedily?

Hart. How impatient you are all of a sudden! You forget it is your own fault that you were not off somewhere long ago. But when I urged it, you always had some pretext for lingering. Will you have the mission, do you ask? There's not a man in the United States that stands so good a chance, I can tell you; so, farewell, and when you see me again, I doubt not I shall bring what *you* desire and *I* can almost promise. Till then, adieu! [*Exit <Hartley>*]

Edw. [*Alone*] Oh, if Belmunda fancied I were about to quit her! But it must be. I trifle with my peace and with her happiness and that of all around me, by remaining. Oh, how blind passion fooled me when I exulted at the accident which delayed her projected return to Naples and flung her as an inmate under my own roof during her new husband's absence! But we are only at the precipice's edge. Be it my care that neither of us fall. [*Flings himself on a chair, where he sits, pensively, while Belmunda gaily enters on tiptoe, gets behind him, and leans over his shoulder. He starts*] Ha!

Bel. What! Have I startled you from your day-dream? Ah, that's an ill thing in anyone as this world goes. What were life but for its dreams, Edward? Since mine has been a dream, it has been happy.

Edw. And are you happy, then?

Bel. Aye, when in the wild whirl of society, when, amid the intoxication of lights and music, eyes may meet unobserved, hands touch unseen, and love breathe its whisper not dreading to be guilty or fearing to be heard. Oh, then, I can for a moment think that I am happy, for then, Edward, I dream. Never had society, never had the gay dance, the romantic play, the crowded promenade such charms for me as now.

Edw. I fear, on the return of my father—

Bel. Edward, that word has waked me! With that word starts up a specter to fright the fairy forms that circled me, and I am left alone and desolate!

Edw. Nay, nay, Belmunda—

Bel. I ought not to have remained in the same country with you. I ought not to have trusted myself with the dangerous delight of society like yours, for I should have known there may be a guilt which in the world's eye is innocence, though that unsinning guilt brings its sure anguish. My heart rebels, although my deeds are loyal. And when they call me exemplary wife, I sicken at the praise—I know I am all hypocrite!

Edw. Be calm. With what can you reproach yourself?

BEL. With this: with giving way to the delirious hope that I might continue the mastery over my feelings which enabled me to resign you at my father's bidding and when I thought you dead, accept another; and that I might continue that mastery without again parting with him whom I had left so lightly. But oh! The consciousness that I am bound for life—for life—while I see you hourly and know you to be lost to me—makes him they call my husband hateful. And then I picture him arrayed in vengeance. Did I not start when last night they sang that touching song—and wildly run to hide me in my chamber? All thought it was the song. I heard no song—<Edward>, it was remorse—

EDW. For what?

BEL. That my heart should be less blameless than my conduct; that I should not have conquered even my thoughts, for erring thoughts are crimes and their retribution, if we repress them not, despair. Mine make me mad with terror—

EDW. Terror?

BEL. Aye, of myself, my husband; of your wife, too, whose calm, clear eye seems fixed on me when none beside can see her, and silently speaks daggers. [*Enter Francis*]

FR. Mr. Morton's carriage is entering the courtyard. [*Bows and exit*]

EDW. Here? Here? And so unlooked for!

BEL. Now you have lost your self-possession, while I am calm and ready for the meeting.

EDW. I am—I am unmanned. Oh, Belmunda, what must guilt be, when but the consciousness of how near we are to guilt, can thus overwhelm the innocent!

BEL. I am the best dissembler. Did I not tell you I was all hypocrite? Go in. Let me receive him. How can he know whether my cheek is red with shame or joy? [*Exit Edward. Morton is heard outside*]

MOR. [*Outside*] But where's Belmunda? Is not Belmunda coming? [*Enter Morton with Estelle*]

EST. Here, father, she is here.

MOR. [*Embracing her*] You might have been kind enough, love, to come down and bid one welcome. Estelle, Lucy, and all the household came, while you—

BEL. I was just going as you entered. I had not expected your return so soon.

MOR. True, true. How unreasonable I was to think you could be on the alert to welcome one you could not have expected. But the truth is I'm jealous even of the suspicion of a slight from you. Ah, I'm afraid I love you more than you deserve, wench! And what's worse, there's no help for it, when you're looking—why you are looking lovelier than ever, darling! I wish I could say as much for Estelle, poor child! Did you ever witness such an alteration! What has been the matter with you, Estelle?

Est. [*With a melancholy smile*] Oh, nothing—nothing—but, look! Here's Edward. This way, Edward, this way. See, here's our father! [*Enter Edward*]

Edw. My dear sir—

Mor. "My dear Mr. Morton—dear Mr. Morton"—how formal! Have you lost your senses, Edward? What have you all been about since I was gone? You seem in a strange way, all of you.

Edw. Oh, my father—

Mor. Why, if anything, Edward, you look more miserable than your wife! How dare you look miserable, any of you, on my Estelle's birthday? 'Faith, when I found I had brought my business to a close, and might by hard travelling get here in time to keep it with you, trust me, I did not spare myself night or day. Come, Belmunda. We must make ourselves interesting for the occasion, and, hang it, love, I've so many things to say to you that I don't see how I am to spare you out of my sight long enough for you to make your toilette. Come along, dearest, or we shall be too late for the young folks. [*Exeunt Morton and Belmunda. Edward is following*]

Est. Edward—*you* are not going to leave me? Leave me thus, too!

Edw. I beg your pardon, I—I—

Est. One word and I release you.

Edw. Estelle!

Est. My father thought me pale and altered, love.

Edw. I, too, have remarked it, and it grieved me.

Est. You never asked the cause.

Edw. The cause, did you say? The cause?

Est. 'Tis this: I'm very, very wretched.

Edw. Ha! How can that be? Wherefore?

Est. Because Edward don't love me as he did.

Edw. Estelle!

Est. No, you don't love me now, Edward, and it must be through some unconscious fault of mine; but I have examined my conduct rigidly and I cannot find that I have not always been the same to you, with this only difference: I love you more than ever.

Edw. And what can lead you to suppose that my affection is failing?

Est. Everything. Do your best to dissemble your indifference, there is an instinct in the heart which will not be deceived, Edward. Even while you listen to me now, your mind is elsewhere, love, and I annoy, I weary you. One sole request—but one—and I have done.

Edw.   Speak.

Est.   Be careless as you will of concealing your coldness from me, but do not, oh, do not let my father see it. It would break his heart. In his presence, be attentive and affectionate as you once were. And then, when we shall be alone, if you do not speak to me, if you do not look on me, I will not ask a question, nor utter a complaint. I will even keep my own apartment and you may remain away from me in yours, provided my father is not allowed to know it and I to see his tears. Yes, I am strong enough for that. I am strong enough to bear anything, Edward, except to see my father's tears. That I could never bear.

Edw.   Estelle, dearest Estelle, you know—you know I love you.

Est.   [*Taking his hand and placing it on his heart*]   Ah, what you say does not come from there—now, does it? It is not spoken with that tone of other days which lent your words persuasion, which would have led me to believe even the impossible. No, Edward. I seek no protestations for myself, I seek no more than I have mentioned. You'll seem to love me before papa, will you not?

Edw.   I will—I will. Pity me, Estelle. Give me your pity and your pardon. There shall be a change, a mighty change, and suddenly.

Est.   You appal me! What's the matter?

Edw.   Nothing—nothing, at least, which you should wish to know. I have a sorrow here. Here let it rest unquestioned.

Est.   If you loved me, you would not keep your sorrows from me, Edward.

Edw.   Again!

Est.   No, no, no, I did not mean—

Edw.   Solitude, love, nothing but solitude can compose me now. For a brief while I'll leave you; but prepare to learn from me arrangements for my future life, which will be sure to heal your broken spirits, to make you happy.

Est.   Whatever plan you arrange is sure to be the best. [*Smiling*] Adieu.

Edw.   Dearest, adieu! [*Apart*] Agony! [*Rushes out. Enter Lucy*]

Lu.   Was not that Edward that went out?

Est.   It was.

Lu.   He seemed strangely discomposed—and bless me! Your eyes are full of tears.

Est.   Tears? No, no. Tears? What should bring tears into my eyes?

Lu.   Why, girl, they are in your very voice. Don't strive to suppress that sob—

Est.   Oh, Lucy!

Lu.   Give way to all you feel. Wretched and not tell your friend the cause? For shame!

Est.   Lucy, darling Lucy—oh, would that I dared to tell it.

Lu.   You will find some relief even in talking of your affliction. Come—what is it?

Est.   Oh, it is a terrible feeling which tears my heart, which tortures me! A torment of which I had no conception. Oh, Lucy, Lucy, I am jealous.

Lu.   Jealous? Of whom?

Est.   Of whom could I be, but Edward?

Lu.   Edward?

Est.   Yes.

Lu.   Has he been false to you?

Est.   Yes, yes. Is it not horrible? I, who loved him so! He loves another. He loves a different person altogether from his Estelle.

Lu.   I can't believe it!

Est.   I'm sure of it.

Lu.   What makes you think so?

Est.   Listen. He receives letters which he conceals from me. The other day I saw one come to him. He trembled as he read it and hurried it into his bosom—next his heart, Lucy! Oh, you can form no imagination of what jealousy is! It freezes up every gentler feeling, and—only to think of it!—prevents our seeing things even as we know they really are.

Lu.   And those letters?

Est.   I have noticed where he hides them; for, twenty times—I am ashamed to own it to you, Lucy, but twenty times have I been upon the point—it would have been wrong, wouldn't it?

Lu.   Where *does* he hide them, then?

Est.   In a secret drawer of the chiffonier in my boudoir. He puts them in a pocketbook where I am sure there are a great many, and he locks up the pocketbook in that drawer.

Lu.   And can you have a jealousy of that sort and not make sure whether you are in the right?

Est.   How can I?

Lu.   I can see but one way.

Est.   Oh, but that would be so mean!

Lu.   Most likely, though, he takes good care not to leave the key in your way.

Est.   [*Taking a key from her bosom*] I have a second one of which he never knew. Indeed, I never thought of it myself until this affair happened, and then I would not name it to him, because he might guess my suspicions of the use he made of that drawer, which, if one can't help having, one can, at least, help exposing.

Lu.   Shall I go help you open it?

Est.   Oh, no, no! If Edward were to come in and find us together!

Lu.   Well, go by yourself, then.

Est.   I should feel so guilty reading letters in that wrong way.

Lu.   Then bring the pocketbook to me unopened. I will look it over, and afterwards I'll tell you what a little simpleton you are to make yourself so uneasy about letters of business, which you have taken for letters of love; and so you'll run back with them and be happier than ever and say that Lucy is the kindest creature in the world for having relieved you from such un-called-for misery.

Est.   You'll not tell, Lucy? Oh, I feel how right you are. I am so wretched that I shall die if I don't put an end to this uncertainty at once. And if I am doing what I ought not, I don't mean any harm; and, oh! may the innocence of my intentions bring me pardon!

Lu.   Courage. I'll wait here. Be sure you bring them. [*Estelle, after some faltering, goes into her boudoir, as Morton enters*]

Mor.   Lucy.

Lu.   [*Who is still gazing earnestly after Estelle, starts*] Ha! Oh, it is you, is it? I was so frightened. I thought it might be—

Mor.   Where is Estelle?

Lu.   Estelle? Oh, I'm sure—I—with her husband, I fancy—with her husband.

Mor.   [*Crossing*] Umph.

Lu.   [*Detaining him*] She's coming back here.

Mor.   [*Turning to her*] I have a question to ask you, Lucy. I have noticed how pale and worn Estelle is grown. I am really very uneasy about her. Has she anything upon her mind?

Lu.   [*Hesitating*] Upon her mind? Y—y—yes.

Mor.   And who can have the heart to distress such an angel?

Lu.   Oh, when people are once married—

Mor.   What do you mean? You don't mean to insinuate that Edward has anything to do with it.

Lu.   Hark. You'll not say a word?

Mor.   Speak.

Lu.   It *is* Edward.

Mor.   I'll seek him instantly and know—

Lu. [*Detaining him*] No, no, don't stir, I implore. Estelle may be mistaken.

Mor. Mistaken or not, Edward is a man of honor and will not hesitate to answer a plain question.

Lu. No, no. Believe me, you had better wait. Estelle will be certain presently.

Mor. How can that be?

Lu. [*Trembling*] L—l—l—letters.

Mor. Letter in the possession of Estelle?

Lu. N—n—no. Not letters that she dare open. She's gone to bring them here to me, and so she and I were—

Mor. [*Angrily*] Leave me, Lucy.

Lu. But Estelle, when she returns—

Mor. Will find a father here in whom I hope she would as soon confide as in her friend.

Lu. Very well, sir.

Mor. Desire the signora, I pray you, to be ready as soon as possible, and order the rooms to be lit up at once.

Lu. You'll not be angry with me?

Mor. [*Less sternly*] No, no, child. But—go—go—go. [*Exit Lucy. Enter Estelle, pale and trembling, not seeing Morton*]

Est. Here, Lucy, here they are. [*Perceiving Morton, she hides the pocketbook behind her*]

Mor. [*Coldly*] Estelle, give me that pocketbook.

Est. That—that—

Mor. I know all, Estelle.

Est. [*Throwing herself into his arms and bursting into tears*] Ah, father, father!

Mor. Dear, dear, unhappy girl! And you think the letters are from a rival?

Est. I am sure they are.

Mor. And thinking so, were about to entrust a child, a mischief-loving, prying, heedless girl like Lucy with a secret of such deep importance! These letters, Estelle, contain some woman's disgrace—it may even be some doting husband's, too—and you would fling their reputation to the winds.

Est. I see my error. I own it. I was mad. I knew not what I did.

Mor. Give me the letters.

Est. Here they are, my father. If they are not a woman's, own all to Edward, and implore him to forgive me. But oh, my father, should the worst be true, give me back the pocketbook. Let me restore it to the place I took it from, but never let me know that woman's name. I should hate her!

Then strain your daughter to your heart, close, close. Let her feel a father's fondness circling her, for I shall have great need, dear father, of your love and pity then! But be it as it may, forgive Edward, as I, in advance, forgive him!

Mor. Fear not, my child. I shall be just and prudent.

Est. One kiss, papa. There—that will bring me good fortune. Adieu! Adieu! If I have wronged him, don't keep me waiting, father. Let me know it soon, oh, very, very soon! [*During this dialogue, the back room, where the servants have been passing to and fro, is lighted up*]

Mor. [*Alone*] Poor child! So young, to have such sorrows! Edward's confusion struck me when I arrived—aye, and Estelle's pale cheek. A secret of such danger so nearly in the power of two rash girls! How fortunate that I should have entered at the moment I did! Now, then, to see—[*Opening the pocketbook*] A miniature! Some female face! [*Taking it to a light*] Belmunda! The picture of Belmunda in the possession of Edward! How chances this? Oh, some mistake—some carelessness of hers. The letters— come, the letters. Heaven and earth! Her hand, too! [*Reading*] "Beware of awakening my husband's suspicions. Your wife is jealous. Make her not unhappy." My curse upon them! [*Sinks on a chair*] But, no [*Laughing hysterically*], no, no, I rave. It cannot be. My sight is failing, and I read it wrong. Come, I'll be sure. These eyes—these eyes—what strange cloud is it gathering o'er these eyes? More in her handwriting. More? "Our feelings must be conquered. Let me bear my own misery as I may, silently, while I drag on this wretched life. When that is over, be even its memories buried with me in the grave." Despair and madness! All now flashes on me! 'Twas she—she was the nameless wonder he had known in some strange way at Naples. 'Twas she he loved, and I have brought her to him! Hell and ruin! Help! Help! Give me something to dash in pieces. I would crush, tear, destroy! Edward Somers, woe, woe upon thy head! Death to thee, Edward Somers! Blood—I must have blood, hot blood! [*Darts towards his apartment and suddenly stops short*] Umph. But an explosion here must be accounted for, a quarrel here must have its cause made public. Fool! Madman! No, no, I'll be revenged but not be jeered at. No coxcomb sneers at the fond, doting fool who could not keep his young wife three months faithful. I'll find a pretext for deadly quarrel which shall not point to the true provocation. Yes, I'll foil the laughing malice of the world and yet not die unsatisfied. Hide here, great vengeance, hide, hide though your serpent coil tightening around my heart even now has taken my breath away. I'm strangling—strangling. [*Falls on a chair, convulsed. Enter Francis*]

Fr. General Drummond, Mr. Montgomery, Mr. Wilson. [*Bows and exit*]

<Mor.> [*Looking out*] What men are those coming hither? What do they want here? [*Observing the dress of the guests as they enter*] Oh! A party? Aye, I remember, my daughter's birthday. Yes, yes. [*General Drummond enters, followed by other guests, male and female*]

Drum. My best congratulations to my friend, Morton. Days like these are proud ones to a father. 'Faith, they almost make me sorry to have deserved your jokes and put me out of humor with myself for never having taken a wife. Morton, I envy what you must feel at this moment.

Mor. [*Laughing wildly*] Aye, do, do. I *should* be envied. Is't not a glorious day? Aye, glorious! [*Enter Francis*]

Fr. Mr. Hartley. [*Enter Mr. Hartley*]

Hart. I meet you on this occasion with more than common pleasure. But where is Edward? I must see him, and then, Morton, I shall have something to tell you about Edward.

Mor. You? You? How should I know where he is?

Fr. Mr. Somers is in his room.

Hart. Excuse me. I'll have one word with him and then return. [*To Francis*] Show me to him. [*Francis bows and exit. Mr. Hartley follows him. Belmunda enters through the center door*]

Bel. Ladies, I am charmed to see you. Gentlemen, you are most welcome. General, will you join them in the next room at whist?

Mor. No, the General remains with me. Look to those ladies. [*A servant at the back announces several ladies. Belmunda receives them gracefully and speaks separately to each*]

Bel. [*To a young lady*] My dear, I never saw you looking half so pretty. Come, ladies, shall we go to the ballroom? Estelle and Lucy are both there and only wait for you to begin the dance. Come, dear. You shall have your old bachelor friend for a partner who is so fond of making—you know who—jealous. [*At the word "jealous" Morton starts and turning, sees Edward, who is just entering with Mr. Hartley and is brought by the changing movements of the groups, directly in face of Belmunda, as she is leading out her friends. They pause and gaze for an instant, as if intending to speak*]

Hart. Signora, I—

Bel. [*Suddenly and confusedly, observing the eye of Morton fixed on her and Edward*] Shall we—shall we—

Mor. [*Aside, noticing her confusion*] Ha!

Bel. Shall we not see you in the ballroom, gentlemen?

Edw. Instantly. [*She goes out with the ladies*]

HART. Gentlemen, I have great satisfaction, and, on an occasion like the present I do it with peculiar pride, in presenting you—the Chargé d'Affaires from the United States to the government of Guatemala.

MOR. Edward Somers—

DRUM. Mr. Somers, from my heart I give you joy.

HART. No longer plain Mr. Somers, but the Honorable—

DRUM. Why, this is magnificent. A brilliant handle, isn't it, for the name of so young a man—

MOR. Honorable, indeed! Honorable—

HART. It is not all of us who can get such a title even in our equal country where everything is said to be alike open to every citizen.

MOR. Oh, brave selection! He—he—honorable! Ah, pah! pah!

EDW. My father, you astonish me. I should have expected you, of all persons in the world, would have—

MOR. Sanctioned injustice, hey? Because he who has taken my dearest blessing from me benefits by a public wrong, I must approve that wrong, and call it noble? You mistake your man, sir.

EDW. This inexplicable—

MOR. Oh, I can explain readily enough, if that's what you desire.

DRUM. But, my dear Morton—

MOR. [Violently] Don't interrupt me, General. I know what I'm about. What? You an old soldier and not disgusted? How? Not a word from you for the honor of the epaulette with which you are yourself adorned? As for the chargéship, one *may* imagine that—yes, yes—when government is importuned to provide for the useless, worried and worn-out by influential friends, it needs must pack him off on some fool's errand, and thus get rid of him and his intrusions.

EDW. Sir! It was not—

MOR. Silence, sir. But when one hears this same—boy—who has done nothing to deserve it, graced everywhere with the title that our country reserves for moral and intellectual worth; aye, such a man as that, as that, called honorable! Honorable—oh, 'tis a bitter mockery of all that's noble and of all that's great!

HART. [Low to Edward] My friend, your father's indignation arises from his recollection of having been thrown out by the opposition in the Senate under the last administration, when the President had nominated him as Minister at St. Petersburg.

EDW. I see, I see—

HART. Tell him what passed upon the subject. That will appease him.

Edw. [*Timidly*] My dear sir, I can understand how annoying it must be to you, who have been so conspicuous as a politician, to see a young man, who, as you rightly say, has had no opportunity of serving his country, receiving an appointment before you; but did you know the motives, motives which must remain forever buried here [*Placing his hand upon his heart*], that prompted me to press for it, you would not view your son-in-law's promotion thus unkindly. For yourself, dear father, the capricious influence of party which prevented your success formerly, can no longer prevail now; for your opponents are out, the mission is again open, and in a conversation my friend and myself had lately with the President—

Mor. Oh, you are kind, great sir! You'll patronize me, will you, *Honorable*—coxcomb!

<Edw.> Father!

<Drum.> You should not forget, sir, that the compliment to Mr. Somers has been earned by his family, if not by him. His father fell in the last war with England—

Mor. Aye, in a battle where his own brother was engaged against him and there also fell. What was his father but his king's betrayer and his brother's murderer? What is he then but a traitor's and a felon's son?

Edw. Hold, sir. If I can brook reproaches to myself, I must not hear my father's name dishonored.

Mor. Indeed. You'll not hear your father's name insulted, was not that the word? I have insulted it. I again insult it. I trample on his memory.

Edw. Great Powers!

Mor. I called you coxcomb. I mistook the term. I should have called you coward! [*Tearing his glove with his teeth*] And if that's not enough [*Flinging the fragments at him*] take this!

Edw. Then thus compelled, sir, have your will. We meet.

Mor. [*Grasping his hand*] Done! [*At this moment Estelle appears and sees her father placing his hand in Edward's. Morton goes on in a low tone*] At six tomorrow. General, you'll settle where.

Drum. But Morton—

Mor. No words. It must be. Aye, to the death. [*Seeing Estelle*] My daughter! She must have no suspicion, gentlemen. Let it be hid from her. Go in—go in. [*They enter the adjoining rooms. Estelle remains at the back*] Now then, I'm easier. I shall have vengeance now! [*Estelle, the moment the others disappear, darts into his arms*]

Est. Dear, dear father, how happy have you made me!

Mor. Happy? Happy? How, Estelle?

Est. Did I not see you give your hand to <Edward>? Oh, I soon guessed the cause.

Mor. You guessed? What cause?

Est. Why, that he was not guilty, of course; or else you never would have given him your hand. Those were *not* letters from a woman. We were all deceived, were we not, father?

Mor. Aye, love, aye—

Est. Oh, I can love him as I did, then. Yes, yes; and now—now I shall love him more in proportion to the regret I feel at having done him wrong. But my past injustice shall be atoned for an hundredfold in the care I will take of his future happiness. Oh, father! Could you but feel how that simple grasp I saw you give Edward's hand has made his wife's heart leap with joy, has filled your daughter's mind with laughing visions of the long years of delight yet reserved for her in the society of her husband and her father—

Mor. [*Wildly and strongly convulsed*] Estelle! Estelle!

Est. Father!

Mor. [*Tottering towards the door*] Air! Give me air!

Est. Help! Help! [*Servants rush in. He sinks in their arms, and they bear him off. Estelle faints and is carried out opposite*]

ACT IV.

Scene: *Another apartment in the same house. Enter Galeazzo.*

Gal. [*To himself*] The open window saved him from my weapon. It passed and struck the ground unheeded; but he has only lived for deeper sufferings, and now his end draws near! [*Speaking at the wing*] Ho, there! The carriage must be ready for Mr. Morton in ten minutes. [*Enter Belmunda*]

Bel. Who gave those orders?

Gal. Mr. Morton, signora.

Bel. And for whose journey are all these travelling preparations?

Gal. I cannot tell.

Bel. [*To herself*] Strange! [*Aloud*] Can you conjecture why Mr. Morton has not been near me since his illness last night?

Gal. He said he was going with the General. I know nothing more.

Bel. Then I'll go to the General and ask him. I cannot be left in this suspense.

Gal. The General is gone out.

Bel. Out?

GAL. Signora, have you courage?

BEL. Tell me the worst.

GAL. There has been a quarrel with Edward Somers.

BEL. A quarrel? Oh, some trifle, soon made up—

GAL. In two hours they fight.

BEL. Fight? Fight? The father fight the son! It cannot be. Galeazzo, you have not heard aright. Galeazzo, you are trifling with me—deceiving me—

GAL. Had I heard nothing, I could not mistake their glances. They meet, and 'twill be mortal.

BEL. Fly to Mr. Morton. Bring him hither.

GAL. Mr. Morton, signora—

BEL. No, no, I rave—Edward! Oh, seek Edward! Tell him I insist there be no meeting. Haste, Galeazzo. Say 'tis Belmunda's charge. Haste—bring him back with you—haste, haste—

GAL. [*Going, stops*] Lady, here comes your husband.

BEL. My husband here! I dare not meet him while thus discomposed! If I could but know—strive to detain him. Make him tell you all, while I, concealed behind this door—oh, I am wild! *He* tell? No, no. He comes to seek him for the battle. But they shall not—no—I will hang upon their steps unseen, and if their swords are lifted, rush—

GAL. He's here.

BEL. [*Darting behind the door*] Remember! [*Morton enters slowly and takes his seat at the side of the stage. After a pause he turns and perceives Galeazzo*]

MOR. Galeazzo—

GAL. Sir!

MOR. What was I going to say? Ah! The company is all gone, is it?

GAL. All.

MOR. The carriage?

GAL. Your orders are obeyed.

MOR. [*Giving him his hand*] Thanks. Thanks, my friend. [*Drops his head upon his bosom. A momentary pause*] Galeazzo.

GAL. Signor? [*Morton looks towards the apartment of Belmunda. He is about to speak, then turns aside and heaves a deep sigh*]

MOR. Tell Mr. Somers I wait for him. Begone! [*Galeazzo starts. <Morton> resumes*] I do not command you, Galeazzo, I entreat.

GAL. It is done, signor. [*Exit through the side door, glancing towards Belmunda's room*]

<MOR.> [*Alone*] It must be so. Woe on me! Woe! But only upon me! What right had I to accept a wife in payment for a service? To cheat my

own heart and usurp the gratitude of others with the false pretense of doing that through magnanimity which was but basely prompted by morbid, insensate, and disproportioned passion! I acted a lie. I now must take the liar's punishment! Woe on me! Woe! [*Rises, walks a few paces and gazes at the door behind which stands Belmunda*] Belmunda! Belmunda! [*Slowly approaches the door, leaning his head against the wainscoting*] How many times have I passed the threshold of this door with a heart jocund as a heedless boy's. Oh, fool that I was! Fool! Fool! No, should I not rather say, happy? Aye, most happy—happy, because deceived! [*Enter Galeazzo*]

GAL. Mr. Somers has locked his door. He does not seem disposed to come to you.

MOR. Tell him, I implore—hear you that? Implore. [*Exit Galeazzo*] Aye. I understand. He is more wretched than I; for mine is but anguish, his, remorse! Come, firmness—oh, how weary, weary, weary I am. Twenty years seem added to my life since yesterday. [*Galeazzo returns*]

GAL. He is here.

·MOR. 'Tis well, friend. Leave us to ourselves. [*Exit Galeazzo. Enter Edward, pale, and in deep dejection. He stops near the side and stands with his eyes bent to the earth*]

EDW. You sent for me, sir.

MOR. I did. Draw nearer. Sit you down. [*Edward remaining erect, bows and declines*] My conduct yesterday must have seemed strange to you.

EDW. [*Falteringly*] I own I have been at a loss to comprehend the causes.

MOR. [*Eagerly*] The cause—you know already. Seek no farther.

EDW. [*Aside, wiping his brow*] I breathe again!

MOR. But these escapes of passion ill suit my years. At my age we should know mankind and not expect to find them treat us fairly. Sir, I was in the wrong.

EDW. Mr. Morton!

MOR. I was in the wrong, sir, and I have sent for you that I may ask your pardon.

EDW. *You* ask *my* pardon? Father! One word of explanation more than extinguishes—

MOR. Sir, I ask your pardon. But as the offense was open, so must be the atonement. As I have insulted you in the presence of persons whose opinions are of importance to your interests, I have written to Mr. Hartley; and you will find, by this letter, which I wish you to hand to him, that I have said everything the nicest honor could exact. Take it.

EDW. [*Repelling it*] Oh, sir, this is quite unnecessary—

MOR. No. Take it, I insist—

Edw. But have I not given you some cause of dissatisfaction yet unknown to me? Speak. Let me explain—atone—I will do anything—anything—

Mor. What there remains for you to do, forthwith you shall be told. [*Rings. Enter Francis*] Is the carriage at the door?

Fr. It is, sir.

Mor. Enough. [*Exit Francis*] You ask what there remains for you to do? There remains this: depart.

Edw. Depart? When?

Mor. At once.

Edw. Estelle?

Mor. Goes with you.

Edw. So suddenly!

Mor. You have a mission for Guatemala. Your credentials were delivered to you yesterday. You depart honored and honorable. What would you more?

Edw. But to depart so suddenly—

Mor. [*Warmly*] I insulted you, and I have asked your pardon. This letter proves that 'tis not you who are the coward, but I. What more would you than this?

Edw. But Mr. Morton—

Mor. [*Still more warmly*] The wrongs which yesterday had burst my heartstrings but for the wrath which came to my relief, I shut within my bosom now. The hate they've kindled, if I cannot extinguish, I can dissemble. Offended as I am, I sink to be a suppliant. I implore you to depart. Again, I ask you, what—what would you more than this?

Edw. I would, at least, be informed, dear father—

Mor. Informed? Of what? Base man, if I had not had courage to endure your conduct, if I had taken refuge from my pangs in my own self-destruction, as at one moment I believed I must have done, his blood, whom you still dare call father, would have been felt, drop by drop, through all eternity, scalding its record upon your traitor soul! Thank my forbearance for having spared you this remorse and hence and question not; for all I now could add would be to curse you! While I live, never let me see you more; but make not my daughter wretched. And at my death hour it may be I can pardon you. Till then [*With a wild laugh*] laugh at me! Aye, laugh. Aye, laugh! Laugh! [*Rushes out. Edward looks after him. Belmunda totters from her hiding place*]

Bel. Oh, Edward!

Edw. Belmunda—my poor father's brain—

Bel. I have seen all—heard all—

Edw. And can you conjecture—

Bel. Aye. But how, or whence, I cannot—

Edw. You know the cause of his strange conduct then?

Bel. There can be only one—

Edw. And that is?

Bel. Jealousy. He must be obeyed, or your life is not safe.

Edw. And yours?

Bel. Fear not for me. Away. I will find means to prove he is not wronged, and I will do yet more. [*Putting her hand to her heart*] I'll kill the rebel here, I will forget you. Go, go, Edward. Go, while I yet can bear it. Farewell!

Edw. But not forever?

Bel. Forever! [*Edward kneels and kisses her hand as Galeazzo enters, when she, seeing him, makes a sign, and Edward starts up and rushes out*]

Gal. Pardon. I thought you might be wanting me, signora.

Bel. When you left Italy for America, say, did you never think that in a foreign land, when far, far, far from yours and all who cared for you, some woe might come which you could not survive?

Gal. [*Feelingly*] I've thought that you might die.

Bel. [*Not heeding him*] And should that withering woe, whate'er it be, come on you, what would you do?

Gal. I always wear two cures for woes like that.

Bel. Name them.

Gal. Poison and this stiletto. [*Showing them*]

Bel. Give me one.

Gal. Choose. [*She takes the phial of poison*]

Bel. 'Tis done.

Gal. One kiss upon that hand. [*Kneels and kisses it. Then, rising, gazes at the door whence Edward departed*] The coward!

Bel. What say you?

Gal. Nothing. I did but think that he who loves you, losing you, should die. [*Apart*] Yet Somers lives.

Bel. Farewell, farewell, good friend. I must go pray.

Gal. Signora, pray for two! [*Kisses her robe and rushes out. Enter Estelle*]

Est. Mama—dear, dear mama—

Bel. Estelle! [*Turns to escape*]

Est. Don't you know I'm going?

Bel. Going?

Est. And won't you bid me farewell?

Bel. [*Kissing her*] Farewell, farewell. May you be happy!

Est. Oh, were it not for leaving my dear father, now might I be happy; for Edward loves me now, I'm sure he does.

Bel. Indeed?

Est. Yes, and I'm not jealous, as I once was. No!

Bel. You were then—once?

Est. More than you'd believe, mama; and it was that which made me do—

Bel. What!

Est. Oh, so wrong a deed! And yet I can't bring myself to be sorry for it, because, but for that, I had been still unhappy.

Bel. What is it that you did?

Est. Edward received letters secretly—

Bel. Well?

Est. Which he concealed in a pocketbook—

Bel. Go on.

Est. I had a second key to the drawer; and yesterday, during the party, I took the pocketbook—

Bel. And opened it?

Est. No. I gave it to my father. [*Dropping her head on the bosom of Belmunda*] Oh, it was very wrong in me, I know.

Bel. [*Bringing both her hands over the drooping head of Estelle*] Child! I pardon thee my death! Heaven bless thee!

Est. What were you saying, mama?

Bel. I say you are a miracle of gentleness and purity; and that those eyes of yours, like eyes of angels, see only what is good and beautiful. May Heaven watch over you! [*Rushes out. Estelle stands, statue-like, looking after Belmunda. Edward enters hurriedly and cautiously, but on seeing Estelle, starts and seems confused*]

Est. Edward!

Edw. Well—

Est. Oh, Edward, the signora—

Edw. Have you taken your leave of her?

Est. These tears will answer you.

Edw. Haste to your father, then. Give him your last farewell. I now wait but for you.

Est. Edward, I feel as if there were something dreadful hanging o'er us—

<Edw.> Dreams—dreams! Go, love, go—

Est. E'en as you will. [*Exit*]

Edw. [*Alone, low*] Now she is gone, I can, without being observed, regain—[*Approaching the door of Estelle's boudoir, it opens, and Morton stands before him*]

Mor. You still here? You!

Edw. Having forgotten something in that chamber—

Mor. Letters, a pocketbook, a miniature, is't not so?

Edw. [*Starting*] Ha!

Mor. Start not. I know it all. Now leave me to my wretchedness. My poor remain of life must wither in solitary anguish, since she to whom I looked for comfort and for love, she—she—[*Belmunda suddenly appears, her hair wildly about her shoulders, pale, but dignified and commanding*]

Bel. Has destroyed both. Is't not so?

Mor. [*Shuddering*] Belmunda!

Bel. Come. Give me curses.

Mor. No. I give you pity, and I give you pardon. The world shall never know your error. Though we must live apart—

Bel. [*Shaking her head, with a melancholy smile*] Apart!

Mor. You shall have all that fortune can bestow; and when my weary years have long been at an end, you will still live, and still be—rich and honored.

Bel. [*Smiling*] Live—with this clammy dew upon my brow? Answer me this, Morton. Did I not tell you ere we wedded that my heart was unalterably devoted to another, who they had told me was no more, one whose name I never would disclose and forbade your asking? My friends deceived me. He was not dead. They knew he was not, and now comes falsehood's punishment: desolation, madness. Answer me this, too, Morton: Did I not ere we wedded tell you that 'twas for my father's sake alone I gave my hand, a hand without a heart?

Mor. [*Sternly*] And promised to be faithful, was't not so?

Bel. That promise I have kept. Though I have told him I first loved all that I felt and suffered, my husband's honor has been sacred with me. But I have still deep crimes to answer for. I yielded to the erring heart's delirious fever, till all around I've made one desolation. Heaven has immutably decreed that the wrong path, even though it lead through sunlight and through flowers, must terminate in ruin. The guilt was mine, and mine be the atonement. 'Tis fit that the disturber be removed. Your hands—support me—do not fear to approach, for now, now comes the awful expiation!

Mor. Belmunda!

Bel. I feel your tears upon my hand, Morton, and they are balm to me, for now, I think, you do not deem me quite the guilty thing you once conceived I was. Thanks—thanks, and, love Edward, for he deserves it richly—richly—richly. I would have told you, had I time, but now—oh, now, the poison—

Mor. Poison! What! Poison!

Bel. [*Wildly*] Aye. Does not the hypocrite deserve it, who bears in her face one love—in her heart, another?

Mor. Within there! Help! [*Galeazzo appears*] Your lady dies—bring help!

Gal. [*Low*] Now then I know my course. [*Exit and shuts the door*]

Bel. All human aid is vain. And as the world recedes, my vision clears, and I perceive this dreadful conflict between love and duty has proved too fierce and hurt my poor brain. Had my mind been right, this last, deep crime at least I had escaped, not rushed unbidden thus a dark intruder in that awful realm whose shadowy shapes now rising frown around. That pang! That pang!

Mor. No help arriving—fly! Fly! Fly, Edward! [*Edward starts up and tries the door*]

Edw. The door is barred.

<Mor.> Then force it. [*Edward bursts it open and starts back*]

Edw. Galeazzo!

Mor. What of him?

Edw. Stabbed on the threshold!

Bel. [*Wildly*] Ha, ha, ha! Has the stiletto done its work so soon, while the poor, drowsy poison—[*Estelle rushes in on one side, Lucy on the other. Belmunda, seeing Estelle, exclaims*] An angel come! An angel come with blessings! Pray for me. Pray—[*Estelle drops on her knees*] Now, I am calm —calm—calm. [*Dies. Lucy supports Belmunda. Estelle and <Edward> rush to <Morton>, alarmed. His hands fall over their shoulders, and his head drops on his bosom*]

CURTAIN

ROMULUS, THE SHEPHERD KING

ROMULUS, THE SHEPHERD KING

THE manuscript of *Romulus, the Shepherd King,* in Payne's own hand, is in the Harvard collection.

The date of composition of *Romulus,* a so-called tragedy in blank verse, which was never acted, is doubtful. Payne's ultimate source is the popular sentimental novel *Romulus* (Strasbourg, 1801), written in German by A. La Fontaine (1759-1831), a French exile who settled at the University of Halle. His direct source, however, is probably the English translation that appeared soon afterwards in London; for he may have owned and annotated a copy of this edition which is now at Harvard. Although he may have completed the play early in his career, there seems to be no evidence that he had done so until after his return to America, when on September 9, 1839, Edwin Forrest sent him a letter of rejection. For this reason the play has been placed last chronologically.

Romulus is far too prolix to have been acted; as Forrest writes, it has "too much narrative" and is "too declamatory." The excessive length is due wholly to Payne's failure to compress enough the long-winded narrative. He does not seem to have expanded the plot of the play by the introduction of details taken from other sources, a method he had used successfully in the writing of *Brutus.* Chief among the many plays which are based on the Romulus legend and which were available to him are the anonymous *Romulus and Hersilia* (London, 1683), De Lamotte's *Romulus,* translated by H. Johnson (London, 1724), and Metastasio's *Romolo ed Hersilia,* translated by J. Hoole (London, 1800). Forrest is correct when he writes in conclusion: "The wrestling scene and several others afford excellent opportunities for spectacle, but I doubt if they would command sufficient interest to repay their 'getting up.'"

CHARACTERS REPRESENTED

ROMULUS ⎫
⎬ *twin foundlings*
REMUS ⎭

AMULIUS, *King of Alba*

NUMITORIUS, *Pontiff and Supreme Judge of Alba*

DOLCAR, *a confidant of Amulius*

IULUS, *High Priest of the Palladium*

VALERIUS, *his son*

FABIUS, *a wealthy nobleman of Tusculum*

POLYMNIUS, *a Prince of Antemnae, uncle of Hersilia*

VULPARIO, *chief of roving banditti*

SILIUS, *son-in-law of Numitorius*

FAUSTULUS, *an aged herdsman*

CENOR, *a priest under Iulus*

LUCIUS, *a subordinate officer of Amulius*

TALTHYBIUS, *a wrestler of Antemnae*

UNKNOWN MAN

HERALD

LORDS, SOLDIERS, ADHERENTS, POPULACE, DANCERS

HERSILIA, *Princess of the Sabine city of Antemnae*

DIOPE, *sister of Fabius*

SEPTIMIA, *a ward of Iulus*

UNKNOWN FEMALE ⎫
⎪
ILIA ⎬ *wife of Silius*
⎪
FLAVIA ⎭

D<small>ANCERS OF</small> A<small>NTEMNAE AND FEMALES OF</small> A<small>LBA AND</small> A<small>NTEMNAE OF VARIOUS</small>
    <small>RANKS</small>

<small>THE EPOCH OF THE PLAY IS 753 YEARS BEFORE THE CHRISTIAN ERA. THE SCENE
VARIES FROM ALBA TO THE HILLS UPON WHICH ROME WAS AFTERWARDS BUILT, TO
ANTEMNAE AND ITS NEIGHBORHOOD, AND TO THE SACRED GROVE OF THE PALLADIUM
NEAR THE NUMICIUS.</small>

ACT I.

SCENE 1: *Splendid antechamber in the Royal Palace at Alba. Fabius discovered with Diope.*

FAB. You will not swear then to renounce him?

DIO. No.

FAB. You then delude yourself with the vain hope
That you may foil the royal vigilance
And gain your freedom, hey?

DIO. No hope for me!

FAB. Your brother would not see his name disgraced—

DIO. Does the same parentage alone make brothers?

FAB. You hate me, then?

DIO. I'm only sorry for you!

FAB. Come, come, I understand your artifice:
You would move pity by this show of meekness,
And by pretended acquiescence, lull
The watchfulness of those who wish you well. [*Enter Lucius*]

LUC. [*To Fabius*]   His Majesty now goes to council, and
Will give you audience there.

DIO. [*To Fabius*]   Have you aught more with me?

FAB. Farewell.

DIO. May the gods change your heart. [*Exit*]

FAB. Was it not kind, good Lucius, in the King
To screen her for me, thus, from prying eyes?
Let not his purposes be baffled, Lucius. [*Giving gold*]
See her well watched. You shall be well rewarded.
[*A flourish heard*] Hark! Is not that his trumpet?
I attend him. [*Exeunt*]

SCENE 2: *The magnificent council chamber of the royal palace at Alba. The King, enthroned. At the King's right hand, seated below him, Numitorius in the robes of office, a table by his side. Opposite to Numitorius are several lords of Alba, sitting in state.*

Am. My lords of Alba, every sun that rises
     Unmasks some cause, more cogent than the former,
     To check the course of this young robber.
Num. Is there
      Fresh news, then?
Am. Yes. A messenger this moment
     Informs me (Impious mockery!) that the upstart
     With solemn rites has set apart some place
     To thieves, incendiaries, outlaws, runaways,
     Come they from where they will, and called it
     The temple of the Asylaean God!
Num. There are two stories of this sanctuary:
      I hear 'twas consecrated to Saturnus,
      Father of peace; to Jupiter, the friend
      Of sufferers and of strangers; to Evander,
      Of hospitality the mirror; and
      To Hercules, the greatest of our heroes.
      I hear, too, that the priests exclaimed, "Be violence
      And sword and spear far from this holy spot!
      Upon this altar may the way-worn wanderer
      Find bread and milk forever; and may Jove
      Strike down the desecrator who shall dare
      To cross this threshold with a bitter thought!"
      And when this invocation was pronounced,
      Upon the altar stone were carved these words:
      "To strangers, kindly cheer; to all who mourn,
      Shelter and smiles, repose and liberty."
Am. A palpable lure to all the disaffected!
     What think you, princes? Is not this rebellion?
Num. Rebellion, brother? And, pray, what allegiance
      Have these young shepherds ever sworn to you
      Or any of the neighboring states? Rebellion!
      'Round seven unclaimed, uncultured hills they built
      Their humble cottages and fed their sheep.
      You called them subjects but because you thought them
      Too poor, too weak to be their own protectors.
      To Pan and Pales with their rustic rites
      They offer adoration; at their fêtes
      Sing with unskilful but with happy voices
      The story of their fathers; equal wants

They satisfy with sharing equally
All that their honest industry can gather.
Their pastoral bells with melodies commingling
Of birds, which found them all so gentle while
Watching their flocks upon the eminences
That they would come and warble at their feet,
Were the familiar sounds of their seclusion,
Until you strove to drag them to your armies
And feed your soldiers with their scanty means;
But their young valor scared your veterans.
You proved them men; though Romulus even yet
Restrained his rural brethren from answering
The wrong you tried, except in this brief message:
"We care not for the shield of Alba, and
Inform the King of Alba that we care
As little for his sword."

AM. And is the King
Of Alba to endure a taunt like this
From nameless vagabonds? Forbid it, honor!
Brother, you give the ruffian boy's rude speech
As though it pleased you in the telling. Brother,
Had it not quite as well become your station
As justicer and pontiff of the state
Not to have smoothed the villanies with which
A robber spurns the law, the desecrations
With which a sacrilegist mocks the gods? [*Enter Lucius*]

LUC. Fabius of Tusculum attends the King.

AM. My honest Fabius! Conduct him in. [*Exit Lucius*]
My lords, these herdsmen as we used to call them
Have flung aside their clubs, and now they drive
Their flocks, unfearing, even to the borders
Of the Albanian lake, protecting *sheep*
With swords and pikes and shields! They will maintain,
Such is their specious cry, their inborn rights
Of pasturage! Their rights, forsooth! And is it
In drawing round them every malcontent
From every neighboring state, that they can seek
Only protection for their half-starved sheep?
Trust to this shallow trick, indulgent pontiff,

And smoking towns and rifled treasuries
Will ere long show how wisely you have trusted.

NUM. Suspicion often makes the wrong it dreads.

AM. Mildness more often but invites presumption.
Who knows but even yet the thirty cities,
With all their subject villages, which form
The league o'er which our native Alba sways,
May shake before these unregarded outcasts
That plant their huts where once the Siculi
Reared the now prostrate village of Saturnia?
Who knows but mighty Alba, which has stood
Four hundred years, may yet be doomed to tremble
Before this daring boy? My lords, when only
Twelve years of age, with his own hand he killed
A wolf from which the elder shepherds fled.
Since then he wears about him for a mantle
The trophy skin; adorned with which, he next
Led on a party who retook a flock
Seized by a wandering troop, to the reprisal
Adding the rifled treasures of the band—

NUM. Do not forget, though, how he used those treasures:
They were divided equally among
His followers, for himself not even reserving
His own proportion—

AM. Subtly to confirm
Himself in their devotedness, for new
Exploits to end in his aggrandizement!
I ask you, lords, should not a youth like this
Be crushed? I ask you if I have not done
Only my duty in dispatching heralds
To every city leagued with us, to join
And give at once a deathblow to the hordes
Of wandering banditti that infest
The whole surrounding forests and wild plains
Between our towns and villages? To give
To each a death blow, but especially
To that of Romulus and to its leader?
Speak, speak, my lords, do ye not all approve?

LORDS. All.

Num.   Though alone, let me once more protest
        Against this provocation, which no wrong
        To us has called for. Recollect, my lords,
        The trampler, though he triumph for awhile
        Must, in the end, himself be trampled on. [*Enter Fabius*]

Am.   [*Rising*]   Fabius of Tusculum, we bid you welcome!
        Now break we up the council. Lords, our course,
        Having your sanction, shall be onward urged
        With vigor and with promptness. Lords, your servant. [*Numitorius
and the lords having risen, they withdraw, and Amulius descends from the
throne to Fabius*]
        My friend, my valiant Fabius! Well, my Fabius,
        You joined the robber troop against which Romulus
        Arrays his herdsmen? You have gathered knowledge
        Of their mysterious leader? You have had your vengeance
        Upon the insult at Laurentum?

Fab.   I can
        Learn nothing of Vulpario's origin.
        He readily received me; doubted nothing
        Of any further object in my coming
        Than that of vengeance for the injury
        Done at Laurentum.

Am.   Is there no one in
        The band he leads, who speaks of whence he came?

Fab.   They merely have a strange, wild tale of how
        They fell upon him long since in the forest
        Where they discerned him on a rock, alone.
        He did not fly. Their daggers glittered o'er him..
        He gave a hideous and a startling laugh,
        And down their daggers dropped. He flung himself
        Upon the earth. They spoke. He bade them
        Trouble him not, be silent and depart.
        And with an awe, to them inexplicable,
        They all obeyed as though he were their king.
        Day after day they bore him food, and thus
        Became acquainted. "Stranger," said their chief,
        "You seem to have no fear of death." "I fear
        Nothing on earth," was his reply. "Then you
        Are like ourselves; for we have not a fear of
        Death, nor the King of Alba. Him we rob

And make his power our laughter." "Say you so?"
Exclaimed he. "I am yours, then." The next onset
Saw their chief slain, and the mysterious stranger
By acclamation planted in his place.

AM. Indeed! You found him then the man
To suit your purposes—a misanthrope
Ready for any mischief?

FAB. No. He gave me
Command of a detachment, and we fell
Upon a band of maidens of Laurentum
Wending their way to some religious rite.
Among them was the girl to whom I owe
My wrongs. We seized them. We were bearing them
In triumph off, when from a covert sprang
A party to their rescue—

AM. By whom led?

FAB. By Romulus.

AM. By Romulus?

FAB. Aye. So sudden
And so unlooked-for was this rush, that ere
I saw a single being, he had struck
My sword away and cried, "For shame!
A warrior armed against defenseless women?
Go and learn better!" Panic-struck, our troop
Yielded without resistance. Romulus
Remained until the maidens were in safety,
Then disappeared.

AM. Nor offered further harm?

FAB. Not even a word was uttered by him. Stung,
I flew to rouse Vulpario to revenge
This insult on our troop. What think you?
"A noble youth," he answered, " 'twas well done!"

AM. There's something in this stranger that—What!
Gives he no clue by which he may be traced?

FAB. None. He is affable but seldom speaks,
Is much alone. He uses for a war-cry
A name for using which he does not give
The best-loved of his troop a cause—

AM. What name?

FAB. Aeghystus.

AM. [*Starting violently*] What? Speak that again?

FAB. Aeghystus.
     That is the battle-cry; at that we rally
     As though Aeghystus were our guardian god!

AM. I have it now! Aha! We'll match him.
     I see your proper course. You must remove
     This leader and no matter how. You must
     Yourself assume his place and wreak revenge
     Upon this upstart Romulus. The way
     Is open—fortune smiles! Yes, you shall have
     All aid from me—all aid, no doubt, ere long
     From all the cities leagued with me. Droop not;
     Watch and be wary, and rewards and honors
     Beyond your wildest dream will smile around you.
     Come with me and receive supplies of gold
     To scatter through the troop, and thus prepare them
     To aid you in your purpose to supplant
     Their insolent leader. You can see your sister
     While I concert some other schemes to aid you
     Among our leaders.

FAB. My good lord, I saw her
     And find her still immovable. If it were
     Only through gratitude for screening her,
     You would command my zeal.

AM. Fabius, we'll turn
     Even enemies now into the means of crushing
     The reptiles that annoy us. I've already
     A spy commissioned against Romulus;
     And if the secret hand should fail, when once
     His rival's troop is yours, we'll strengthen it
     With power which nothing earthly can resist,
     And thus make sure work with both robber chieftains.
        Come on, brave friend! You'll not wait long for Vengeance. [*Exe-
unt*]

SCENE 3: *The flat represents the mouth of a noble cavern near Mount Palatine, occupied by Romulus. It is draperied with vines. Trees and shrubs are
picturesquely grouped around it.*
   *Day has not yet dawned. Dolcar rushes from the cavern, alone, with a
drawn dagger in his hand.*

Dol. 'Tis scarce a moment since I left him sleeping
      Upon the moss, at which I struck my dagger,
      And yet its point is broken by the rock,
      And I find not my victim! Three times foiled!
      'Twould seem as if some unseen power watched o'er him!
      Curse on the coward fear that he might not
      Be found asleep, and so detect the dagger,
      Which made me hide it in the grass behind
      His cave and give him time to rise (while I went back
      To seek for it and bring it), and so thus
      Elude me! Shall I back then to Amulius
      Report my observations on the force
      And the positions of this shepherd band?
      But how will he receive me, leaving thus
      The most important duty unfulfilled?
      Dagger! I'll give thee a new edge, and then
      Once more attempt, and when I strike, strike home! [*Remus enters
unobserved*]
Rem. When would you strike, friend Dolcar?
Dol. [*Starting and alarmed*] W—W—Whom?
Rem. Aye, truly
      You seem aroused against some enemy.
Dol. Not
      Of my own; no, no, but him to whom I owe
      Shelter and kindness—
Rem. Romulus?
Dol. Aye. I would rid him of this robber foe
      Vulpario.
Rem. This place and hour seem strangely
      Chosen for warring against one so distant.
Dol. True; but the news I heard this night
      Possessed my fancy and I could not rest.
      Day is not far from dawning; therefore, here
      I waited for the rising of your brother
      To tell him that Vulpario arms his troop
      With fresh accessions, to take vengeance on him
      For the affront of thwarting his attack
      Upon the maidens of Laurentum. Then, thought I,
      What were my ecstasy could but this dagger

Strike to Vulpario's heart and rid my friend
Of this bold rival—
REM. Soft. 'Tis that a robber
Should be ranked with him and be called his rival,
As you now call him, that has galled my brother.
But I lose time here. I must see my brother;
For news is come that forces from Antemnae,
Lavinium, and Laurentum arm against us—[*As he approaches the cave, Dolcar stops him*]
DOL. You'll not find him there.
REM. [*Suddenly and pointedly*] How know you that?
DOL. [*Disconcerted*] I—I—I—
I saw him gliding yonder.
REM. Spoke you? Spoke you to him?
DOL. No, he was wrapt in thought. I feared to give him
Displeasure. But I detain you. Fare you well. [*Exit*]
REM. [*Alone*] Farewell! The knave prevaricates: my glance
Has long been fix'd on him and must not sleep. [*Exit*]

SCENE 4: *In the background, the square summit of Mount Palatine. A hut, thatched with reeds, and formed of logs and ruins is seen upon the Mount, and is surrounded with olive and fig trees and various shrubbery. At the foot of the Mount appears a deep grotto, the entrance to which is embellished with ancient oaks. The Tiber is discovered through the opening between the grotto and the Mount, on the right of the audience. Nearer the front, in the center of the stage, stands a statue of Hercules, with poplar trees around it. Opposite to it is that of Pales, the goddess of shepherds. A third, representing Pan, appears on the path leading up Mount Palatine. Behind Palatine rise the double peaks of the Capitoline Hill and several other and smaller elevations crowned with rude cottages. In front, on the right hand, appear various scattered ruins and the entrance to a forest.*

Day begins to dawn. Romulus is discovered by the statue of Hercules, his eyes rivetted devoutly upon the statue. He is alone.

ROM. [*Alone*] Guardian of dreams, this vision breathes of thee!
Thanks, mighty Hercules! Its ecstasy,
Which makes my heart bound in its earthly prison
And lifts me out of my own being, speaks
The influence of the god. Are not
Feelings like these the germs of immortality?

Temper these longings, deity, or show me
Whither they're meant to lead me; else my senses
Will reel beneath their aching vagueness. Am I
Destined to be remembered with the mighty?
Why is it that strange raptures as I ramble
Quicken my pace and make me feel as though
I trod in air, present me scenes I dare not
Even name, lest I be laughed at; but which fill
Eyes that scarce know the way to weep with tears
Of exultation; and when I'm entranced
In this delirium, so thronged appears
Each spot with faces, voices, and events,
That, with a stare, I wondering start to hear
Men ask me why I am so much alone! [*He stands absorbed in medi-
tation. Remus enters unperceived, pauses a moment, then advances and
touches Romulus on the shoulder*]

REM. Brother!
ROM. [*Starts*] Ha! Remus—well, well—Remus, well—
REM. You have risen early, yet still seem to dream.
ROM. Brother, a dream which will not vanish roused me.
      It follows me where'er I go. I strive
      In occupation to extinguish it;
      But still 'tis there—
REM. You stir my curiosity
      What was the dream?
ROM. I'll tell it to my brother,
      For he will not disclose a brother's weakness.
      It has come o'er me often, but yet never
      Before, so like reality as now.
      Remus, I found a scepter in my hand—
      Nay, smile not; though 'twas nothing but a dream,
      I will not have it mocked, no! Remus, where
      Now the rude huts shaded by mighty trees,
      Planted when first Jove laid the earth's foundations,
      Are the sole objects that salute our eyes,
      I saw a marble city! Alba? 'Twas
      A pygmy to the city of my dream!
      Astonished Tiber quivered as it took
      The impress of this wonder on its wave!
      I looked upon the glorious picture in

The mirror of its bosom, and there shone
Upon my brow a diadem! I know not how,
But, brother, something told me that my voice
Had called this city into being, and
I spoke again, and lo! Upon yon hill
Towered up a glorious temple, and before me
A conquering people bent in adoration;
And there pressed round me crowds from every corner
Of the wide earth for shelter; and I heard
Millions of voices call that noble city
By my own name; and walls uprose around it,
And it was filled with chiselled images
Of immortalities that fate has destined
To guide, astonish, and delight the world,
Until the world itself shall be no more.
I sprang forth from my couch to pour my rapture
Before my god, my Hercules, and looked round
To feast my eyes on these unheard-of grandeurs.
The shepherd's hut was all that met my view,
And I myself was only Romulus!

REM. Brother, the dream was kindly given—

ROM. Ha!

REM. Aye, for without it, you might, possibly,
Have now been less than Romulus.

ROM. What mean you?

REM. Did I not tell you when you consecrated
A spot to shelter strangers, there was peril
In thus admitting them unquestioned here?

ROM. Oh, you are ever fearing ambuscades.

REM. When serpents glided toward the cradle where
The infant Hercules slept, what had befallen
But for the cries of Iphiclus, his brother,
Awakening him and all who were around him?

ROM. When Hercules felt the danger, it was o'er.
He did not even wait to be awakened.
True valor has an instinct when to act
And needs no prompter but the gods. This child—
He only crushed the serpents and slept on.

REM. Had you slept on a moment since, my brother,
You would have never waked to scorn my warning.

I found a stranger with his dagger drawn
Before your cave—

ROM. A stranger?

REM. Dolcar—

ROM. Ho! So, even
The honest Dolcar wakes your apprehensions!

REM. I know Amulius calls us shepherds, rebels;
Threats with death whoever of us may
Fall in his hands. I know, too (and the news
Has been but now confirmed by one who came
While you reposed), that all the Latian cities
Are arming to o'er whelm us; while Vulpario
Is on the march with his ferocious troop—

ROM. [*Impatiently*] I'd rather meet this robber chief, Vulpario,
And him, no less a robber, though not called so,
Amulius, with his thirty Latin cities,
I'd rather meet them all, alone, unarmed,
And brave their fury, then be startled by
Each leaf that stirs and fancy it an army!
As for this Dolcar, what is there in him
To tremble at? Friendship for Numitorius
Exposed him to Amulius' jealousy—
His life was threatened—he sought here a shelter—

REM. Easy pretext!

ROM. Are we to call around us
The sorrowing and suffering and insult
The dignity of their afflictions by
Low, prying curiosity? For shame!
Be it enough for us to know the world
Has stung the mourner who implores our aid.
If he's compelled to say he needs our aid,
We cannot ask a bitterer cup for him
Nor more endearing homage for ourselves.
'Twere mean to gall him farther.

REM. I repeat,
We are in danger if we do not question,
Nay, more than question,—if we do not watch
These strangers who thus throng our sanctuary
And will, ere long, outnumber us. If you
Refuse to give due care to your own safety

As well as ours, I will myself appeal
To all the shepherds for a wiser course.

ROM. Appeal? Appeal? My brother, do not make me
Forget myself and you.

REM. Must I forever
Become subservient to your orders, even
When I am certain you are in the wrong?
What are you more than I am? We have lived
And grown together; and, we think, are twins
Of the same mother. Both alike, unfriended,
Were cast to perish on the naked wild
Where the fierce wolf proved gentler than our kind
And lent our helpless infancy protection.
Alike we suffered and alike we triumphed.
What has given either of us right of mastery
Over the other?

ROM. Brother, hold. Debates
Like these are full of danger. Knit as we are,
Or, ought to be, together by the bonds
Of common origin and common struggles,
If we ourselves cannot ourselves restrain
From bickering for nothings, how are we
To dare exact a more discreet forbearance
From the incongruous and unconnected
Spirits we have to govern? What becomes
Of us, of them, if once the poisoning seeds
Of jealousy should ripen in our hearts
And even madden us to lift our arms
In hideous warfare each against the other?
I shudder at the thought. We are alone,
And let us strangle even in the birth
This serpent discord. Mastery! What
Mastery? The powers above that form us
Form every man for some peculiar sphere,
Not one for all. You've qualities which I
Have not the vanity to dream that I
Can ever rival: forecast, order,
And, spite of now and then an outbreak such
As this, which galls your brother, you are gentle, ah!

That starting tear betrays your character
More truly than your brother's words can speak it.

REM. Hold—hold—oh, hold—

ROM. No, for we now must end
Such strife as this forever. You or I
Must be supreme. We're born to fearful trials;
They thicken all around us. Thirty cities,
Troops of banditti, startled villages,
All, with one common shout, cry, "Crush the robbers!"
Look upon this: brother, you remember
When the fierce wolf sprang from the thicket, Remus
Turned pale and stood amazed; but I plunged onward,
Darted my staff deep down his yawning throat,
And having slain him, tore away this skin,
Which since has been my mantle. Then, a stripling,
Thy deeds, oh Hercules, had filled my mind,
And then I thought of thy Cythaeron lion.
That folly's past; but from the moment when
This mantle first hung on me, all our shepherds,
Unsought, unlooked for, owned me for their leader,
Until, I know not why, I've brought myself
To look upon it as a monarch does
Upon his robes of state, and to regard it
As the insignia of my station here.
Brother, I cast my mantle to the earth
Before the statue of our guardian god.
Look down, O Hercules, and now direct us!
If, Remus, you can feel you have the force
To guide the fiery coursers of Bellona
Through the fierce battle-clouds that now are gathering,
Take up the mantle, wear it! Romulus
Will kneel and own you for his chief. But if
You deem you're fitter for a milder sphere,
Restore to me with your own hands the mantle,
For, from no hand but yours will I receive it.
To you I leave the choice. Whichever way
It turn, I swear before this shrine, that I
Will ever pay it honor and obedience;
But whether Romulus or Remus rule,
Remus and Romulus must never quarrel.

REM. [*Falling on his knees*] Brother, I feel my error. Take the mantle
And with it, my allegiance. At your feet—

ROM. [*Raising and embracing him*] No, in my heart—Come to my
bosom, brother!
No appeal [*Smiling*] now, dear Remus, to the shepherds?

REM. Forget—forget—

ROM. No, I'll remember
Forever and with joy, the hasty words
We both have uttered, for their blows have only
Welded our loves more firmly than before. [*Enter Dolcar*]

REM. [*Aside*] That villain! Soft—I'll watch but must be silent.

DOL. My friend, my benefactor! As I crossed
The path conducting to your cave, a stranger
Accosted me.

ROM. What seeks he here?

DOL. He brings
A private message from Vulpario—

REM. What
Business in private can this robber chief
Have with you, brother?

ROM. Oh, I see, I see.
When some days since I freed the prisoners we
Had taken from his band, I bade them tell him
That I was ready, hand to hand, to meet
Their vaunted leader and to settle thus,
By single combat, who should be the lord
Over these forests. Here's no doubt, his answer.

REM. [*Aside to him*] You would not meet this stranger, above all
When thus announced by Dolcar, unprotected?

ROM. [*To Dolcar*] Conduct the stranger. [*Exit Dolcar*] Brother, hold our
men
In readiness, if they should hear my horn,
To show themselves on every side. But see
That we are not intruded on, unless
You hear the signal. [*Exit Remus. Enter Dolcar with Vulpario. To
Dolcar*] You may retire.

DOL. [*Aside as he goes*] Not far!
I must learn whither all this mystery tends. [*Exit Dolcar*]

VUL. You are Romulus?

ROM. I am. You bring me
    A message from Vulpario?

VUL. Yes, I
    Come to address you in Vulpario's name.

ROM. To name the day, the place, he has selected
    In answer to my challenge?

VUL. He invites you
    To come yourself alone and unescorted
    And meet him in his forest.

ROM. Thinks he, then,
    I am so easily fooled?

VUL. Fooled? Fooled? How so?

ROM. He has a right, oh, I will not dispute it,
    To set what trap he will; and if he can
    Succeed in wheedling me within his trap,
    I'll let him laugh at me and not complain.

VUL. What! Do you deem Vulpario so base
    That he would violate—Romulus, if he
    Once pledged his honor, could you feel unsafe?

ROM. Vulpario would not place such faith in mine.

VUL. You wrong Vulpario. He would come, alone,
    Even to the heart of your retreat, hemmed round
    By all your forces and your hate, and ask
    No guarantee for his security
    But his own courage and your plighted word.

ROM. Then let him come.

VUL. Behold him.

ROM. Whom?

VUL. Vulpario.

ROM. You have judged me truly.

VUL. And you have
    Not less untruly judged Vulpario.

ROM. We'll speak,
    Vulpario, of your errand here.

VUL. You long
    To measure strength with me?

ROM. I do—
    Upon the open plain, my men and yours
    Circled around us—

Vul. Romulus,
You have a settled scorn of me and mine?
Rom. I have.
Vul. And for what reason?
Rom. You are robbers.
Vul. Robbers? Is that your only motive?
Rom. Yes.
Vul. You are mistaken, Romulus. You know
For many years that Alba and Laurentum,
Lavinium, and all the country round
Have ever stilled their crying children with
The whisper of our name. Think you that I
See not the motive better much than you
Yourself can see it, why you are inuring
Your shepherds to adventure? You would make them
Robbers, as we are.
Rom. Miscreant!
Vul. Be calm.
You view me as a rival—
Rom. Rival? You?
I hope we seek a very different path
To glory from the one which you have chosen.
Vul. And what's the object, think you, that impels me?
Rom. Insatiate, sordid, selfish thirst for booty.
Vul. You do me wrong. A stronger, nobler passion—
Rom. Name it—
Vul. Revenge against a base oppressor—
Rom. Whom do you mean?
Vul. Amulius—
Rom. The King of Alba?
Vul. So he calls himself.
Rom. You wake my curiosity. Speak on.
Vul. I will, young man, for I can trust you. Yes,
I'll tell you all, and you, perhaps, may give me
Respect as well as sympathy. Then, learn:
My name is Silius and not Vulpario—
Rom. There was a Silius who once led the Sabines—
Vul. My father was that Silius. When the late
Monarch of Alba, Procas, broke the league
Formed with my father's state, I myself fought

Against the Albans. From the camp I went
One day, alone, to reconnoiter, and
I met a foe and fought him. Heavy groans
Stayed our uplifted swords. We made a truce
And joined to aid the sufferer who had fallen
The night before in battle—

Rom. Bravely done—
And your antagonist?

Vul. He saw that I
Was fainting from a wound and from my effort
In bearing the poor soldier, and he cried,
"We'll meet some other time—"

Rom. And did you?

Vul. At the next onslaught, at the very next,
Our party charged a troop and in its leader
I recognized my foe. The fray was hot,
He was unhorsed, his people fled, and he himself
Made prisoner. I gave back his sword. "Take," cried he,
"Thanks from Aeghystus, son of the next heir
Of Alba's throne, Numitorius." And he sprang
Upon the horse of one of his slain followers
And in an instant vanished from our view.

Rom. Come, let me press thee to my bosom for
This gallant act. Did not your people shout
And bear you home in triumph?

Vul. No, they frowned,
And factious spirits called me and my father
Traitors for having freed a hostile prince,
And we were banished.

Rom. Banished!

Vul. And when cast out
From our own state, Aeghystus came and made
A home for us in Alba. We grew to be
Such friends as seldom live except in dreams
Of poets' fancy. One day when I went,
As was my custom, to his father's house,
Cast on the floor, haggard and desolate
Before his household gods sat Numitorius;
Aeghystus on the altar leaned, his lip
Curled with a smile of bitterness and scorn.

Upon her knees, her dark and trailing hair
Veiling her face, Ilia, his sister, breathed
An ardent prayer, then, with a comforting glance
Cried to her father, "All will yet be well."
Young man, a tone, a look, can sometimes fix
Our fate, when all the strength of all the world
Might work on us in vain. That glance, that tone
Fixed mine!

ROM.   I grieve to see you weep. Tears are
Only for women, deeds for men. No tear
Should wet his eye whose arm can wield a sword.

VUL.   You have the notions of a boy, on what
Is fitting for a man.

ROM.   What meant the scene
You have described?

VUL.   Procas had just expired.
Amulius, with subtlety and gold
Had won the army to declare him King
Instead of Numitorius, the successor;
Who, in the hope that he might save his children,
Ere long assented to the usurpation
And took the judgment seat and place of pontiff
Under his brother.

ROM.   Now, ye gods, I thank ye
That in my breast ye planted a detestation
Of this Amulius, though his wrongs to us
Were petty to these crimes. Go on—go on—

VUL.   Poor Numitorius thought to save his children!
Romulus, mark this arrow. Nineteen years
Nearest my heart I've worn it. See you there
The stains of gore upon it? Listen, youth:
Aeghystus and myself had hunted. I
Was walking by his side, as he discussed
His chances of the throne: "My uncle has
No son; my uncle lately grows so kind."
Just as he spoke, an arrow whizzed. He fell,
Uttered a shriek, and never spoke again.
I saw the assassins. They were trusty slaves
Of the usurper. I perceived the bow
Of one, prepared to make a second shot.

I flung my spear. He fell. His partner fled.
This is the arrow from Aeghystus's corse!

Rom. Well, and further—

Vul. I took the body up
And on my shoulders bore it to the gates
Of Alba. What dost think? Throngs poured forth
As slowly I approached. They yelled, "Look! Look!
There comes the murderer!" I had deeply sworn
Vengeance for my Aeghystus, or I would
Have let them tear me into pieces; but
I fled into the forest—

Rom. Vengeance for wrongs
Like these, was worth the living for—

Vul. Like these?
Like these? Ah, Romulus, were these the only
Woes I endured, I would have dashed at once
Through the insulters, found the tyrant's heart,
And perished o'er the sacrifice exulting.
But there's a passion stronger than revenge,
Stronger than even hope, for it will live
When hope itself is dead—

Rom. And that is?

Vul. Love.

Rom. And have the gods bestowed these iron hands
To play with women's tresses? Have they given
These sinewy arms to strive with feeble girls?
The manly ear is formed for trumpet's clangors,
Not for the cooing of the timid dove.
The manly grasp was given for the sword,
Not to entwine the silly maiden's fingers.

Vul. Boy, you may live to see the hour when you
Can understand the spell which Ilia flung
Around me from the moment when I saw her
Cast down and desolate before the altar.
Enough that now I tell you, when Amulius
Knew that we loved, Ilia was snatched away
(We were already wedded secretly,
Unknown to any but my friend, Aeghystus).
Amulius had extorted from her father
An oath that she should join the vestal train,

Hence even Numitorius was not told it.
I missed her on the morn Aeghystus fell.
By chance I learned she had been forced among
The vestal guardians of the holy fire
Treasured within the groves of Troy's palladium.
I lived but to regain her, found a way
Within the walls, watched there her turn to fill
The vase for sacrifice where gushed a fountain
Hidden within a consecrated bower.
We met, and often, thus, but every outlet
Was too securely guarded for her flight.
I dug a passage from a distant wood
To stretch beneath the wall and thus release her.
'Twas finished; and, on her accustomed day,
I flew with rapture to the fountain—

Rom.   Well—

Vul.   I heard a priestess singing as she came.
'Twas not the voice of Ilia! Again—again
I went—the form of priestess after priestess
Glided along, but not the form of Ilia.
In desperation once I made a spring,
Meaning to seize the vestal who that day
Had come in place of her and force from her
News of my Ilia. But the tangled branches
Flung me to earth, and the scared vestal shrieked.
Succor arrived; and, as I laid in covert,
I heard the trembling maidens mourn their sister
Who, for oblivion of her vow, had been
By order of Amulius doomed to—

Rom.   What?
The slow murder of a living tomb? Shut down
Forever from the light of Heaven, within
The bowels of the earth, to die by inches?

Vul.   I know not how, but I—I—I—pardon—
A moment's patience—I—I found myself
Surrounded in the forest by the band
Of which I afterwards became the leader.
Of this, hereafter. By one master feeling
I was absorbed: to crush, annihilate
The throne of this Amulius. This arrow

I swore should flash before him as he fell,
Stung with the shriek, "From Ilia and Aeghystus!"

Rom. Your woes are mighty, and I pity them.
I would I could do more.

Vul. You can. At first
I thought the tyrant's death would be revenge
Enough; but that were mercy to him if
Compared with wrenching from him what with crime
Heaped upon crime, he has sold every hope
Of Jove's Elysium to possess on earth.
His kingdom must be taken. He must see
The brother he deposed rise over him.
For this have I so many years unceasing
Toiled to exhaust him, seize upon his treasures,
Augment my forces, till I might at last
Sweep o'er him like a whirlwind!

Rom. Wherefore
If his chastisement only were intended,
Thus gall his subjects, ground to dust already
By his extortions?

Vul. You, like others, think then
That heaps of treasure slumber in my caverns?
I am the poorest of my troop. The only
Joy that e'er comes within my breast is kindled
By rifling this usurper's ill-got wealth.
But what I openly thus wrench from him
Is given, in secret, back to the oppressed
From whom his crimes have wrung it.

Rom. Is't indeed?

Vul. Yes, and has gained me many a secret friend
Even in the midst of Alba, where they stand
Prepared to second any step I take
To set them free. Amulius trembles at me,
Although he knows not the deep cause he has,
For he thinks Silius has for years been dead.
Your name, too, he of late begins to fear.
Romulus, this despot would exult to see
Implacable hate between your troop and mine.
We can destroy each other; but, united,
We and we only can destroy Amulius.

Young man, an impulse strong as fate has long
Turned my whole heart to you. I have intended
These many months to seek you. I have watched
Your course from its first dawn, and each new act
Has but eclipsed the admiration
Its predecessor kindled. Your late message
Supplied the opportunity I wished.
You know me now; you know my history.
Instead of fighting, let us join our forces;
And be the only rivalry between us
Which shall most firmly be the other's friend.

Rom. I have not sought for this alliance, nor
Can I accept it.

Vul. Shall I tell you why?
You wish to sway alone. So did Amulius,
And thus became a villain.

Rom. Ha!

Vul. Aye—tremble
At that desire for power which masters you
Unknown even to yourself, and take the counsel
Of one who feels for you as would a father.

Rom. A father!

Vul. Yes, and only as a father
Desire I to remain among the bands;
I seek not to partake your power.

Rom. You would resign
All governance? All? Ev'n that of your own troop?

Vul. Swear to give all your soul to the dethronement
Of the usurper, and—I abdicate.

Rom. I swear!

Vul. Come to my heart, and as a father
I will watch o'er, advise you. All my host
Are now encamped on the Numicius's banks
Beside the forest of Lavinium.

Rom. Near
Where the Lavinium forest shades the ashes
Of great Aeneas? And where the palladium
Borne from expiring Troy is guarded by
The great high priest Iulus?

VUL. Yes, and where
      The garden of the vestals rears its walls,
      Go with me to that river's bank and there
      I will present thee as their future leader
      To all our forces—

ROM. I'll attend thee there,
      For I must see those hallowed groves; and after
      A secret mission calls me to Antemnae.
      That city threatens us—I go alone
      To reconnoiter. I must check their pride
      With some bold show of power. We will confer
      Upon our way; concerning further measures—[*Romulus sounds
the horn. It is instantly answered from various points, and, at the same moment, from behind every bush and tree, at every part of the stage, to the far
distance, armed groups spring up, some with arrows drawn and some with
spears levelled, all directed towards Vulpario. Remus rushes in on one side,
and on the other, Dolcar. Romulus makes a gesture, and the groups drop
their weapons and their hostile attitude*]

REM. My brother!

ROM. Remus, strange events have passed.
      This is Vulpario.

REM. and DOL. Vulpario!

ROM. Yes,
      My friend, my father!

REM. How!

ROM. No more
      Our foe, his men unite with ours. I go
      To take command of them. I must depart
      For a brief time and must not be pursued.
      Conduct our forces to the neighboring plain,
      Where I'll acquaint them with what has befallen,
      Then leave instructions with you for my absence.
           On, brother, on. [*Remus goes out. Romulus beckons to a couple of
officers, who approach him, and he converses with them, while Dolcar speaks
aside*]

DOL. He leaves them! Now's the time!
      Alliance with Vulpario? To Amulius
      Then, on the instant. Romulus, farewell!

When I return to your possessions, carnage

Shall herald me. [*Dolcar goes out on one side, and the officers of Romulus on the other. At the same moment the troops of Romulus enter, in procession, headed by Remus. Each detachment is headed by one of the Manipuli, bearing a handful of grass and shrubs upon a pole. As the troops pass the statue of Hercules, they drop their banners and spears as a military homage to it. Doing the same to the other statues, Romulus and Vulpario stand, unseen by the troops, at the front of the stage in the corner, till the procession is off, and then they advance*]

ROM. I could not love a woman

As you loved Ilia, but can understand

And feel such love as yours was for Aeghystus.

Stretch forth your hand. Friend, I am yours forever! [*They follow the procession*]

ACT II.

SCENE 1: *The interior of the consecrated Lavinian forest. On the left, under a splendid arch sustained by marble columns, and on an elevation approached by numerous wide steps of marble, appears a square block of white marble inscribed "PALLADIUM." On the top of it is a vase of flame and behind it rises a white marble statue of Minerva, seated and in armor, with a spear in her hand. At the back of the stage is the sarcophagus of Aeneas, surmounted by a statue of Aeneas bearing Anchises from the burning of Troy, and holding by one hand his little son Ascanius. Trees of cypress and myrtle surround it. At the right hand and nearer the front is a small altar, almost hidden with flowers and inscribed, "TO PIETY." At the far distance, part of the walls of the garden of the vestals appears in the horizon.*

The scene is so lighted as to give it a solemn and mysterious air. The High Priest, Iulus, enters, followed by Cenor.

IUL. Alone, you say?

CEN. Disguised and all alone.

Even his small guard, alike disguised, he leaves

Beyond the outskirts of the sacred forest.

IUL. What can Amulius have to do with me?

The day of annual sacrifice which brings him

Hither with all his train is yet far distant—

CEN. But coming as he does, alone, there's surely

No danger from his coming, to be feared.

IUL. From those we doubt, the worst is ever feared.
        Were Numitorius on the throne, from him
        There would be nothing that we ought to fear.
CEN. Soft—who is this? [*Enter Romulus, in a dark mantle. Cenor with-draws*]
IUL. Stranger, we bid you welcome.
        Your errand? Speak! A follower of the King?
ROM. No follower of any king.
IUL. What then
        Seek you within these sacred solitudes
        Inhabited by the unseen immortals?
        Where the primeval and majestic oaks
        Have never heard the echo of the axe;
        And from whose shades the awestruck traveller
        Turns on his journey, to a longer road,
        Dreading to pass where dwells the earliest gift
        Made by the gods to man: the blessed shrine
        Which even the robbers that are prowling round us
        Dare not profane with their unhallowed presence.
ROM. I come to look upon the tomb where slumbers
        All that is left of great Aeneas.
IUL. Behold it.
ROM. Shrunk to this narrow spot! A life of toils
        Paid but with empty honors, when 'tis o'er,
        Of which thou sleep'st unconscious!
IUL. Who art thou?
ROM. One who would earn such fame as blest Aeneas;
        Which shall not, like the shadow flung by yonder
        Cloud, on his tomb, be seen but for a moment
        And then forgot.
IUL. Say rather, you aspire
        To kindle glory which, like Etna's flame,
        Shall make the world turn pale; for such ambition
        Your manner would betoken.
ROM. Well, and if so?
IUL. Suppress it. Such is the ambition which
        Has given those reckless rovers of our wilds,
        Vulpario and young Romulus, their throngs
        Of mischief-dealing followers.
ROM. What say you?

IUL. Children in mind think power is built on fear,
     And so, through fear, they seek the path to greatness.
     The red volcano at the distance charms,
     But death and horror stream forth in its brightness,
     And those who know it, fly from it with curses.
     Young man, I saw this mighty Etna once. Beneath it
     I saw an altar reared to the Destroyer
     Wielding the thunderbolt. 'Twas guarded by
     Richly appointed priests; and once each year
     Thousands from all the neighboring regions flocked there
     To view a sacrifice. But, on an eminence,
     I also marked two simple rustic altars.
     No grandeur graced them, and by glittering priests
     They were not guarded; yet even for a moment
     I never saw them empty like the other.
     Parents and children hung their garlands there
     And o'er them poured smiles, tears of joy, and blessings.
ROM.   And what has this to do with fame or Etna?
IUL. Stranger, there was a time when Etna, pouring
     Its fiery torrent, in one wide sweep drowned
     Cot, village, city, all that came within
     The deadly gush. While the scared multitudes
     Wildly ran to and fro, striving to shun
     The crimson deluge, there appeared two youths.
     One of them tottered underneath the weight
     Of a sick mother; and one of them reeled,
     Threading his way among the tides of lava,
     Bearing an aged father on his shoulders.
     The very terror-stricken fugitives
     Stopped short, astonished at the noble sight.
     "You cannot save them, let them go!" they cried.
     "Sons, leave us here, leave us and save yourselves!"
     Implored the parents. The youths gained the height,
     And a fresh flood of flame, that, at the moment
     Rolled o'er the vast expanse, beneath them parted,
     Flowed in two streams down past it to the sea
     And left the parents and their children safe!
ROM.   'Twas right to build those shrines to such a deed.
IUL. And in the homage of the heart, which brings
     Thousands and thousands hourly to these shrines,

While the more splendid reared to the Destroyer
Is all forsaken, till through fear attended,
Say, in that homage of the heart, what read you?
Does not that show you where true influence dwells?
Where true fame should be sought? Mark yonder sculpture:
Some few recall, perhaps, the fights Aeneas
Waged with Achilles, Diomedes, Turnus;
Some few recall his sufferings and his patience;
But all the world recalls exultingly
That single deed recorded in yon sculpture
Which shows him with Anchises on his shoulders
And which alone has placed him with the gods.

Rom. You have perplexed me. I have ever scorned
   A baseness; yet I own I have not cared
   To win men's love, but rather sought to make them
   Tremble before me. I would know you better.

Iul. Your frankness gives me hope. May I not learn
   From whom I hear it?

Rom. One without a name.
   One who could ne'er perform such deeds as you
   Have pictured, for he never knew a parent.
   A man brought up with rustics—[*Cenor re-enters suddenly*]

Cen. The King! [*Enter Amulius. Cenor retires. Romulus recedes to the palladium and the tomb of Aeneas, unobserved by Amulius; but never departs so far as not to overhear the dialogue between the King and the High Priest*]

Am. Iulus, that through paths beset with dangers
   I thus should visit you unguarded, speaks
   At once my faith in you and the importance
   Of the occasion which has brought me hither.

Iul. I thank your highness for your confidence
   And humbly ask the motive of your visit.

Am. Both you and I, Iulus, are descended
   From the same ancestry: both of us from
   Aeneas. When the foreign son, Ascanius,
   Who came with him from Troy, and Sylvius Posthumus,
   His only son by Latium's native princess,
   Lavinia, whose father's hospitality
   Had given the homeless wanderer a shelter;
   When these two sons agreed to reconcile

The troubles which their jarring claims had caused,
You know what then resulted?

IUL. Yes.
      On the descendants of Ascanius,
      From whom you spring, the royal crown was settled—

AM.   And on the sons of Sylvius Posthumus,
      From whom it is your blessing to descend,
      The guardianship of yon palladium, which
      Aeneas brought from Troy, yon mystic shrine
      Of which the oracle pronounced, while that
      Is held in reverence, will Aeneas's race
      Preserve the majesty of Troy, where'er
      Fate may decree for it a resting place.

IUL. And if his sons dishonor it, then Troy
      Is indeed fallen! 'Tis now four centuries
      That each successive monarch has respected
      The privileges of this sacred place
      And, as enjoined in the beginning, sought
      From each successive pontiff holy counsel.

AM.   You do not mean that all have held the *place*
      As so inviolably sacred? Sure
      You rather mean to speak of the palladium
      Which it enshrines, for all our annals tell
      That when Ascanius founded Alba, thither
      Was the palladium removed—

IUL. What followed
      Upon this desecration by Ascanius?
      Big drops of sweat poured from the marble brows
      Of great Aeneas's statue; and the columned
      Gates of Ascanius' palace toppled down;
      And showers of meteors from the welkin gushed.
      The earth in awful fissures open yawned;
      Strange, deformed beasts ran bellowing to and fro;
      And yon Minerva, although but the emblem
      Of the mysterious wonder that's enshrined
      Within that marble, as before, when stolen
      By sacrilegious hands from Troy, mark, monarch!
      Whirled her spear wildly, sent forth from her eyes
      Lightnings at which the gazer on them dropped
      Dead on the instant; and a voice exclaimed:

"Till its own priests recover the palladium,
And Latium's kings are ruled by their advice,
The wrath of Heaven hangs heavy o'er the realm!"
AM.   True, true, and 'twas restored; and ever since
The kings of Latium have sought counsel of
The priest of the palladium. Holy father,
Still they would have your counsels, still would they
Preserve to your possession and forever
This mystic guardian and yon sacred tomb.
But in Ascanius' time, the space between
These groves and Alba was not full of danger
As in these difficult, dishonest days,
When I require instruction daily, hourly,
And need yet more the blessing Troy's palladium
Must bring on any spot where it may dwell.
IUL.   Surely these doubts that flash on me are false.
You cannot mean to ask—
AM.   I mean to promise,
If you will take these holy treasures hence
To Alba, now, rewards and honors more
Than your imagination can conceive
Shall shower on you and them.
IUL.   Forget not, Prince,
The horrors which have twice ere this attended
Their violation—
AM.   'Tis to rescue them
From threatened violation that I now
Seek to remove them.
IUL.   They are never, King,
To be removed until the gods themselves
Pronounce the order.
AM.   And is't only then
In earthquakes and in thunderbolts that we
Can hear the voices of the gods? Events
Are, to the wise, voices with which the gods
Speak louder than in hurricanes: events
Tell now their mandate. Bands of robbers gather
Around you. What! And shall these holy treasures
Become the prey of robbers! No! They *must*
Obtain a safer shelter.

IUL. *Must?* They *must?*
      Must? And is this a language for Amulius
      To hold with Jupiter's vicegerent here?
AM.   The gods themselves suspend their ministers
      When they forget their duty to the gods.
      Go hence to Alba, and e'en Numitorius,
      Already subject to your supervision,
      Shall yield his local power, and you shall sway
      In Alba even as here. But if you still
      Persist in waiting till these robbers come
      Tear up your groves, insult Aeneas's tomb,
      And cast down your palladium; if you will not
      Cheerfully listen to my pleadings, I must
      Find out a way to *make* you listen to them.
IUL. *Make* me, Amulius! *Make* me! There's no power
      The world e'er yet beheld will ever *make* me
      Forget my duty here.
AM.   When you shall see
      My veterans bear yon tomb and yon palladium
      To Alba, sure you'll not refuse to follow?
IUL. You dare not order them—
AM.   Who'll aid you
      When you behold them here? Vulpario? [*At the name of Vulpario,*
Romulus starts and listens intently]
      No doubt, no doubt. Aye, and perhaps there'll come
      To your assistance, too, this other braggart,
      Young Romulus—[*At his own name, Romulus is still more excited*
and darts forward, facing Amulius, who starts]
ROM. And if he did?
AM.   Who's this?
ROM. That braggart Romulus of whom you prated.
AM.   Reptile!
ROM. Put up your sword. I would not have you
      Arouse the lion here that I would tame.
AM.   An ambuscade? Conjoined with robbers, priest?
      My confidence betrayed, and I surrounded
      By wretches hidden in these groves to slay me?
IUL. Wonder and indignation both unite
      Almost to rob me of the power of speech.
      Shame on you, King, for this suspicion, shame!

          I do not know this stranger. He came hither
          Professing that he only came to pay
          His adorations in this sacred grove.
          I hope he harbors no concealed design, to
          Offer it insult.

Rom.   Never; nor will he
          Permit its desecration by that man
          Who calls himself a monarch.

Am.   How!

Rom.   Great King,
          This little horn can call a swarm around you
          Upon the instant, in whose presence you
          And all your majesty would shrink to nothing,
          Vanish from earth and be no more remembered.

Am.   You do not mean to sound it?

Rom.   'Tis not long
          Since all the world would not have had the power
          To hold me back from doing so; but the voice
          Of that good man, the holy influence
          Of these august and sacred solitudes,
          They have been inspiration to me. No,
          I will take no advantage. I will not
          Resign you to the power of the man
          You most have injured, though with him I've sworn
          To give you deadly battle. You are free.

Am.   [*Aside*] My courage withers at that voice, that form.
          Whence, why is this? [*To Iulus*] I am not well. Conduct me
          To where my guard awaits.

Iul.   [*Calling Cenor, who enters*] Cenor! Conduct
          The King.

Rom.   Avoid the pathway at whose entrance
          The oak, by the late tempest overthrown,
          Tosses in air its widespread, earth-clogged roots.
          Pass o'er the stream bridged with the fallen poplar.
          Keep to the left across the eminence,
          And you are safe. Should any stragglers, armed,
          Attempt to intercept you, say the word
          "Aeghystus," and fear not. [*He eyes Amulius closely*]

Am.   [*Starting*] Aeghystus!
          Lead, lead me hence. [*Exit Amulius with Cenor*]

Rom. That awful password
    Struck the villain home. I thank you, pontiff,
    That you have taught me there's a nobler triumph
    In saving than in slaying those we scorn.

Iul. Young man, I thank the gods that they have wrought
    This change in you.

Rom. You have done yet more:
    You've shown me how the upright, even though helpless,
    May soar beyond the mighty; made me feel
    'Tis only love of justice that lifts man
    Above the brutes; for brutes possess with us
    In common life, abundance, strength, nay, even
    They oft are our superiors in all these,
    And none of these are at our own command.
    But love of justice is within our power.
    Nor chance, nor death itself, can take it from us,
    Nor any share it with us, but the gods.

Iul. With thoughts like these how much must it be mourned
    That you should not possess some station where
    They might do service, and not thus be wasted
    On wanderers without a home or country.

Rom. Is not the whole wide wilderness our home?
    Where'er our flocks find pasture is our country.

Iul. And yet ye are but wanderers, merely *living*
    In this wide world; only a grade above
    The brutes who, like you, rove and feed, are dreaded,
    And die, unknown, unhonored. 'Tis for man,
    Created with the power to make himself
    Next to the gods, to lead his brother man
    The way to all their nature can attain.

Rom. I see! The difference bursts on me at once,
    And my o'er-dazzled fancy aches with its
    Effulgent glory! Oh, in feverish dreams
    Something of this has come o'er me before,
    But undefined, a formless fantasy,
    A selfish hope—but now—I do but dote!
    Oh, pontiff! If it could be possible
    That I should ever be the founder of
    A country! should be destined to make millions
    Happy and great; to send through far, far time

(When even this region where we range shall wear
Another countenance, the very names
Of all the mighty cities of our day
And of our mighty men, become confused
In the perplexing mist of years), oh, should it be
My destiny to send beyond all this
To far, far time, the enviable fame
Of being the beginner of a country,
Where every man untrammelled may enjoy
All that the Heavens intend for all alike!
Father! Forgive me that the very thought
Should overcome me with its vastness, bring
The woman into eyes unused to tears;
And on my knees, oh holy father, let me
Offer you thanks for lessons which have so
Enlarged and purified my untaught mind.

IUL. Temper these feelings and the torrent may
Be guided to much good. Youth's dreams are always
Excessive, but time sobers them. I'll not say
That you can ever found a name or country
To live forever, but 'tis in your power
To be to many a blessing. Come with me,
And I will show you happy cottages,
Where love and labor each on each confers
A new delight; where many of my sons
Can tell you how much greater is the joy
Of conquering the thirst for power, than power
Itself can yield. For all my sons in turn
Went to adventure in pursuit of that
Which men call glory; and they have come back,
When it was gained, to seek for happiness
Here in their native homes; yes, all but one:
Of him we have lost sight. We heard indeed
That he was at Antemnae, but since then
No trace is found of him. We apprehend
He has been slain by robbers.

ROM. Father, I
May not attend you to the Elysium
Which you have pictured, now. I have an errand

Hence, to Antemnae. There, I'll seek your son.
His name?
IUL. Valerius.
ROM. Often will I come
When I can steal alone from my companions
Into your hallowed grove. I bless this hour.
Believe me, Romulus will cling to you
Whate'er betide, will shield you from Amulius!
Farewell. Perhaps I yet may find your son.
Perhaps I yet may live to have a country. [*Exeunt at opposite sides*]

SCENE 2: *The suburbs of Antemnae. Trumpets and shouts are heard. Multitudes rush by, shouting. Enter Polymnius, who calls to one of the crowd.*

POLY. Ho! Doltima! Tell some of them to mount
The piles of stones, gathered to build yon temple.
Range others on the steps of all the buildings
(For many still seem yet unoccupied),
Between this and Antemnae; others on
The strong, wide walls which screen the public walk;
But bid some careful guard keep down the climbers
From the tall scaffolding there upon the right,
Else 'twill be overwhelmed and toppling down
Upon the heedless multitude, in place
Of gladness at our festival to Ceres,
Antemnae will be wrapped in tears and mourning.
Haste! For the train's already on the march. [*Exit. The procession begins to enter. It is opened by a group of females dancing. After them follow gorgeous banners and a band of music, principally flutes; then a plough, drawn by oxen, decked with flowers. A magnificent chariot led by lines of men garlanded bears a female representing Ceres. Soldiers again follow. After them a tall, splendid canopy is sustained on four poles, entwined with vines and roses, over the head of Hersilia, who is attended by Polymnius and followed by ladies of the court and soldiers. As Hersilia reaches the center of the stage, the procession stops, and she comes forward from under the canopy, having previously appeared to mark intently some object which she had passed on the way*]

HER. [*To Polymnius*] Did you not mark him, uncle? I am sure
He is no common person. On his spear

         He leaned, as one accustomed to this symbol
         Of princely sway.

POLY. A Volscian helmet, say you?

HER. Yes, uncle. As a stranger, 'tis our duty
         To give him honor. He appears alone,
         All unacquainted here; and since, to me
         The duty is appointed of presiding
         Over the festival, is't not fitting that
         I should invite this stranger to partake
         Our pleasures?

POLY. Bravely thought! You're right.
         Who knows but he may be some prince disguised?
         Ha! Ha! Yes, yes, perhaps some foreigner
         Come to seek what the oracle has promised—

HER. Uncle! Uncle!

POLY. Well, well, I'll bring him.
         'Tis wisely thought. The gods themselves sometimes
         Have stolen from Heaven to test us mortals. Aye,
         I'll bring the stranger. [*Exit Polymnius*]

HER. [*Apart*] Young—stately—and absorbed in meditation.
         He seemed not even to cast a glance on me.
         Soft. He is here. [*Polymnius returns with Romulus, clad in a white tunic, scarlet robe, Volscian helmet, and bearing a spear. Hersilia makes a move towards them and addresses Romulus*]
         Stranger, at a moment
         When all around is revelry, when every youth
         Is happy in a smiling partner, much
         I grieve that any here should be alone.

ROM. Lady, it may be that even if I had
         A partner, I might not be less alone.

HER. So! A misanthropist! Has some fair damsel
         Played the coquette and made you cheat yourself
         Into a fancy that you scorn the sex?

ROM. Not so, fair lady, but I think men born
         With objects nobler than to lose themselves
         For beauty's selfish trifling and caprices.

HER. [*Smiling*] Come, come, you are too young for thoughts like these.

ROM. But old enough to know that seriousness
         Becomes a man.

HER. And so does cheerfulness,
Especially at such a festival
As this we celebrate.

ROM. And prithee, what
May be the festival?

HER. To Ceres, she
Who plenty, health, and joy returns for labor;
Who, when she gave our ancestors the plough,
Gave them the source of that, the only, wealth
Which strengthens men and nations. On this day
We gather all the country, far and near,
To strive for prizes in such sports as rouse
Our youths' ambition. Say—is not this wise?

ROM. Yes, it is right to be ambitious. Still,
How rarely is ambition's aim accomplished!
Life is so brief, that when our goal is only
But half attained, we are ourselves extinguished
Like the bright star which midway in its course
Drops from the firmament.

HER. *Must* we attain?
Is't not enough to strive?

ROM. That is a question
Fit only for a woman, by whom nothing
Can be attained, because she wants the courage
For what is difficult.

HER. The strongest courage
Can only will. To gain is for the gods.
You said my question was a woman's. Are not
You of the nobler sex so very eager
To gain your purposes, because you prize
The glory of a deed, and not the deed?

ROM. Ha! True—it may be so. Pray—pray go on.

HER. We mortals are but drops. We fain would claim
The force of showers, whose influence can change
The face of nature, yet we never can
Be more than single drops. And what one drop,
However large, can fertilize the earth,
Though each one does its part? And even when
Our mightiest purpose is attained, what is it
But the beginning of a new creation?

Rom.   Of which another age, another race
        Must reap the glory and enjoy the gain!

Her.   What if they do? Our part should still be acted.

Rom.   Young woman, you have spoken like a man.

Her.   I've only spoken as all men should feel.
        I myself strive to do whatever good
        The gods permit and think not of myself;
        Though what I do attempt, I strive as much for
        As though 'twere only for myself I wrought.

Rom.   You mean you are thus zealous when you find
        Occasions promising a fit return?

Her.   I think not of return. Whate'er I deem it
        Worthwhile to undertake, I also deem
        Worth my best zeal. The rest I leave to chance.
        Said a philosopher who visited
        Antemnae once, "Let that which is most easy
        Be undertaken as though difficult,
        Lest unforeseen impediments should make
        The effort irksome; and let that which is
        Most difficult be undertaken as
        Though it were easy, for fear courage wither."

Rom.   He was a good man, and his words were wise.

Her.   You have not heard the wisest, for he spoke
        About the motive of our undertakings
        And bade us recollect that the great gods
        Bestow not benefactions for applause,
        Nor even withhold them when they are not thanked;
        The only heralds of their bounties are
        The cheerful hearts of those whom they have blessed.
        Shall mortals ask more than immortal gods?

Rom.   [*Apart*] Is she of earth? Or some intelligence
        From the bright worlds of yonder welkin?

Her.   Stranger,
        You plant your spear-staff in the earth and still
        Lean on it and look grave. Cheerly, cheerly,
        Come and partake our sports. Dispute, if so
        You will, for any prize you wish to win.

Come, stranger! Hospitality commands
That, as a stranger you should share the best
Our city yields. Take, then, your place with me.

On! Let the train proceed! On to Antemnae! [*Romulus takes his place under the canopy on one side of Hersilia, whose uncle, Polymnius, is on the other. The procession resumes its march. After the ladies and soldiers following Hersilia, the procession closes with a group of dancers, as it opened*]

SCENE 3: *An open square in the city of Antemnae. The columns of a noble temple appear on one side on the horizon. In the center of the stage, a lofty platform, splendidly carpeted, a number of wide steps leading up to it. It is surmounted with one raised seat, two steps higher than the top of the platform. At the right of this seat and a little behind it, is a slight column of marble, hung with beautiful wreaths. On a range with this seat, but one step lower, are two seats, one on each side; and behind them, are elevated standing-places on a level with the second step of the central seat. From each side of the platform are amphitheatrical ranges of benches, branching off in the form of a quarter-circle towards the front corners of the stage. When the scene opens, these seats are entirely filled with male and female spectators.*

The procession enters. Hersilia, attended by her uncle, ascends to the raised seat in the center of the platform. Two females place themselves, one on each side of Hersilia, upon the elevated standing-place behind her, at the outer edge of which, on each side, a soldier stations himself with a banner. The seat at the right hand of Hersilia is taken by Polymnius. The soldiers of the procession dispose themselves, with their banners, on each side of the stage, from the footlights to the beginning of the amphitheatrical rows of seats. Romulus remains standing at the foot of the platform.

The characters being all placed, Hersilia rises.

HER. We hail the stranger! [*She makes a gesture to Polymnius, who rises, descends to Romulus, and conducts him to the vacant seat at the left of Hersilia, which she herself has indicated. Romulus, on reaching it, bows to Hersilia, and they are seated. During all this action, there is music. Hersilia now rises again and exclaims*]

HER. Let the sports begin! [*Hersilia resumes her seat. There is a loud flourish of trumpets. The dancers dart in. The youths are all armed and with spears in their hands. They dance apart at first, then fling up their spears threateningly, point them, and are rushing together, when the girls spring between them with garlands and lure them asunder. In the next change of the dance the youths cast away their spears, draw their swords, clash them furiously together, and afterwards catch the blades on their shields, forming*] *a series of picturesque attitudes and groups. The girls again interpose as before. After this has been repeated, and the youths are once more dashing with renewed fury upon one another, each girl flings her garland around a youth and entwines herself also in it; thus paired, all dance off together.*

This being ended, the trumpets sound again. While they are sounding, a soldier ascends to Polymnius, delivers him a scroll, and withdraws. Polymnius, after reading the scroll, rises and turning to Romulus, says:]

POLY.   Young man, Talthybius, a famous wrestler,

Defies the stranger to a struggle with him. [*Romulus springs up. Hersilia, agitated, starts from her seat and puts forth her hand to restrain Romulus*]

HER.   Do not accept the challenge. Friends, this stranger

Is travel worn, and he is out of practice—

POLY.   Talthybius by long training is prepared.

The stranger is not. Let the challenge be

Withdrawn—

ROM.   I never yet was unprepared

To meet a challenger. Let the man stand forth. [*Talthybius the wrestler, a gigantic figure, appears. There is a flourish of trumpets and shouts, as he presents himself. Romulus springs down the steps, throws his helmet across the stage to a soldier, his spear to another, his mantle to a third, and presents himself with his simple tunic. Talthybius approaches with overbearing defiance. Romulus closes with him, undaunted. At the first violent onset Romulus is nearly overpowered. They close together again for a firmer grasp. After a few struggles, they remain foot to foot, immovable, each equally unable to stir the other. Romulus at length is beaten back, but he rallies and Talthybius gives way. Talthybius lifts Romulus. Romulus grasps the shoulders of Talthybius, bends him downward, and lifts him; but neither is subdued. They part a moment for breath, then spring upon each other with renewed vigor. At length both fall; but, almost at the same moment, both rise, Romulus entirely, Talthybius instantly sinking down upon one knee, in evident pain. He still defies Romulus, and as Romulus does not approach him, he makes his way to him, seizes him, and is not overthrown by Romulus, who drags him on his knees across the stage. At length he springs up to make a desperate rush on Romulus, but staggers and sinks back exhausted into the arms of soldiers, who dart forward to receive him.*

Throughout this encounter there is music adapted to the changes of the fight and the emotions of the spectators, who, although occasionally shouting and waving scarfs for Talthybius, evidently incline to Romulus. Hersilia watches with obvious interest for Romulus. She springs up when Talthybius sinks, catches a wreath from the column, and exclaims]

HER. The stranger wins! [*She unconsciously darts down the steps and cries to Romulus*]

        Young man, receive the crown!

ROM. Lady, his ankle has been wrenched. And yet
        For all its agony, I can't o'erthrow him.
        The crown by me has not been fairly earned.
        [*He takes the crown from her hand*]
        Talthybius, it is yours! [*He advances to Talthybius, places it on his brow, as Talthybius revives, makes a gesture of delight, sinks back in the arms of his supporters, and is borne out*]

HER. Stranger, you merit
        Honors and praise beyond the best our chaplets
        Can wreathe around your brow. [*To a female in attendance*] Fly, Flavia!
        And bring me information if Talthybius
        Revives. [*Exit female attendant. Romulus resumes his mantle, helmet, and spear*]

POLY. [*To Hersilia*] How different is the conduct
        Of this young man from that of Fabius!

ROM. Who
        Is Fabius?

HER. One from Tusculum. He passed
        Some time here with his sister, who was loved
        By one Valerius.

ROM. [*Starting*] Valerius?

HER. Yes,
        A worthy youth. I was at Laurentum
        With his betrothed and him and Fabius;
        And by the maidens of Laurentum I
        Was chosen to bestow a crown of oak leaves
        Inwove with gold, formed by them, to be given
        To him who had achieved the noblest deed.
        Fabius had slain, in many a desperate fight,
        Some twenty foes, had gained ten lances and
        Two suits of armor; but Valerius had
        Tended a wounded foe, when his own life
        Was deeply perilled, and had given him back
        To a despairing, helpless wife and daughter.

Valerius won the crown, and Fabius swore
Eternal vengeance on him, snatched away
His betrothed sister—

ROM. And Valerius, now?

HER. Has wandered, none know whither, in despair.
Nay, we much fear, he in a neighboring torrent
Was drowned; for, when last seen, 'twas on its brink
Adventuring wildly. It is thought the sister
Of Fabius sunk beneath the awful shock.
Fabius himself, a prey to evil passions
To wreak his vengeance upon those who had
Baffled his vanity, straight joined a troop
Of roving robbers. The knave watched his time:
Ere long, upon another visit to Laurentum
I went to mingle in a solemn rite
Where none but females were admitted, and
Where those were mostly the same maidens who
Had given the festival which galled this Fabius.
The villain lurked till we were far from succor.
Then, with his minions, plunged upon the throng
And me among the rest.

ROM. You!

HER. Yes, and we
Should all have been the victims of his troop
But for one Romulus, the leader of
Another band of robbers, who disarmed him
And drove the rival robbers—

ROM. [*Eagerly*] Know you aught
Of Romulus?

HER. They say he has a statue
Built to his model, Hercules—

ROM. And could he
Honor a nobler shrine?

HER. Poor savage!
I doubt if even he can tell for what
Hercules should be honored. He adores
The power, and not the benefactions to the world
For which that power was used, in Hercules.
He saved the maidens to defeat his rivals.
Both he and Fabius are like those we talked of

Who do bold actions for the gain it brings
Themselves, not all mankind, as other brutes do
That prowl the forests; but ere long Antemnae
Will find a way to tame such troublers. Stranger,
I would that you were only with our people
Who now prepare, in concert with Amulius,
An expedition which will end at once
This Romulus, this dark cloud that comes
Upon the midnight slumberers, with his lightnings
Crushing them unprepared. [*She sees Flavia re-entering*]
Ha! Flavia!
Pardon me while I ask about Talthybius
And give instructions for the care he needs. [*She crosses to Flavia,
with whom she remains in conversation during the ensuing dialogue between
Romulus and Polymnius*]

Rom. [*Drawing Polymnius to the front, and apart to him*]   May I dare
ask who this fair lady is?

Poly.   She is the daughter of Antemnae's King.
Her name, Hersilia. An oracle
Pronounces that she's destined for a stranger
And to be queen of a most powerful nation;
But must not quit Antemnae until called
By one whom Fate marks out to be its ruler.

Rom.   Has such an one appeared?

Poly.   Dorax,
A neighboring prince, aspires to win her hand.
Her father, now at Alba, sanctions him;
So does Amulius.

Rom.   And the lady?

Poly.   She
Cares not for love, and less for Dorax; but
We fear Amulius will yet win her father
To force her to consent, for Dorax is
A creature of Amulius—

Rom.   Force consent!

Poly.   Yes, for the oracle's in part fulfilled:
Three brothers stood between her and the throne,
And all are dead. If Dorax weds her,
Another state is added to Antemnae,

And Dorax, as the favorite of Amulius,
If his survivor, may add Alba, too,
So make the powerful nation that's predicted. [*Hersilia returns
from Flavia and accosts Romulus*]
   HER.   Stranger, the man by whom you owned yourself
Conquered implores that you will wear this chain
To mark his gratitude for magnanimity,
Which tells him you are born for destinies
Nobler than common mortals. [*Romulus takes off his helmet,
kneels, and Hersilia places the chain around his neck. While she is doing it,
Polymnius exclaims*]
   POLY.   Would he were
But born for what the oracle has spoken!
   HER.   Uncle! Good stranger, there appears a cloud
Even yet upon your spirits. You alone
Seem not to have partaken in the joy
Which has made all of us today so happy.
It is not right, I know, to ask a question
Of any stranger; for a host should wish
For nothing from a guest but what a guest
Of his own will unasked discloses. But
We still would know by whom we are thus honored.
   ROM.   By one whose name's not worth the knowing: one
Without a parent and without a home.
   POLY.   Wherefore without a home, when our Antemnae
Would glory in possessing such a son?
   HER.   It would indeed.
   ROM.   It would? It would? Say *you*
It would? But no, no, no—I must away.
My heart, my wishes, must not speak within me.
I live not for myself.
   POLY.   Excellent youth!
   HER. [*Apart*]   Indeed, most excellent! And yet the oracle
Has not designed him for Antemnae's throne!
[*To Romulus*] Stranger, you <surely> can stay to see the rest
Of these our revels—chariot races—
   POLY.   Throwing
The discus, fights of gladiators, and—
   ROM.   It may not be. Farewell. Perhaps ere long
We'll meet again.

HER. It cannot be too soon. [*Romulus bows. Hersilia curtsies. Romulus turns at the wing and bows again. Hersilia again curtsies, gazing after him fixedly, and then starts, as if from a trance, exclaiming*]

On to the circus for the chariot race! [*Triumphal march, and the scene closes*]

ACT III.

SCENE 1: *A wild scene of precipice and waterfall. At the back of the stage, over a raging torrent, falling from a great height, stretches the trunk of a tree. On the right hand, facing the audience, a steep, winding path leads from the top of the precipice to the rocks at the foot of the waterfall. The stage is perfectly dark. A violent storm of thunder and rain rages. The flashes of lightning are incessant, broad and vivid. Enter Romulus.*

ROM. [*Alone*]   What spell has changed me thus? This frame inured
To toil, when but a little moment resting
Upon the earth, surprised and lost in slumber
Until loud thunders shook it from the dream
Of empire, glory, and Hersilia's smile!
'Tis well—a retribution merited—
That I should only wake to be bewildered
In the deep darkness and to lose my path,
Wander the wilderness, while war prepares
Havoc against my troop. [*Loud thunder*] Flame on, great Jove,
Flame on. I feel, I feel the fierce rebuke
Inscribed in those forked streaks of fire that flash
Wildly through yon black clouds. It is deserved:
I, who have sworn that if all Italy,
Nay, all the nations of the peopled earth
Combined to bribe me to forsake my shepherds,
I still would share their fortunes, be their guide,
Yes, I forgot them for a woman's smile!
[*Violent thunder again*] Aye, threaten mighty Jupiter. I own
The apostate thought; I know I should have been
Upon my native hills, among my men,
Ready to meet the onset of our foes,
Not here! No cottage window in the distance
Twinkling compassion? Is not that a glimmer
From some lone dwelling shining through the trees?
I'll grope my passage that way and discover—

No! 'Twas no cottage taper—'twas the flash
Of lightning in th' horizon. Soft—my horn—
Perhaps some peasant's ear—[*Sounds the horn. A violent peal of
thunder follows*]
The bellowing thunders
Have even scared the echo from the hill,
And the horn dies unheeded. [*Thunder*] Fiercer yet!
Look on the majesty of scenes like this,
Proud man, and own thy littleness. Again! [*A tremendous burst of
thunder. The lightning strikes into the ground by the side of Romulus. He
shrieks and falls. At this moment from the side of the scene opposite to the
winding path, a female figure appears and passes to the center of the bridge.
A broad and continued flash of lightning discloses her to view. She is clad in
white and with long and trailing black hair. She descends the winding path,
the lightnings plainly showing her as she descends. When she reaches the
center of the stage, she speaks*]

Un. Fem.   Yes! 'Twas in this direction—shrieks—a horn—
            Distress. Who seeks for succor? Not a word!
            Is't he who calls himself the Desolate? Whom
            I have watched o'er so long—he lost at last! [*Another burst of
thunder, followed by a broad red glare of light, which falls directly upon
Romulus and the Unknown Female*]
            That startling thunderbolt has set on fire
            Yonder lone clump of trees, and by its light
            I now can search. My fears are true! Struck down
            Behold him here! But no, he is not dead—
            Still his heart beats. Rise, sufferer. Your friend—[*Enter Un-
known Man*]

Un. Man.   My guardian spirit's voice!
Un. Fem.   Ha! Can that be—
            Why, who is this, then? My fears pictured thee—
            Quick, quick—your aid to lift this fallen man—
Rom. [*Reviving*]   What voice is that? Where am I? Do I live?
Un. Fem.   Yes, thank the gods, you live and are with friends.
Rom.   What friends? Who is it speaks?
Un. Fem.   Be calm.
Rom.   Nay, I am well, quite well. I was but stunned
            By lightning which struck near me. I'm well now—
Un. Fem.   Blest be the gods!

Rom. Aye, blest! Inscrutable
      Yet kind even in their rage. They strike us down
      Amid our noblest aspirations. Be it so,
      For, after all, what's life!
Un. Man. Aye, truly, stranger,
      What is it? Seems it not the brand of slavery
      Burnt on the brow by a hard master? Yet,
      Though 'tis our only chain, we have not courage
      To break it and to end our woes and follies.
Rom. You speak like one who has been tortured deeply.
      You speak a hurt mind's language.
Un. Man. Why, what are joy
      And grief and hope and fear, but airy phantoms,
      Which we ourselves laugh even at ourselves
      For ever deeming real, as the gods
      Laugh at our constant though our varied forms of
      Love for these nothings! Tell me, don't each age
      Smile at its antecedent? The youth smiles
      At that which pleased his infancy; the man
      At that which charmed his youth; the old
      At the delusions of his prime. And just
      As three score thinks he only is awake
      And knows the real happiness of life,
      The grave takes him to its oblivion; and
      The gods themselves then smile at all the follies
      Of all the ages which have mocked each other.
Un. Fem. My sons, life disappoints you thus, because
      You view its purpose from too low a point
      And have unwisely failed to ponder that
      Whate'er regards the individual man
      Is perishable as man himself:
      His bliss or woe, his triumph or defeat,
      All that exclusively belongs to him
      Must die before or with him; but his wisdom,
      His justice, truth, humanity extend
      O'er the immortal race of human kind
      And are, like that, immortal. Cherish then
      These only true distinctions, and the lures
      To those delights which center all in self,
      Forever changing and forever stinging

The heart that leans on them, will lose their power;
And you will live content with the ambition
Of imitating those who, having lived
Not for themselves alone, but all mankind,
By all mankind are ranked among the gods.

Rom. What mystic monitor art thou, who seem'st
Descended from the radiant spheres above
To succor the forlorn, and thus between
The pauses of the howling tempest, lulling
The wounded spirit with such heavenly music?
Art thou a guardian goddess from the skies?

Un. Man. That is the word: in truth, a guardian goddess;
For so to me she has been. Kneel and worship.

Un. Fem. No matter what I am—

Rom. Now I remember—
Aye, and 'tis hereabout, in some mysterious
And unapproachable seclusion, stands
The Temple of Carmenta; and they say
She never died, but since full many an age
Visits her nymphs and teaches them those verses
Of prophecy, which have amazed the world.
And when Jove's wrath o'er disobedience thunders,
She turns aside the bolt, or gently softens
To means of wisdom, lightnings, meant to kill.
Say, that benevolent spirit, art thou she?
Art thou that blessed one? Art thou Carmenta?

Un. Fem. Inquire not. If I *am* Carmenta, let
My words sink deep. Whoever I may be,
I have bought wisdom from deep woe, and now
Am not of this world. You have said you're grateful;
Then show that you are grateful by avoiding
To seek all knowledge of me. [*To the Unknown Man*] Son, you have
Forgotten that the shower has drenched the stranger.
Guide him to your cave.

Un. Man. Lo, benefactress,
The flame which lit us from the blazing tree
Has ceased to shine. I'll hurry to the cave
And bring a torch to guide the stranger thither. [*Exit*]

ROM. Spirit, if such thou art, inform me who
    Is this young man, whose griefs appear so heavy?

UN. FEM. Heavy indeed!

ROM. What are they?

UN. FEM. Thwarted love.

ROM. Love! That base passion, given by evil powers
    To turn man from his duty?

UN. FEM.   Rather say
    The star to guide away the young from paths
    Of wretchedness and wrong; the spell that tames
    The tiger in the heart; the great inspirer
    Of everything that's great.

ROM. Indeed. Then what
    I have deemed love, must be some other passion;
    For when I've seen it, it was full of anguish—

UN. FEM. Have not you loved?

ROM. I—I hope I have not.

UN. FEM. I think you have.

ROM. And wherefore do you think so?
    How is love known? Say, is it whereso'er
    The eye may turn ever to see one image?
    To meet it in our walks, our visits, dreams?
    To feel no joy complete without one sharer?
    No triumph fame without that one approver?

UN. FEM. Have you felt thus?

ROM. I meant but to inquire
    Whether this youth gave you such marks of madness?
    Who is he? Whence? What name?

UN. FEM.   He withholds
    All clue to whom he is or what or whence.
    I found him wandering, almost a lunatic,
    And I have watched him closely, soothed his grief,
    And raised him, as I hope, to fortitude. [*The Unknown Man
returns with a lighted pine torch*]

UN. MAN. Stranger, the fire is lighted in my cave,
    And I have spread a couch and frugal meal
    For your refreshment. When you will, I'll guide you
    Upon your way from these wild solitudes.

UN. FEM. My duty then is done. Farewell. [*Going*]

Rom.   When and how
       May I again hear wisdom from a voice
       Which seems to come to me from Heaven itself?
Un. Fem.   If you desire my counsel and respect
       The secret of my solitary dwelling,
       Come hither by yourself, thrice sound your horn.
       Whene'er you hear it answered thrice, be sure
       Ere long I will appear. Farewell. [*She goes up the winding
path. On the bridge she pauses and makes a parting gesture to Romulus and
the Unknown Man, whose eyes are fixed on her from below, until she dis-
appears*]
Rom.   Oh, stranger,
       How full of wonders has this day been to me!
       It seems a strange, delirious dream. There's something
       In this last apparition which affects me
       With deeper, holier feelings than e'er yet
       Trembled in this firm soul.
Un. Man.   Your agitation
       From the wild storm and from your fall—
Rom.   Perhaps.
       Why do you dwell alone thus in a cave?
Un. Man.   Because the spirits of my better days
       Inhabit there. Know you a blessing greater
       Than all the rest that mortals can be robbed of?
Rom.   The resolution to resist misfortune?
Un. Man.   Much more: the inclination to be happy.
       I have none now.
Rom.   What have you lost then?
Un. Man.   To the cave. [*Exeunt*]

SCENE 2: *Near Mount Palatine. Enter Remus with Vulpario.*

Rem.   Oh, you have nobly conquered! Romulus
       Will bless the hour he met you.
Vul.   There's another
       And a more difficult conquest I must now
       Attempt to gain: To take from these insulters
       Who came on us at daybreak from Antemnae
       Those of your flocks they captured from us were
       And easy task, to quelling disaffection
       Among ourselves.

REM. How say you? Disaffection?
VUL. Hush. Not a word. You shall know all anon.
      I hope when Romulus returns, he'll hear
      The danger and its overthrow at once.
      Till then, it must not be suspected. Flames
      Spread when they take air. Am I understood? [*Exit Vulpario*]
REM. [*Alone*]   What disaffection? Oh, my brother, where
      Can you thus loiter? Ever in your absence
      Some strange disasters gather. Master spirits
      Like yours seem armed by something more than earthly,
      Which mischief dare not meet. Ha! Romulus! [*Enter Romulus*]
      Brother, dear brother! Oh, ten thousand welcomes!
      Such troubles, Romulus—
ROM. Upon my way
      I heard them all. I heard how nobly, too,
      You dealt with those disturbers from Antemnae;
      And proud I am, indeed, of the discretion
      Which held our forces back from farther vengeance
      Than to claim restitution of our flocks. [*Enter Vulpario*]
      My friend! Aye, like a friend and like a hero
      Have you sustained our honor in my absence,
      For I have heard it all.
VUL. Would there were no more
      For you to hear.
ROM. How say you? Out with it.
VUL. One of my chiefs, one Fabius—
ROM. Of Tusculum?
      He that once lost the oak wreath at Laurentum?
VUL. He is of Tusculum. The rest I know not.
ROM. Well, what of him?
VUL. Brave but wayward, he
      Refuses to receive you as a leader.
      He was away when the rest swore allegiance.
      He says you once affronted him. He led
      My men against some maidens of Laurentum,
      And you released the maidens, took his sword,
      And sent him back insulted.
ROM. True, 'tis true.
      Aye, I remember—true—I should not thus
      Have chafed the morbid pride of him I'd baffled.

Vul.　He had been absent and returned with treasures.
　　　These he has scattered; and with these has lured
　　　Numbers away from us, who have been joined
　　　By troops of strangers. He has ranged them all
　　　And shouts defiance.

Rom.　Let them all come on.
　　　What say you now, Vulpario? I seek peace,
　　　And it flies even from my longing. Tell me,
　　　Have I desired this battle?

Vul.　You rejoice
　　　That it has come to you without desiring?

Rom.　How? How? Thanks—I—I own—that—I—*did* feel
　　　The exultation which in other days—
　　　Pardon me—guide me. But they shall have war
　　　If they deny us justice, shall they not?

Vul.　Soft. Here's a messenger from Fabius. [*Enter a herald*]

Rom.　Herald,
　　　What is your errand?

Herald.　Fabius, who heads
　　　　　A numerous troop, sends me to offer peace—

Rom.　Peace? Peace?

Herald.　To Romulus, provided he
　　　　　Will bring his shepherds and give up their arms.

Rom.　Who is this Fabius? Is not this the man
　　　Whose sword and shield I at Laurentum took
　　　And sent him home rebuked for waging war
　　　On women?

Vul. [*Apart to him*] Gently—

Rom. [*The same*] Thanks—thanks—thanks—

Herald.　And this same Fabius through me commands
　　　　　That you shall now give up your arms to him.

Rom.　Tell Fabius that instantly I'll carry hence
　　　My arms and those of all my men, to where
　　　His followers encamp.

Herald.　You've accepted then
　　　　　The olive branch?

Rom.　The olive branch? Great gods!
　　　Go. I will meet this Fabius with my men. [*Exit Herald*]

Rem.　My brother, what is this? I never saw you
　　　Thus moved before.

Rom. Nothing, nothing. Yes, I must
     Brook it, for I have drawn it on myself.
     'Tis hard—so much the better. Pride? Aye, pride—
     My pride it was provoked it, and my pride
     Must suffer for the injury to his.
     It was enough to have disarmed him. Why
     Added I taunts to humiliation,
     Which of itself would have galled me to vengeance
     Greater than this he seeks? Down, paltry longing
     To triumph with the sword; prefer the nobler
     Triumph of being just. Why don't the world
     Give shouts and honors only for exploits
     Of virtue, not of mischief? Brother! [*To Vulpario*] Friend!
     Lead forth our forces to confront the troops
     Of Fabius. On the way I will unfold
     The rest of my intent. Come. We must bustle. [*Exeunt*]

Scene 3: *An open plain near the forest of Laurentum. The soldiers of Fabius are drawn up diagonally on one side of the stage in several rows, each of which is lost to view in the wings, giving the appearance of a display of only the heads of the corps.*

   At the front of the stage are several chiefs with Fabius, before whom stands his herald to Romulus.

Fab. [*To the herald*] Is that his answer? [*To the officers*] Friends, I know the man—
     There's nothing like submission in this answer.
     'Tis vague that he may take us unprepared.
     But we'll be ready for him, thank him, too,
     That he affords us opportunity
     For signal vengeance. [*To the soldiers*] You there of the vanguard,
     You were my followers before Laurentum.
     You lost your lovely captives there: you, in a panic,
     Cast down your arms before him, saw yourselves
     By this young robber packed like schoolboys home.
     But now you are again once more yourselves;
     And he who will not wash off this affront
     In the heart's blood of the boy-chief and all
     His ragged train, why let him to Laurentum,

There to be scourged, like a detected urchin
Even by the girls who saw his first disgrace.
Ready, brave followers! [*The troops of Romulus appear on the oppo-
site side, forming themselves like the others*]
Lo, the enemy!
But where's their leader? [*Enter Vulpario*] How! Vulpario!
Your errand, recreant.

VUL. I come from Romulus
     To offer peace.

FAB. Peace! With these hosts in arms?

VUL. I come, the friend of Romulus, to beg
     Peace.

FAB. And from me?

VUL. With Fabius.

FAB. And what
     Thin stratagem is this?

VUL. No stratagem.
     Romulus begs for peace, because he deems
     That it is due to justice; but in arms
     He asks for it, that Fabius may feel
     He asks it but for justice, not through fear.

FAB. Have I to you, who, of all men on earth
     Ought of yourself to feel my injuries,
     To bring them to your mind? You know he took
     My sword and shield, disarmed my men, reviled
     Both me and them. By the eternal gods,
     Until I see him on his knees before me,
     Unarmed as I was, I'll not even listen
     Though he should beg with voices from Olympus.

VUL. He owns that the presumptuous vanity
     Of youth misled him and he galled your pride.
     He feels 'tis fitting that *his* pride should suffer
     In retribution; hence he sues to Fabius.

FAB. He would not sue unless he knew himself
     Conquered already. Let his men cast down
     Their arms before me, take me for their leader,
     And then, perhaps, I'll deign to hear his suit.

VUL. No other answer?

FAB. None.

VUL. I will convey it. [*Exit Vulpario*]

FAB. Now then my turn is come! Now shall I revel
In all the luxury of sweet revenge!
Ha! He is here again. [*Vulpario re-enters*] Well, sir, and now?

VUL. Romulus bids me supplicate that you
Will pause and not expose the lives of hundreds
For a mere personal pique. Shall helpless women
Be rendered widows, children be made orphans,
But because Romulus has hurt the dignity
Of Fabius? Romulus implores for peace.

FAB. If Romulus deems this a personal pique,
Why does he skulk behind his desperadoes
And not come forth to meet me like a man?

VUL. In single combat?

FAB. But he dare not do it!

VUL. Are you content to rest the issue on
A struggle hand to hand?

FAB. I am. My men
Shall be restrained if he can keep back his,
And he who triumphs shall be lord of both.

VUL. He shall be told.

FAB. If when our trumpets sound,
His does not answer to the third salute,
I shall command my men to charge for battle.
Pass the word, officers. See it fulfilled. [*Exit Vulpario. Officers go up
the stage*]
Now we shall see! [*Pauses*] No signs of battle yet. [*Listens*]
The brave man quails! He dare not come unbacked
By his fierce band of thieves and murderers.
First I will string the rascals on these trees
And then parade their leader through our cities
Crowned with a paper wreath inscribed "The Coward!"
Sound there! [*A flourish of trumpets*]
Again! [*A second flourish*]
Again! [*A third flourish*]
[*Exultingly*] No answer!
[*A flourish from within*] Ha! [*A second flourish is heard from
within, after which Vulpario, Remus, and others enter*]
My shield! [*Impatiently*] My shield!
[*A third flourish from within*] A better sword!
He comes! [*Enter Romulus in full armor*]

Rom. Fabius, again—

Fab. I stand not here to parley.

Rom. Come on, then. [*After a furious and well contested encounter the shield of Fabius is broken. Romulus, observing this, flings his own away, and they renew the battle. At length Fabius closes with Romulus, who, in the struggle, wrenches away the sword of Fabius, flings him down upon one knee, and stands for a moment with his own sword suspended over his head*]

      Fabius, take your life,

      And with it, take your sword and keep your power.

      Wear all to better purpose. [*Having restored the sword of Fabius, Romulus departs, and Vulpario and Remus give a signal to their troops, who withdraw also*]

Fab. [*Rising*] Forever,

      Forever is this Romulus to triumph!

      Unheard of plagues upon his head! Men! Soldiers!

      Will you be trampled on by outcasts? Forth

      And fall upon these renegades and robbers,

      And Alba will reward you with her richest

      Honors and treasures. [*The soldiers, in order, march over and go out by the side where the troops of Romulus departed*]

      Ha! They move! No answer!

      What means this strange and sudden march towards

      The quarters of the foe? They are ascending

      The hill—they pass its summit, disappear

      Upon its further side—I see no longer

      Even the last banner top! What spell detains me?

      Aye, I will on and rouse them to resent—[*As he is rushing out, he meets Vulpario and recoils*]

    Again Vulpario here!

Vul. Fabius, Romulus

      Once again tenders peace and friendship to you.

      You are forsaken, and your men even now

      Have joined with ours.

Fab. 'Tis a falsehood. [*Shouts heard*]

Vul. Is it? That shout may answer. You are now

      Entirely in the power of Romulus,

      And yet he offers peace and friendship to you.

Fab. Let them all go. Let hope go. Aye, let nothing

      Remain to me but hate of Romulus.

Impotent hate, to gnaw my brain to madness!
In my despair he is even more detested
Than with an army round me. Say—I curse him! [*He rushes out on one side, and Vulpario departs on the other*]

SCENE 4: *A part of the sacred grove of the palladium. Septimia rushes in, greatly agitated.*

SEPT. [*Calling*]   Friend! Guardian! Come, oh, come to my relief! [*Enter Iulus*]

IUL.   Septimia, whence is this alarm?

SEPT.   I saw him here!

IUL.   Saw? Whom?

SEPT.   Fabius.

IUL.   He from whose addresses
    You fled at Tusculum?

SEPT.   I saw him stretched
    Beside the tomb of Ilia. I am sure
    'Twas Fabius. Though 'tis more than twice twelve moons
    Since we have met, and he is changed by woe,
    I cannot be mistaken.

IUL.   Were you seen?

SEPT.   I gazed on the forlorn, despairing figure;
    All on a sudden, he upraised his eyes,
    Sprang from the earth, and stood like one entranced,
    Wildly exclaimed, "Septimia!" and I fled!

IUL.   If he is suffering, he must be soothed.
    Suffering discreetly dealt with purifies;
    Used harshly or neglected, it destroys.
    Show me the place where you beheld the mourner. [*Exeunt*]

SCENE 5: *A picturesque part of the grove, with a monumental tomb surmounted by an urn, containing the representation of a flame ascending. The marble slab forming the front of the tomb is inscribed "Ilia of Alba." The tomb stands on a raised bank in the center of the stage and is surrounded by shrubs and decorated with climbing vines and flowers.*

Fabius is discovered upon the ground, his elbow on a fragment of rock embosomed in foliage, his chin upon his hand; and he is looking off wildly at the side. As the soliloquy proceeds, he rises.

FAB. [*Alone*] Are all the furies leagued to drive me mad?
  At such a moment to have seen her specter!
  For so it must have been. If she, how here?
  Yet wherefore should I cherish any thought
  Of one whose deep pledge was so lightly broken?
  Where is the honest indignation which
  Should banish even her image from a bosom
  She stung to desperation? Where's my pride?
  Ha! Steps! Let me avoid them! Let me fly
  All miscalled human and go herd with beasts! [*As he is departing on one side, Iulus enters on the other, led by Septimia. She points to Fabius. Iulus crosses to him past Septimia and catches the arm of Fabius, who turns suddenly and sees Septimia, just as <she> is departing*]

IUL. [*Catching his arm*] Hold!

FAB. [*Gazing after Septimia*] What form is that which fled as you approached?
  A moment since I saw it—give the truth—
  Say—does it live? For, if it lives, to that
  And that alone, I'll listen. Hence! Bring back
  That form, if you would save a desperate wretch.

IUL. Septimia!

FAB. It is, it is, and I was not deceived! [*Enter Septimia*]
  [*Kneeling*] Oh, if thou hast descended from the skies
  To bless me in my desolation, kneeling thus
  I pour forth my thanksgiving!

IUL. Speak thy woes.

FAB. We met at Tusculum. I loved her; but
  Her friends were startled at my heedless thirst
  For glory and at my ungoverned temper.
  My suit was thwarted, and she disappeared,
  Though she had sworn to live for me alone!
  Since then in strange adventures have I sought
  To bury my devotedness to her.
  A desperate gambler, my last die was thrown.
  Friendlessly, hopelessly, I wandered forth,
  Found myself here, I know not by what means;
  And in my hour of anguish she appears—
  She glances by me like a meteor and
  Leaves me in darkness deeper than before.

SEPT. [*Tremulously*] Fabius, when in these sacred solitudes
    I fled the world, determined to prepare
    With my kind guardian's aid, for the subduement
    Of an ill-omened passion, by devotion
    To the pure shrine of Vesta—[*Emotion chokes her voice*]
FAB. Oh, speak on!
IUL. My children, come with me, and let us speak
    Of matters better suited to the moment.
    If disappointment, Fabius, has taught you
    To hate ambition, it will prove a blessing;
    But wintry disappointment may but freeze
    The serpent passions, which the brighter sun
    Revives with tenfold venom. Time alone
    Can prove if they be truly dead within you.
    Till then, I dare not teach your love to hope.
SEPT. Methinks we heard you were with Romulus?
FAB. Romulus!
SEPT. Nay, it may make you wonder,
    But of that name we feel not here the horror
    You seem to apprehend.
IUL. He is our friend,
    My pupil, our protector.
FAB. Romulus!
IUL. Romulus knows you better than we can.
    If he approve, Septimia may be yours.
FAB. And have you lifted me thus high in hope
    But to ensure a fall that must be death?
SEPT. Fabius!
FAB. The very name of Romulus
    I curse, detest! If, in destroying him,
    I should pull ruin upon all the earth,
    I would exult in crushing Romulus.
    Away! Away! I see you all are leagued
    For my despair! Oh, let me hide forever
    Deep in the deepest of all earth's recesses,
    No matter where, so it be where the name
    Of Romulus shall torture me no more. [*Rushes out*]
IUL. You see, Septimia, my apprehensions
    Were not unfounded. He is still the victim
    Of the same whirlwind passions.

SEPT. [*Hiding her face on his bosom*] Beloved guardian,
　　　My heart will break.
IUL.　Go in, my love. I see
　　　A visitor's form glancing among yon trees.
　　　Go in—be comforted. Send one that's trusty
　　　To watch, and unobserved, the steps of Fabius.
　　　Ha! Romulus! [*Enter Romulus, passing Septimia as she departs*]
ROM.　Septimia in tears?
IUL.　She has deep cause; and you shall know it all.
　　　But, first, your mission? There's upon your brow
　　　Business of import.
ROM.　May it prove so!
　　　Pontiff, you named to me some time ago
　　　Your son, Valerius.
IUL.　I did.
ROM.　You said
　　　He went hence to Antemnae. What heard you
　　　Of his adventures there?
IUL.　Nothing distinct.
　　　There was a story of a foolish passion
　　　For some girl there; but 'twas confused,
　　　And those who might have known about it seemed
　　　Inclined to hush it up, for the girl's sake.
　　　Valerius himself wrote nothing of it
　　　To us; and hence we doubt 'twas more than half
　　　Mere city gossip. We fear he may have been
　　　Waylaid by robbers; though 'tis possible
　　　He may have gone to some far distant clime
　　　In hope hereafter to surprise his friends,
　　　Who did their best to wean him from ambition
　　　With glory won abroad, to shame their counsel.
ROM.　What was his person?
IUL.　Wherefore would you know?
ROM.　Don't ask me yet.
IUL.　Indeed! You make me tremble.
　　　His mother has a bracelet of his hair.
　　　His sister, too, modelled a bust of him
　　　With clay—
ROM.　And can I see it?

IUL. Yes,
      'Tis in her cottage. Come. Go with me thither,
      And on the way I will unfold to you
      Some other matters of deep interest, touching
      Septimia, whose weeping you remarked
      As you came in.
ROM. On, father! Let me hear. [*Exeunt*]

SCENE 6: *An arch of rock stretches across the front of the stage, forming a frame through which appears a wild, rugged, and rocky background, interspersed with shrubs, trees, fallen trees, and a stream of water. Enter Fabius.*

FAB. [*Alone*] Her look, her interest in my sorrows, show
      The constancy she promised is unbroken,
      Though fate is yet inexorable. Oh,
      I thought I had forgotten in the storms
      Of busy battle weaknesses like this;
      But now they rise as if refreshed with slumber
      And seize with tenfold fury on me. Thou,
      Star of my soul! and hast thou but been shown
      By jealous gods, amid my desolation,
      Only to make me feel there was one treasure
      Greater than all the rest, and even that one
      Must be kept from me and by Romulus!
      [*Gazing around*] Well chosen retreat! I like thy loneliness,
      Broken and savage as my fortune; shunned
      And hated, too, like wretchedness: for fear
      Peoples thy crags with phantoms, from which all
      Hold themselves, trembling, far aloof; so, here
      I may prowl, undisturbed, unless by beasts
      As much the haters of mankind as I.
      Here let me dwell, alone. Here let me curse
      My wrongs and agonies, while famine slowly
      Gnaws and consumes its solitary victim. [*Enter Romulus, muffled in a dark mantle*].
ROM. Fabius.
FAB. [*Starting on seeing the figure*] Who art thou? Who? My evil genius?
ROM. [*Flinging off his mantle*] Behold!
FAB. Romulus? Romulus? Indeed
      My evil genius! Presumptuous wretch,

How darest thou dog me thus to my seclusion?
Am I to find no place upon the earth
Undarkened by thy presence? What dost thou
Here?

Rom.   I would seek the friendship of a man,
 By chance and misconstruction made my foe.
 Your followers and mine embrace already
 In brotherhood. Shall we, their leaders, do
 Less than our followers?

Fab.   Do not provoke me
 Longer by mockery like this. Forlorn as is
 This place of ruggedness, 'tis now my home,
 And I would not be goaded to a madness
 By which a guest, even in a home like this,
 Might deem the household gods had lost their power
 To make a sanctuary of any dwelling,
 However rude, where they are held in honor.
 Hence then, and tempt me not to sacrilege.

Rom.   That very thought shows Fabius to be generous.

Fab.   The acts of Fabius yet shall make you feel
 That he is firm. Hence, for I hate you, hate you
 With an enduring, an implacable hate
 Which will not let the thought of Romulus
 Enter my mind unmingled with the longing
 To see you writhe—aye, at my feet—imploring
 For mercy, unregarded, agonized—

Rom.   My hope of you is quenched. They who informed me
 Your soul was great have been mistaken in you;
 For you not only are not great, you are not
 Even brave, Fabius, and that makes you envious.
 If you will have it, let us then be foes,
 And so remain. But ere we part, I would
 Perform an act of justice. There's a voice
 Whose music is endowed with all the power
 Of all the harps that play around the thrones
 Of great Olympus; at its thrilling tone
 The evil passions hurry from the heart;
 It turns impetuosity, which else
 Is oft a desolating flame, to sunshine
 Which draws forth every health-bestowing fruit

And all the sweetest of the flowers of life!
Innocent youth, that hears its accents early,
Is, by their magic, kept from tangled paths,
Lured to a round of excellence. Baffled age
May by its potency be even recalled
From crime and wretchedness and feel a joy
As his sun sets, he never felt before
Even in its gay meridian. Fabius,
In leaving you, I leave with you that voice;
And here is one will show you where it is.
[*Calls*] Come forth!

FAB. What mummery is this? [*Enter Iulus from behind the rocks*]

IUL. Fabius, I told you that on Romulus
Depended my approval of your suit for
Septimia's hand. Romulus has pleaded
The cause of Fabius, and Septimia
Has my consent to be the bride of Fabius. [*Romulus leads Septimia
forward, veiled. Her uncle removes the veil, and Romulus passes her to
Fabius*]

FAB. Real! Aye, real! Living hands and brow—
It is no dream, and I am blest at last!

SEPT. Oh, Fabius, shall Septimia attempt
In vain to mediate between her husband
And him to whom she owes her happiness?

FAB. Romulus, thou has conquered me at last;
And on my knees I ask thee to forgive—

ROM. Hush. Rise. Let this embrace convince you
That all is now forgot.

FAB. How can I ever
Repay this boundless bounty? From this moment
I only live to execute your orders.
Speak them.

ROM. When good Iulus has pronounced
The nuptial benediction, I will show you
How you can more, much more, than pay for all.
You are in favor with Amulius. Seek him.
Persuade him to withdraw his army. Lure him
To give us peace, to leave us unmolested.
That done, perhaps, I may yet have to ask
Another favor.

Fab. Be it what it may,
            Count it as granted. You have bound me to you
            By that strong power resembling most the power
            Of the great gods—
Rom. [*Smiling*] Which is?
Fab. The power of gentleness. [*Exeunt*]

ACT IV.

Scene 1: *A wild picturesque defile walled by precipices. Enter Romulus and Vulpario.*

Rom. I know this pass. And are you certain that
            Hersilia on withdrawing from her escort
            Went thitherward? [*Pointing off at the side*]
Vul. With my own eyes I tracked her.
Rom. And there's no other path for her return?
Vul. Our men have well examined. There's no other.
Rom. Nor any danger of surprise?
Vul. No, none.
            She had no sooner left her guard, than they,
            Alighting, tethered all her steeds, and leaving
            Near them their arms, not dreaming there was danger,
            Stretched themselves carelessly along the grass,
            Some sleeping, some intent on games of chance,
            Awaiting her return.
Rom. But may not someone
            Have dodged, unseen, when you and your brave men,
            Creeping between these thoughtless guards and their
            Horses and arms, made them your prisoners?
Vul. For
            Each horse we had a prisoner. They were counted
            Ere we permitted them to take their steeds
            And go their way to Alba. All their arms
            We thought it prudent to retain.
Rom. And when
            You told them that Hersilia's life and safety
            Would be as sacred as their own had been,
            Provided no attempt were made to follow her—

Vul. They promised, if they could, they would prevent,
  Upon our solemn oath no harm should come,
  Attempts to follow. Yet I've placed a guard
  At the sole entrance to this pass, lest they
  Prove false when reinforced, and so pursue us.

Rom. Let them; for my great object will be gained
  Before they can have time to rouse Antemnae.

Vul. Yes, and your love be certain of possessing
  The goddess it adores.

Rom. I have not questioned
  My heart, Vulpario. Her happiness,
  And not my own, impels me to this act.
  If she remain another day within
  The power of those who should be her protectors,
  She is forever wretched.

Vul. 'Tis your love
  That makes her happiness so precious to you.
  This love is an ingenious self-deceiver
  And can provide pretexts for good or evil,
  Impelling those who often are themselves
  Unconscious of the motives which direct them.
  But oh, my son, beware how you allow it
  To gain a power which reason cannot check;
  For, if ill-fated, it is agony
  Even when as stainless as the snows from Heaven!
  You wondered, once, how it could rule the strong.

Rom. I'm not so mad as to hope for Hersilia;
  But never shall she, while I live, be driven
  To give her hand where her heart goes not with it.
  As for myself, to others I am bound
  And may not even dream of my own wishes.
  Vulpario, I must make myself a country.
  All must be sacrificed to rearing blossoms
  Whose fruits cannot appear till Romulus
  May not enjoy their beauty and their sweetness.

Vul. If you can make this sacrifice, you merit
  The adoration of all future ages.
  To give up fortune, honors, power, the world,
  Has been achieved by thousands; to resign,
  For future blessings we can ne'er partake,

When within reach, the heart we can subdue,
And when the torrent of young passion pleads
For warm desire with eloquence by which
The gods themselves have oft been turned to wrong,
This is a heroism to entitle
Him who can boast it to the highest throne
On great Olympus.

ROM. Soft. Heard you not a footfall?
A light tread in the distance? Stoop your ear
To earth on that side, while on this, I listen. [*They stoop*]

VUL. Aye, it is she returning. Stand aside,
And all shall be conducted as you ordered. [*Romulus goes out on one side and Vulpario on the other, as Hersilia enters alone*]

HER. [*Alone*]   Yes, dearest friend, this last, this solemn promise,
Has been fulfilled. Let your beloved manes
Repose in peace! Now then to join my escort. [*As she is going, Vulpario appears*]

VUL. Lady, your escort are departed.

HER. [*Alarmed*]   Hence!
What man art thou, who thus would intercept
My passage to my guard. Hence. Let me pass.

VUL. Lady, you go no further. I would not
Wish to seem harsh, but lady, you're my prisoner.

HER. Your prisoner, miscreant! [*Draws a dagger*] Stand aside, or this—

VUL. Nay, lady, all your efforts are but vain.
Behold! [*Whistles, and armed men dart in from every side*]
Resistance must be fruitless here—

HER. Hemmed in by ruffians! In the toils of wretches!
Oh, powers that watch o'er innocence, protect me
From these barbarians! Save me, save me from—
Ha! I am heard! [*Enter Romulus*] The stranger guest! You here?
You here? You? You? [*Running to him*] With you I am in safety!
[*Romulus waves his hand, and Vulpario and the armed men disappear*]
Why, what is this, and who art thou? A god,
That at thy presence even hardened robbers
Start back appalled and lose their savageness?

ROM. I am a man who fears not death itself,
If he can give Hersilia happiness.

HER. And who are these that fly at your command?

Rom. The troops of Romulus.

Her. Recall that word!
Oh, stranger! Do not let my worst of fears
Be realized. Yet, give me yet the truth,
For I will bear it, though I dread to hear it.
Are you a vassal of that robber chief?

Rom. No, lady, I am not the slave of Romulus,
Though I have found it hard to free myself
From his control and own no lord but justice.

Her. I will believe you. Oh, say on, say on—

Rom. I may not tell you, yet, or how or wherefore
I gained consent from Romulus, that you,
Who might have been detained by him to check
The movements now preparing by Antemnae
Against his shepherds, were resigned to me,
And that the guard which was your escort hither
Were suffered, without injury, to return—

Her. My guard in safety? Wherefore then am I
Claimed by a stranger—

Rom. Only as a shield
From threatening peril—

Her. From what peril?

Rom. Tomorrow Dorax, with your father, comes
From Alba; and your father's word is pledged
To force you to accept the hand of Dorax.

Her. Me? Sooner will I wed the grave!

Rom. I saw
Only one mode of rescue. 'Twas to fright
Your train away and to make you a captive.

Her. A captive in the power of Romulus?

Rom. No, lady. By the immortal Hercules,
I swear that you yourself shall be the mistress
Of your own movements and no more a captive.
Whate'er you bid, I execute. You know
The peril I would guard you from. If you
Would brave it, I restore you to Antemnae;
But if you would be screened from an alliance
From which your heart recoils, I'll find you here,
With a Heaven-gifted priestess, an asylum.

> I know not who she is. By chance I met her.
> But this I know, if she's indeed of earth,
> Heaven has given earth an image of itself.

HER. Stranger, I'll trust you. When the danger ends,
> Restore me to Antemnae. Where's this wonder
> Of whom you speak?

ROM. 'Tis near a cave o'erhanging
> The neighboring waterfall she comes to meet me
> In answer to a signal prearranged,
> When I would seek the wisdom of her counsel.

HER. I know that cave. 'Twas thither that my vow
> Just now conducted me.

ROM. What vow?

HER. A maiden,
> The partner of my studies at Antemnae,
> Gained a young stranger's love, which she returned.
> The lover, in some sports held at Laurentum,
> Bore off the laurel from the maiden's brother,
> Who swore revenge; he even forbade his sister
> To see her lover; so 'twas but by stealth
> The pair could meet, and this lone cave was chosen
> For these stolen interviews, to which I myself
> Often attended her—

ROM. Proceed, proceed!

HER. We passed one day happier than all the rest.
> It was her birthday. On that very. eve,
> As we went homeward, we discoursed of friends
> Whom nurses tell us will rise from the grave
> To visit after death the places where
> They have been happiest; and just then a cloud
> Glanced o'er her brow; and Diope began
> To twine a wreath of evergreen and round it
> Twisted some braids of her luxuriant hair,
> And cried, "Hersilia, when this day again
> Returns the coming year, should Diope
> Be in her grave and may come back to view,
> Unseen, the places dearest to her, here
> My spirit shall be present. Take this wreath,
> If what a sad presentiment foretells
> Befall, come to the cave, Hersilia,

On my next birthday; hang the chaplet there
In memory of her who loves you, and
Of hours of ecstasy we've passed together.
And think your friend beholds it and is blessed!"
You'll deem this childishly romantic; but
Had I not kept my secret vow to her,
I should have felt that I had earned the scorn
Of every honest heart for slighting such
Devotedness as only women know.

ROM. Tell me: this maiden, is she not the same
You mentioned at Antemnae?

HER. What! The sister of—

ROM. Fabius.

HER. The same.

ROM. The young man's name?

HER. It was Valerius.

ROM. Thanks, ye blessed gods!

HER. Thanks? Wherefore thanks? Say, did you know the youth?
Was he a friend of yours? If he were, mourn,
For he is lost to you. Awhile he wandered
Around these solitudes, until one night
A peasant saw him on the precipice
Outraving the vexed torrent's wildest roar;
And ever since, the cave has been avoided
Through terror of his ghost, which many say
Is seen to glide by moonlight and in storms
Around the hallowed refuge of his love.

ROM. Ask me not why your words have given me joy
And not the sorrow which you think they should.
But take my thanks, my blessings. [*She makes a gesture of in-*
quiry] No, I cannot
Reveal the mystery yet. A time will come.
Your safety only now must claim our care.
For this inscrutable woman, to whose charge
I shall entrust you, do not seek to learn
Her secret. I've scarce dared conjecture,
Though in some unexplored recess of these
Beautiful solitudes there stands a temple
Built to Carmenta—

HER.   She who to our shores
        Came with her son Evander, long before
        The war of Troy? She who, by worth and wisdom,
        'Tis said was shielded from the doom of death
        Which strikes all other mortals; she who some deem
        One of the Destinies? She whose holy words
        Enshrined in verse, are echoed by all lips
        And ever prove prophetic?

ROM.   I have thought
        That she I speak of may even be Carmenta;
        For, like a goddess, she's unseen except
        In acts of mercy; nor is heard unless
        In oracles of wisdom. She forbids
        Her bounties to be published; she enjoins
        Concealment of her being; and will only
        Appear when called forth by such prayers for aid
        As Deities alone consent to answer.

HER.   I tremble at your picture. Awe and wonder
        Make me at once both long and dread to see her. [*Romulus sounds
the horn. Hersilia listens intently. The horn is answered. Hersilia starts. At
each peal of the response she seems to be more and more appalled, and Romulus lifts his hands in exultation*]

ROM.   'Tis answered! [*To Hersilia*] I attend you; and, be sure
        Evil beneath her wing can never come;
        Nor, from her gentle converse aught arise
        But wisdom and delight. Come, cheerly, cheerly.
        Nay, droop not. Be not fluttered. Come, come, come. [*Exeunt*]

SCENE 2: *A wildly picturesque view among precipices interspersed with trees,
vines, and shrubbery; and including the front of the cave alluded to by Hersilia in the scene preceding. Valerius appears, gazing on an evergreen wreath;
and violently agitated.*

VAL. [*Alone*]   'Tis hers! 'Tis hers! I know the tress. 'Tis hers!
        And with the cypress wreath entwined, it speaks
        Her fate and my despair! She's gone! She's gone!
        Whence these dire emblems and how came they here?
        Has some bad spirit done this to torment me?
        Might I not even retain the doubtful hope
        That still, by miracle, she had escaped? [*Romulus enters unobserved
and approaches him*]

ROM. Forgive me, friend. Disturbed?
VAL. Nay, wonder not
    To find me thus convulsed. No, wonder only
    That I am still so heartless as to live.
    Look upon this. What think you this conveys?
    Spirits from other worlds have sent this chaplet.
ROM. I've heard about that chaplet.
VAL. Whence it came?
ROM. It came from one you know: one from Antemnae.
VAL. Eternal gods!
ROM. A maiden, who had promised
    A fondly cherished friend to hang it here
    On the returning birthday of her friend
    In memory of persecuted love.
VAL. You mean Hersilia. Do you know Hersilia?
    What said she of the friend she honored thus?
    What was her fate when she was wrenched away
    From her adorer? Answer. Does she live?
ROM. Of that she did not speak.
VAL. Not speak? Not speak?
    Why did you wait for her to speak of it?
    Unfeeling man, you should have forced it from her!
    What! Come you here pretending interest
    In my affliction, yet not think to ask
    Whether its object were alive or dead?
    Out on such spiritless, unmeaning friendship!
    An insult to the name! Away, away!
ROM. Hersilia knew nothing of her fate.
    But arm yourself with patience. It may come
    Within my power to satisfy your doubts.
    I know the brother—
VAL. Speak not of the monster!
    I will not listen even to his name.
    Man! Do not, do not goad me into madness
    By reference to the miscreant whose envy
    Could force him even to sacrifice the purest
    Of all created beings—his own sister!
    Man! Do not tempt me to forget the promise
    I gave her on the eve before I lost her
    Ne'er to resent her wrongs. Aye, let him live,

For she implored he might. I, too, must live.
Beloved! I gave my oath that I would live
Nor seek to join thy spirit in the skies!
Oh, wherefore is it that I may not die!

Rom.　Valerius, keep your promise. Live, and since
　　　　Fabius is now my friend—

Val.　He cannot be the friend to any.

Rom.　Fabius is wedded
　　　　To your own father's ward.

Val.　Septimia?
　　　　Gentle Septimia given to such a wretch!
　　　　And yet—and yet—had this alliance been
　　　　A few months earlier, it might have opened
　　　　My path to happiness. 'Tis too late now!
　　　　Oh lost, lost, lost! Cursed be the light that beams
　　　　First on the sufferer from within the tomb,
　　　　Shows him the raptures that he might have shared
　　　　And on his other anguish, heaps despair!
　　　　Oh, my adored! One friendly ray had saved you,
　　　　But all was dark and the flower drooped and died!

Rom.　If she be dead, shall not the dead be honored?
　　　　How can you honor her, but by fulfilling
　　　　Her last desires. You say she bade you live?

Val.　Do I not live?

Rom.　Valerius, existence
　　　　Given up to sorrow is not life. To live
　　　　Is to be active. Say, did not your father
　　　　Rear you for usefulness? Oh, how that wise,
　　　　That good old man would blush to see his son
　　　　Living as though life were but made for tears,
　　　　Squandering his days to gratify himself,
　　　　To gratify his grief, and not to aid
　　　　His brethren with his talents and his time!
　　　　Think you, by tears, to show you had a right
　　　　To such a heart as hers for whom you mourn?
　　　　For shame! A heart like hers would deem itself
　　　　Insulted by such weakness. Mark that chaplet.
　　　　Read in that evergreen what man should be.
　　　　Believe it sent to you by her you've lost

To teach your virtue to preserve its beauty
Brightest amid the snows of fortune's winter.

VAL. To him who wears no wound on him, 'tis easy
To talk of fortitude.

ROM. No wound? No wound?
I have a heart, Valerius, whose longings
Are fierce as the wild hurricane. I love,
And fortune does not frown upon my love;
But I think man, the image of the gods,
Was formed for nobler, better uses than
To immolate himself for such desires.
My vow is pledged to render thousands happy;
And can I basely give up all for one,
Even though that one's myself?

VAL. Oh, spare me!
I fear my power of usefulness is gone.
Instruct me what I yet can undertake.
Tell me. I'll do it, do it, yes, and die!

ROM. Do what you can, and you will die in peace;
But opportunities misused or lost
Will make your death an agony beyond
All that your life has suffered. Your afflictions,
You say, have taken you from all the world.
Your own afflictions! Oh, Valerius, think
What deep afflictions you have brought on many
A tender heart in your dear father's home,
And who now grieve as deeply over you
As you o'er her you think that you have lost!
You did not apprehend your selfish passion
Would make you cruel; but it has. Even now
It wrings the bosoms at your home with anguish.
I know them all. Your father is my guide,
My counsellor, my oracle! Oh, friend,
But let me make you feel as I feel for you;
Render you worthy of the father who
Has taught me what man should be. Grant, oh grant
That I may have the blessing of returning
Some of his kindness by restoring you
To him, to virtue, to the world—

VAL. 'Tis done.
    I yield me to your guidance. I am yours.
ROM. Then come with me. Ere long you will confess
    That he who merits happiness can never
    Be permanently wretched. Come—and—hope! [*Exeunt*]

SCENE 3: *Splendid apartment in the royal palace at Alba. Enter Amulius, meeting Dolcar.*

AM. Ha, Dolcar! From the hills? The news? The news?
DOL. You have no more to fear from Romulus:
    A sudden change has come upon him. He
    Now prates of peace instead of violence.
AM. Of peace? How came the change?
DOL. Some spell
    Flung o'er him by Iulus. Now his fancy
    Is filled with visions of a nation framed
    On the fantastic notions of the priest.
AM. Then we can conquer him without an effort.
DOL. Aye, and possess yourself of the palladium.
    But arm your soul for startling news: Hersilia—
AM. What of her?
DOL. Has disappeared.
AM. Hersilia?
DOL. 'Tis thought, a captive of the robber chief
    And in concealment at the sacred grove—
AM. Hersilia captured!
DOL. Hence Dorax has arrayed
    A powerful force and swears to bring its treasures
    To Alba with Hersilia.
AM. Bravely done!
    And opportunely, too; for, as I hear,
    The neighboring states begin to cool in fury
    Against this Romulus. Nay, some even dare
    To give him praise and countenance! The fools!
DOL. Their countenance will soon avail him little.
    His downfall is at hand. This very day
    His robbers celebrate a festival,
    Brought by Evander into Italy,
    To Pan, the shepherd's god, for his protection

Over their flocks from wolves. 'Tis at a cave
Below Mount Aventine; and Remus has been
Named by his brother high priest of the rites.
They call them, if my memory is faithful,
The Lupercalia, or some such name.

AM. But say, how aids this festival our plans?

DOL. While Romulus' men are busy there, Iulus
Is unprotected; and our troops will pour,
Part, on the grove, and part upon the band
When without arms and unprepared, engaged
In their devotions.

AM. Mars inspired the thought!

DOL. 'Tis well that some are loyal, when perhaps
Those who are trusted most may first betray.
Fabius—

AM. And what of him?

DOL. Soft. He is here. [*Enter Fabius*]

AM. Well, Fabius, we soon shall see this upstart
Chained, like a wild beast, in an iron cage,
Borne through the cities he has long made tremble,
A common show, to be scoffed at and scorned!

FAB. Prince, let me rather think the time may come
When these proud cities, great as now they are,
May in his glories be themselves forgotten,
As the sun's coursers, in their radiant rise,
Extinguish all the lesser lights of Heaven.

AM. Fabius!

FAB. I know, for I myself, my lord,
Have shared the error that has made the traveller,
Affrighted by the tales of slandering rumor,
Turn from the path that passes near their hills.
But I have lived among them; I have witnessed
Virtues in those poor cottages which here
In Alba's palace would in vain be sought for—

AM. You've grown a warm defender, sir—

FAB. I do not
Assume the gift of prophecy, but, mark me!
A people yet may rise beside the Tiber
Who, although born unfriended, without laws,

Commerce, or agriculture, without even a home,
May give a home and laws to all the world!

AM. If you have found so great a people, wherefore
Not plant yourself among them? Why return
To these decaying states, so soon to be
Forgotten and forsaken?

FAB. Prince, I come
To tell you I *have* done as you advise;
And I now visit Alba on a message
Of peace and kindness from this rising power.

AM. Impudent traitor!

DOL. [*Apart to him*]   Spoke I not the truth?

FAB. No traitor, Prince; for I would save your state
By making you the friend of Romulus.

AM. The friend? The friend? Call in my veteran guard!
Seize this acknowledged rebel!

FAB. Hold. I'm protected,
Being his herald, by the shield of Heaven.

AM. Skulk and be safe beneath your shield, then, till
Upon the battlefield by vengeance crushed.
Back to your Romulus and bid him bring
His arms and yield himself and them to me.
And he and his shall be protected. Failing
In this, I swear eternal war against him.
Fetch his submission, and I grant you pardon.
Till then, I am your foe. [*Fabius is going*]
Stay, sir! There is
A certain hostage in my hands—a sister
Of this most loyal Fabius, is there not?

FAB. My lord, you cannot dare—

AM. If in three days
You do not bring me favorable news,
Your sister dies. These are no times to trifle.
Some great example must stop further treachery.
Hence! Hence!

FAB. Perfidious villain!

AM. And
Be grateful for my clemency, that you
Yourself have thus escaped.

FAB. I shall perform
What duty bids. The rest is with the gods. [*Exit Fabius*]
DOL. My liege, 'twas wisely done to bid them bring
Romulus here, for Romulus' twin-brother—
AM. What? Say that again! Twin-brother? Whose twin-brother?
DOL. Romulus'! Remus, although twinned with him
Is of another stamp—gentle, unwarlike.
AM. Hold. Said you twins? Who were their parents? Answer!
Their age! Some nineteen years? Their parents?
DOL. Sire,
I thought you knew of Remus.
AM. So I did.
I knew there was some reptile called the brother
Of this young miscreant. But what thought I
Or any, whether they were twins! The countenance
Of Romulus awakened withering doubts
Which this twin-brother story would appear
To turn into a maddening certainty.
DOL. You speak in riddles. What can it import
More to your majesty, their being twins?
AM. True, true, true. Forgive me, Dolcar. Recollections
Of a disastrous tale of years long past—
Forgive me for this folly. A sad story
And it bewilders me when it returns. [*Enter Numitorius*]
[*To Numitorius*] Your eye foretells strange news. Out with it.
NUM. Dorax, your friend, is slain.
AM. By Romulus?
NUM. Yes, in defense of the palladium.
AM. How came the robbers there? Was it not today
They were engrossed in their religious rites?
NUM. A scout from Romulus saw the advance
Of Dorax, and the chief withdrew his men
From their devotions.
AM. Then Antemnae is
No longer ours. Hersilia's hand is free.
On me the odium falls of an attempt
To desecrate the holiest of shrines
Which Romulus gains the glory of defending!
DOL. But now, my lord, you named him with contempt—

Am. Slave! The contempt was only on my lip,
    Not in my heart! That shudders at his name.
Num. Let not your heart sink yet. There's further news.
Am. More ruin? Let it pour!
Num.   No. Remus and
    A party of the robbers are your prisoners.
Am. Remus within my power! Thanks, thanks, thanks!
    Well, on, go on—Oh, my kind brother, say—
    How came he in our power? Remus our prisoner!
    Tell it again! 'Tis music to my soul!
Num.   His brother bade him linger at the cave
    And, with a chosen few, protect its shrine
    And pay the honors of the Lupercalia,
    While he, with thousands of his veterans, flew
    To meet the force of Dorax.
Am. So the troops
    Despatched against him there, made sudden work—
Num.   Hundreds to one they poured upon the shepherds
    And yet the shepherds fought them to the last.
    But all in vain. Hark! [*Shouts and martial music heard*]
    Shouts! Dost hear?
    The prisoners are entering the city!
Am. Never to quit it more! Dolcar, see Remus
    Brought to my presence! Leap, leap high,
    My heart, so long unused to throb with joy!
    Now I shall know it all. Prove what it may,
    At once I'm sure of safety and revenge! [*Exeunt*]

ACT V.

SCENE 1: *A new view of the cave of Romulus, so disposed as to show in the distance several distinct summits of hills. Enter Romulus with Valerius.*

Rom. Valerius, it gives me joy to see
    Your eye begin to brighten and your ear
    Conscious of what it hears. Employment,
    New scenes, and stirring objects, not the cant
    Of schoolmen's precepts, are the remedies
    For the bruised heart. If one despotic passion
    Bring man to woe, fill his imagination

With some new idol to drive out the former,
Whose fate will be a warning to the last
To leave a mind resolved on independence
The master of itself. I trust, ere long,
To find you worthy of your noble race,
The hero they would make you. There are reasons
Why I defer restoring you; you'll know them
Early and honor them. On my return
From a most painful and a secret mission
We will together to the sacred grove. Till then—
But soft. There's one approaching who must have
Some private orders from me. In, Valerius,
I'll be with you anon.

VAL. When you are with me,
The spell of a superior energy
Drives back my sorrows; but when you are gone,
They rush, again, like furies to torment me. [*Exit Valerius into the*
cave]

ROM. [*Alone*] False counsellor! Am I myself less feeble
Than he whose feebleness I thus upbraid?
Like thee I sleep, and I forget and wake
Free and a moment happy; when the sense
Of all I have to yield, with tenfold fury
Comes back to goad me, like the criminal
Whose eyes unclose in smiles, but to behold
The world depart for which he lost himself. [*Enter Vulpario*]
Vulpario, tell me, how could you outlive
The loss of Ilia?

VUL. What means, my friend,
That strange inquiry in that tone of anguish?

ROM. Nothing, Vulpario, nothing. Dorax, friend,
Fell, as you know, in his assault upon
The sacred grove. No motive now remains
For the detention of Hersilia.

VUL. True.

ROM. You know I promised, when she could return
In safety to her home, I'd set her free.

VUL. 'Tis well remembered.

Rom. On the instant, therefore,
    The wretch who would have taken her hand by force
    Having thus paid for his presumption,
    I must repair to her retreat. While absent,
    To you, Vulpario, I entrust—

Vul. Hold. See who comes. [*Enter Fabius*]

Rom. From Alba? Well! Amulius? Speak, what tidings?

Fab. The worst. That despot drove me from his presence
    With execrations; but it is not that
    Which thus disturbs me.

Rom. Why, what more
    Can have befallen?

Fab. The party who remained
    To celebrate the Lupercalia, crossing
    On their return such foes as had escaped—

Rom. Well—

Fab. Arm yourself with fortitude. As I
    Departed from the palace, I beheld—

Rom. What? What?

Fab. Your brother Remus—

Rom. Dead? In battle dead?

Fab. No. He was entering Alba as a prisoner!

Rom. Praised be the gods, for I will break his fetters!
    My gentle brother captured! That meek spirit
    That looked on war but as the imposition
    Through which the bad usurp renown, he, he
    Become the earliest victim of the war,
    Loaded with fetters and exposed to scorn,
    Not for himself, pure heart! but that he is
    The brother of rough Romulus! Their triumph
    Shall be a brief one! Yes, unhappy Remus,
    Before the tyrant can prepare his insults,
    This arm shall make thee free as the young eagle.

Fab. Do not indulge a hope which must be foiled.
    Prepare to hear that Remus is no more.

Rom. Great Hercules avert it! What! Destroy
    A youth from whom he can have nought to fear;
    Of whom he never has heard aught but what
    Even in the tyrant's flinty breast should waken
    Tenderness? Why, when I myself have struck

These Alban villains to my feet, poor Remus
Would bind the wounds I gave them. Fabius, no!
Amulius could not look upon that face
And not relent; that pure and feeling eye
Would rein back even the tiger. He's not dead.

FAB. He who can murder in cold blood a woman
Would scarcely spare a man, whate'er his worth.

ROM. A woman? Who? What woman?

FAB. My own sister.

ROM. Ha!

FAB. Yes, Diope, whom he consented,
Through a pretended friendship for her brother,
To hide from one whose love—

ROM. Did you indeed say
Your sister, Diope—

FAB. You ask as if—

ROM. No matter why or how I ask, lives she?

FAB. I hope she does, but yet I fear to hope.
The tyrant holds her as a guarantee
Against attack. He swears that if his city
Should be assaulted, Diope shall fall.

VUL. Pardon me, Romulus. I see how much
You are perplexed. I have heard all. I know
The proper course.

ROM. Go on.

VUL. There's not a corner
Of Alba with which I am not familiar.
Nay, more: I told you once the treasures
My followers took from this Amulius I
Gave back in secret to <his pl>undered subjects;
And hence have form<ed f>ull many a secret friend
Within his city walls. Numbers even now
Of my own followers lurking in disguise
Among these Albans every hour are adding
Strength to a powerful party, who now stand
Ready to rise, whenever from without
They can be certain they may be sustained
Against the tyrant. By concerted signs
I soon can gather them. I have the means
Of access to the city unperceived.

Disguised, I'll hasten thither. I'll array
My friends to watch o'er Diope and Remus.
Meanwhile, let all our forces be assembled
And with all speed. While I prepare within,
Do you rush on the city from without,
Release the prisoners, and avenge Aeghystus!

ROM. Bravely devised. As you pass, give the order
For every beacon fire, on every hill,
To flame at once and call our warriors hither.
Go, friend; go, father! And the gods watch o'er you! [*Exit Vul-*
pario]
Stay, Fabius. A word before you join
Your band for battle. Fabius, you once promised
That you would grant whatever boon I asked—
I said there might be one which I might ask.
The time is come for me to ask it now.
The lover of your sister, yes, Valerius,
Lives, aye, he is here; nay, more, he is my friend.
Start not, he must be yours. He must be more,
Fabius. He must, if Diope escape,
Be, and with your own consent he must,
Your brother. Hang not back. Your oath!
There, there, I knew it! Your hand on the pledge.
'Tis done! I shall not yet inform Valerius
Of what I have accomplished for him. Go.
Prepare your bands to join in the assault.
Valerius shall lead another party. [*Fabius is going*] Hold.
Send hither fifty of our choicest horsemen
With two spare horses, carefully accoutered.
Now, hasten, Fabius—[*Distant shouts and the music of an alarm
among the troops. At the same time the beacon fire blazes on the nearest
hilltop, and, after a very short delay between each, a blaze from each of the
other hilltops answers it. From this point to the end of the scene the hum of
the gathering continues in the distance*] for, hark! Shouts and trumpets
Proclaim the stir begun. And lo! where fire
From every hilltop quickly answers fire,
And valor flies to arms! Away! Away! [*Exit Fabius*]
Valerius, ho! Valerius, I say! [*Enter Valerius*]
See you those glancing flames, Valerius? Hear you
The murmurs and the trumpet calls of thousands

Gathering for vengeance? Oh, events have passed
Within the little moment of your absence
Which it would cost a lifetime to record.
Attend, Valerius, for among them are
Matters of awful import to yourself,
As well as me. Did I not just now tell you
That I myself had sorrows of the heart?
And that the time must come when I must lose
All hope of her I worship? I had meant
Myself to give her freedom. Other claims
Prevent me, and to you I delegate
That sacred office. Fly back to your cave;
See that mysterious and inspired unknown;
Inform her that the prince who sought Hersilia
Has fallen in battle and Hersilia now
May go in safety to Antemnae. The unknown
Will understand your meaning. Guard Hersilia.
A troop of fifty horse will meet you here.
They shall attend you. But, beware, my friend,
Of naming who it is that sends you thither;
And, when Hersilia's safe, then back to join me
Before the walls of Alba. If you there
Encounter Fabius, know he is your friend;
And know, besides, if you observe all this,
Perhaps, you may regain your Diope.

VAL. How! Does she live? Lives Diope?

ROM. Perform your orders faithfully, and if
Diope lives she only lives for you,
And with her brother's will; but, slight them,
And she is lost to you forever. [*The tumult and trumpets are louder and nearer*]
Hear you?
War howls on every side. The army gathers.
Away! [*Exit Valerius*] Now, Remus, rescue or revenge! [*Rushes out*]

SCENE 2: *Elegant apartment in the royal palace at Alba. Enter Amulius meeting Dolcar.*

AM. No signs of troops approaching?

Dol. None, my lord;
      But all is silent.

Am. As the hour preceding
      Earthquakes!

Dol. But you have naught to dread, even should
      They come with all their powers. The city walls
      Glitter with steel. Legions in every square
      Pant for the call to battle. Even the women,
      Crowding the windows when they see a soldier
      Run from his brother soldiers at some stall
      To snatch a cup of water, even the women
      Smilingly cry, "When shall we view the robbers
      Marched through our streets in fetters?" Thus, you see,
      Each heart beats high with certainty. Alarm
      Pales not a cheek in Alba.

Am. There's more cause, though,
      Than if the foe were battering at our walls.
      The beacon fires were seen on every hill;
      The hum of gathering thousands, and their trumpets
      Startled the dwellers on the forest's edge
      Full many an hour ago. When they delay
      Mysteriously thus, it is portentous
      Of deep-laid plans. Soft. Here comes my guard
      With Diope. Hasten to the walls again
      And bring me tidings. See you mark each movement. [*Exit Dolcar.*

At the same time Diope is brought in guarded]
      Lady, your brother has betrayed my cause,
      And you must suffer for it.

Dio. I?
      Did I e'er offer homage to your cause?
      Am I within this palace by my choice?
      'Twas by your own suggestion that my brother
      Brought me, against my will, a prisoner here.

Am. I hold you as his hostage. A hard fate!
      But you must thank him for it, not blame me.
      Still, although wronged, I would be merciful;
      And you shall hear how you yourself may grant me
      The joy of saving you.

Dio. *You* merciful!

AM.   You have been guarded here to wean you from
　　　Some silly fondness hateful to your brother.
　　　His ruling passion is to see that fondness
　　　Extinguished; and all hope forever torn
　　　From him who shares it, whom he abhors.
　　　Swear to fulfill his wish, if he return
　　　Back to his duty here; and let me send
　　　A herald to inform him that you will,
　　　On that condition, solemnly renounce
　　　Your love for this Valerius, and—

DIO. I see
　　　Your scope. You'd purchase, with the sister's perjury,
　　　The brother's bondage to a tyrant's will.

AM.   You have your choice. If you refuse my boon,
　　　These guards conduct you to the city wall,
　　　Place you on high before the hostile army,
　　　And the first blow of Fabius against Alba
　　　Is answered by their daggers in your heart.

DIO. Then let them strike. The blow will be but death.
　　　And what is death? The little moment which
　　　Changes the form of life but does not change
　　　The soul that wears it. King of Alba, vision
　　　Dwarfed by this world may shrink back with dismay
　　　From that whose brightness makes it seem to such
　　　A stinging void; but, King, my different view
　　　Welcomes that little moment which transfers me
　　　From a distorted, falsely-colored scene,
　　　Where all I value withers, to a sphere,
　　　Where purer eyes will see me as I am,
　　　Where baseness cannot thwart the honest purpose,
　　　Where despots cannot break the virtuous heart,
　　　And where his spirit, without whom existence
　　　To me were wretchedness, no longer may
　　　By envy and injustice be restrained
　　　From joining her whom not even you, great King,
　　　With all your threats, will scare from her allegiance.

AM.   What! Still unmoved in obstinacy, though
　　　Your brother's blood—

DIO. King of Alba, mark me!
　　　My oath of constancy is pledged. If Fabius

        Could stoop to take his life as a reward
        For the base forfeit of his sister's oath,
        He were not worth the saving.

AM.   Take the fruits
        Of your perverseness. [*To the guards*] Bear her to the ramparts.
        Hence! Hence! Nor supplication, nor reproach—

DIO.   Oh, I make no reproach. I go as gladly
        As to a march of triumph o'er the world. [*Diope goes off, guarded,*
on one side, as Dolcar enters on the other]

AM.   So, Dolcar, so—the enemy?

DOL.   Clouds of dust
        Shade the horizon. On the forest's border
        No light appears between the trees; but darkness,
        And seemingly, from forms in motion, fills them;
        And a deep buzz, and now and then a trumpet,
        And multitudinous tramps that shake the earth
        Proclaim the war advancing.

AM.   Oh, Nemesis,
        Let not the hecatombs of victims offered
        For many a year upon the shrine I reared
        To deprecate thy scourge have bled in vain!
        Fight on my side, and if thy will be blood,
        It shall outstream in torrents! And, scorn not,
        Oh, awful goddess, to sustain my courage,
        Withering before the portents of this hour!

DOL.   Pardon me, King, but wherefore should it wither?
        Some of your foes already are your captives;
        And with them, Remus—

AM.   There's my agony!
        Oh, Dolcar, could you know what in that Remus
        I shudder at! But I will have the truth!
        He answers warily, seems to know nothing,
        Although I threatened torture if he did not
        Reveal the secret of his birth—

DOL.   His birth?
        What is the secret of his birth to you?

AM.   True—nothing, nothing. But I ordered him
        To Numitorius. Who can tell but he
        Knows the dark truth already? By the gods,
        If but one look betray even a suspicion,

His grey hair shall not save him. Dolcar, pardon
This frenzy. 'Tis to none but you, my Dolcar,
I would lay bare the anguish that I suffer.
If you betray me, tremble! But on you,
On you alone, can I rely; and honors,
And countless treasures, Dolcar, shall reward
Your zeal, if it remain untiring—

DOL. My
Most honored sovereign.

AM. Yes, my friend, yes, Dolcar,
That cry of war, "Aeghystus," which the robbers
Combined with Romulus are said to shout;
The look of Remus, nay, ten thousand shadows
Gather to drive me mad! Oh, Romulus!

DOL. Once, chance alone preserved him from my dagger.
The chance may turn, my lord, when next I try.

AM. Chance? From his infancy, a guardian genius
Has thus made chance his shield. But gentle Dolcar,
If Numitorius change color when
He questions Remus, if he cast one look
Of kindness on him; though I know he can
Dissemble, for when his Aeghystus fell,
He did not shed a tear, no matter, mark!
If his voice tremble, be on the alert—
But break we off. He comes. Withdraw
And watch you for the judgment. [*Exit Dolcar on one side, as
Numitorius enters on the other*]

NUM. Brother,
What is the duty you exact from me?

AM. Remus must be condemned. The rest I pardon.

NUM. Why except Remus? Gentle and unwarlike,
None ever heard of him except in deeds
Of mercy and affection.

AM. By his fall
At least I touch his brother [*Eying Numitorius intently*], his twin
brother.

NUM. Amulius, when you robbed me of the purple,
'Twas at the instance of your daughter Antho,
And in the hope that I might be a check

On your despotic temper, and thus guard
My country, I consented to accept
The throne of pontiff and of sovereign judge—

AM.   And Antho's gratitude rewarded you.
When your own daughter, Ilia, forfeited
Her life by the desertion of her vows,
Through Antho's intercession, I preserved
Your daughter.

NUM.   How preserved her?
You took her from the vestals; you denied
Her father, your own brother, even a sight
Of his poor daughter. And the gods took Antho
From an unworthy parent, and no sooner
Was Antho in her grave than Ilia followed.

AM.   I screened your Ilia from ignominy,
And you reward me with these base surmises.
Why am I twitted with the grievances
Of times almost forgot?

NUM.   Only to lead you
To think how little your security
Has been confirmed by harshness. Let me not
Say 'twas through you my son, Aeghystus, fell,
And Ilia followed; and that through you Silius
Was basely exiled; although your severeness
Has made your subjects charge you with these crimes,
And 'tis my gentler policy alone
Has kept their indignation from rebellion.
Your throne stands on a smouldering volcano,
Which, at one tyrant trample more, will burst
And swallow you and all your boasted power.
Beware! Your people love this Romulus,
Remus, and all their shepherd warriors. Harm them
Without a better cause, and you are lost—

AM.   You have some secret reason for this zeal
To save the robber boy. Declare it.

NUM.   I?
What reason can I have, but to preserve
The innocent? This Remus is to me
A stranger, but a wronged one, I am sure.
As such, I would befriend him.

Am.   If within
      This very hour his head falls not beneath
      The executioner, your own shall answer it. [*Exit Amulius*]
Num. [*Alone*]   Now to the throne of judgment. Take my life?
      Let him. With gladness shall I yield it, if
      It can preserve the guiltless. Powers of justice,
      Come to my succor, guide me, give me light! [*Exit*]

Scene 3: *The place of judgment. In the foreground, a large, open space, on the right hand side of which, as the spectator faces the stage, stands a platform raised several steps and surmounted by a judgment seat, which is backed by a large, square block of marble, sustaining a statue of Nemesis. Beyond this open space appear beautiful gardens; and along the back, in the distance, rise part of the city walls of Alba.*

Crowds of spectators are discovered as the scene opens. A solemn march ushers in Numitorius with his official suite. Numitorius ascends the judgment seat, and the officers of his suite take their respective places at the foot of the steps.

Num.   Officer! Call the prisoner. [*An officer goes out and returns followed by Remus, chained and guarded. Dolcar follows and watches Numitorius intently*]
Off.   He is here.
Num.   Shepherd, your name!
Rem.   Remus.
Num.   Of what crime
       Stand you accused?
Rem.   I know not.
Num.   You are the brother
       Of Romulus, the robber, it appears;
       So you, no doubt, are charged with robbery.
       Where's your accuser?
Rem.   Sir, I am no robber.
       The Alban troops surprised me and my friends
       At a religious festival.
Num.   Then wherefore
       Are you brought here for punishment?
Rem.   Because
       I cannot name my parents. The King threatened
       To put me to the rack, although I answered
       The truth and all the truth.

Num.   'Tis very strange, though.
        Do you, indeed, not know who were your parents?

Rem.   'Tis now some nineteen years, since, as we learned,
        A herdsman found my brother and myself
        Cradled within the scooped-out fragment of
        A fallen forest tree beside the Tiber—

Num.   If this be true, 'tis strange that the report
        Should not, ere this, have reached us here at Alba.

Rem.   The herdsman, Faustulus, who found us there,
        Enjoined us not to speak of it. He made us
        Pass for his children and was proud of being
        Esteemed our father.

Dol.   Pardon, gracious judge,
        But do not these fantastic tales appear
        Inventions, framed by Romulus, to give
        Factitious interest to his vulgar birth?
        He strives, upon the influence he has gained
        Among the shepherds, to exalt himself;
        Forms daring projects, and even now arrays
        His powers against our city.

Rem.   Wait his coming;
        And, if you dare, then charge him with a fraud,
        And you will have your answer.

Dol.   Mighty judge,
        Mark you the prisoner's tone? Is this the accent
        Of one without ambition to be more
        Than a mere shepherd?

Num.   Dolcar, 'tis for me
        To deal with this young man. In truth, you seem,
        Shepherd, to use a tone and bear yourself
        As ill comports with your supposed condition.
        And if you have shed Alban blood, or robbed
        The citizens of Alba, you must not
        Look to escape unpunished.

Rem.   With my head,
        For any murder, any robbery
        Committed by our troops, my lord, I answer.
        If these alone endanger me, I need
        No better safeguard. [*To Dolcar*] But before what judge,
        Can you, vile mercenary traitor, answer

For your offense to us? To us
Who, with most unsuspecting confidence,
Received you to our arms? Gave you the shelter
For which you humbly begged, and would have perished,
Each of us, all of us, ere the pursuer
You said you dreaded should have looked upon you!
[*To Numitorius*] Yes, my lord, Romulus and I and all
Would have done this for him who now stands by
To slander us and ours when in peril
And give the very life, which might have fallen
A sacrifice for his, to the vile headsman.

DOL. I've served Amulius. If I have incurred
Hatred upon your hills, 'tis on your hills
Alone I can be punished. Here, I've earned
Nothing but gratitude. My lord, you called
For an accuser. You have heard, my lord,
The prisoner unconsciously declare
That I once chanced to fall among these robbers.
What better evidence than mine, then, can
Be offered to convict him? I pronounce him
Guilty and meriting the axe. The gods
Sent me to be a witness of these robbers'
Insatiate thirst for power; to fling the light
Of truth upon the covert winding paths
Of their ambition; and the King himself
Commissions me to utter what I know
And call on you for judgment. [*A great stir appears in the crowd. A voice is heard clamoring for admittance, and at length Faustulus breaks through the center of the throng and stands between Remus and the judgment seat*]

FAUS. [*Without*] Back, I say,
Stand back and let me pass. I *will* be heard. [*Enters*]
Are you the judge? I, sir, am Faustulus.

REM. [*Stretching forth his arms to embrace him*] My father! Oh, my father!

FAUS. Fettered, my poor boy!
Fetters on limbs formed only to be free
As the young hart that bounds among the hills!

REM. Those tears, my father, make me mourn your coming.

FAUS. You do not envy me the mournful joy
    Of weeping for you, if I cannot aid you?

NUM. [*Aside, much moved*] Peace, peace, my bursting heart.

DOL. [*Observing him impatiently*] Officious dotard!

REM. I should have died more firmly, had you left me
    To die alone.

FAUS. Die? No! It cannot be!
    What said you? Die? At that word die, I feel
    These white hairs rise with horror. Oh, my son,
    I'll save you, now, my son, a second time;
    For look! the tears are standing in the eye
    Of your just judge! My lord, you need not hide them,
    For I will prove that pity is your duty,
    And I command you to arrest the judgment.

DOL. Hear you the arrogant insolence of this
    Imposter! Tear the villain hence! The course
    Of justice must not be obstructed thus.

FAUS. Not all the powers of earth shall stir me hence
    Till I have uttered the disclosures which—

DOL. Stop the knave's mouth!

NUM. Disclosures? What disclosures?

FAUS. Touching the birth of Remus and his brother.

DOL. What is their birth to us?

NUM. True, Faustulus,
    How can their origin affect the judgment
    Which 'tis my duty to pronounce on Remus?

FAUS. One word; and that, my lord, with you in secret,
    Is all I ask.

DOL. Dismiss the meddling dotard!
    Guards, do your duty!

FAUS. On my knees, great judge—

NUM. Speak before all. 'Tis for all Alba that
    I sit in judgment. It is right all Alba
    Should hear the cause in which I am to judge.

FAUS. Then thus compelled, my lord, I will reveal
    A secret which I thought would slumber with me
    Unspoken in the tomb; but then I thought not
    To see the subject of it in a danger

From which he only can be rescued by
Warning you, judge, to pause and to beware
Of shedding blood whose source—
REM. What says he?
DOL. [*Rushes forward, seizes the arm of Faustulus, and says to him, aside*]
Escape, old man, or tremble for your life!
FAUS. [*To Dolcar*] Shall I be silenced by a wretch like you?
Albans! The mystery which shrouds the birth
Of Romulus and Remus touches even
The realm itself—
DOL. Liar and slave!
FAUS. I swear
They are the offspring—
DOL. Hence with the impostor! [*The guards make an advance towards
Faustulus*]
REM. [*Attempting to screen him*] Oh, Faustulus, my friend, my father!
NUM. [*Starting up*] Guards,
Stand off, stand off; nor lay a finger on
That aged man. [*To Dolcar*] By what right, Dolcar, dare you
Command this violence where I preside?
DOL. My lord, the crisis calls for promptitude.
My head shall answer for it to the King.
Permit me, then—
NUM. [*Indignantly*] Permit that my authority
Be thus insulted!
DOL. [*To the guards*] In the King's name, soldiers!
On your allegiance, advance, come on!
NUM. People of Alba, guard the sanctuary
Of justice; and protect your judge! [*Vulpario, disguised as an
Alban, darts from the crowd and is supported by a number of the citizens
and others*]
VUL. [*Aloud to Numitorius*] Be firm!
The people are around you. Who shall dare
Resist the people? [*Shouts. Vulpario exclaims, aside*] Now, ye gods,
Now prosper Romulus! [*Amulius rushes in, followed by soldiers*]
AM. What's this confusion?
Is't not enough that armies from without
Beat at our gates? Shall we become a prey
Of anarchy within?

Dol. Sire, there are those
      Who mock your power.
Am.   Let them be punished.
Num.   Then
      Punish this fellow, whose effrontery
      Has dared to bid defiance to my office.
      You wear the crown. Uphold the rights of justice.
Am.   Dolcar was here to watch, at my request—
Dol. My lord, this is no question of the rights
      Of justice. 'Twas but to protect the rights
      Of your own royal crown I interposed;
      For infamous imposture might have shaken
      The throne itself by a feigned story of
      This robber's origin. 'Tis for you, my lord,
      To probe the treason to its root; but Faustulus,
      So earnestly upheld by Numitorius,
      Is made the instrument of loftier traitors,
      And it was my attempt to seize the knave,
      Which wrought this shameful riot.
Num.   'Tis not so.
      Your effort to control the course of justice
      Produced it; and, Amulius, I invoke you,
      And call on all the gods to second me,
      To see that justice reassume its reign.
Am.   It shall; and its first lesson shall be written
      In the heart's blood of that impostor, Remus.
      Guards, seize the prisoner. Let some trusty sword
      Be buried in his heart. [*Guards approach him*]
Rem. Oh, brother!
Dol. [*Drawing his sword*] Mine
      Be that sword! [*As the guards attempt to seize Remus, Vulpario and
some of his associates attack them, rescue Remus, and drive back the guards;
but these last rally and regain Remus; and Dolcar and another engage Vulpario, who disarms the assistant and grapples with Dolcar, who loses his
sword in the struggle but flings Vulpario from him upon his knee. The antagonist who was first disarmed, and another soldier, grasp Vulpario on each
side and hold him down. At the same moment, guards, one on each side of
Remus, draw him into a position to receive the thrust of Dolcar, who, as he
regains his sword, exclaims*]

Dol. Thou'lt not escape me now! [*As Dolcar is preparing for the plunge upon Remus, Vulpario, struggling with the two guards, exclaims loudly*]

Vul. Where, where is Romulus? [*At this moment there is a violent shout and commotion. The crowd of Albans falls back and leaves the center of the stage open. The distant walls are covered with armed men climbing from the outside. The gates fall and Romulus, with a large body of troops, dashes forward, exclaiming*]

Rom. Here! [*As Dolcar is rushing upon Remus, Romulus strikes down his sword, stabs him, and Dolcar falls into the arms of soldiers, who bear him out. Amulius starts, violently agitated, at the sight of Romulus and exclaims, unconsciously*]

Am. They live!
  They live! And, Ilia, even yet thy wrongs
  May be avenged!

Vul. [*Darting towards him*] Ha! Ilia! Who's that
  Named Ilia? Tell me all—speak—Ilia—

Am. Immortal gods! That voice! Can that be—can—

Vul. Aye, tyrant, let that voice in thunder tell thee
  Thou'rt in the power of thy deadliest foe.
  Villain, by thee my friend Aeghystus fell;
  Through thee, my Ilia found an early grave;
  Through thee, I've roved for years, a banished man,
  Deprived of every treasure but this one. [*Drawing the arrow*]
  Look on it. See you the red gore that stains
  Its venomed point? It is Aeghystus's blood!

Am. Spare me! Spare me!

Vul. No, from the cloud of years
  In banishment, I now emerge to shout,
  "Ilia! Aeghystus!" in your ear! To see you
  Unthroned and grovelling at my feet; to plant
  The venomed point which basely slew my friend
  Deep in the heart—[*As he is rushing toward Amulius, who has fallen despairingly upon his knee, with the upraised arrow, Numitorius comes between them, catches his arm, and exclaims*]

Num. Hold! Think you not the gods
  Punish the criminal? Why snatch the lightnings
  From the Omnipotent?

Rom. Life, life will scourge him
  More bitterly. You swore that in his fall
  That dart should flash before him, and it has:

Its sight has roused the worm that gnaws the heart,
Whose tooth will make each instant of his life
A death of hopeless agony!

VUL. [*Giving the arrow to Numitorius*]   Take the weapon,
And let him feel the bitterness of owing
His own escape to those he has most wronged. [*Numitorius flings the arrow at the feet of Amulius*]
Tyrant, we spare you! Profit by our mercy!

AM.   Thus, then, is that mysterious cry, "Aeghystus,"
Which broke my slumbers, haunted me with terrors,
Explained at last! [*Catching up the arrow*] Thou wert the instrument
Of my first murder, and thou com'st to tell me
After the lapse of many a checkered year
The catalogue of all my crimes! Oh, Silius,
This hour you deem so full of horror to me
Is luxury to all the agonies
Of apprehension, doubt, uncertainty,
Which, for it seems an age, have made my throne
A splendid curse! Now there is nothing left
To hide, to fear. Oh, what a weight is gone!
I have not even the shame of knowing that
I perished by the hand of him I hate,
Or lived for his contempt, for thus—[*Stabbing himself with the arrow*] And thus—
I free myself and laugh ye all to scorn! [*Falls*]

NUM.   Brother, oh, brother! 'Tis too late; he bleeds.
What meant you when you said, "They live?" He's gone!
And by his death I lose the only knowledge
Which could make life supportable.

ROM.   Some one raise him,
For he would speak. [*Soldiers raise up Amulius*]

AM. [*To Numitorius*]   Brother, spies had told me
That Silius, unknown to you, had wedded
Your Ilia. To prevent their meeting more
I placed her with the vestals and by chance
Discovered that which gave me a pretext
For dooming her to punishment. My daughter
Pleaded to have her spared; so she was taken
To an unknown retreat. When she became

A mother, Antho died, and I decreed
That Ilia and her offspring should be slain.
The slave to whom the duty was entrusted
Died with the secret, and—

SIL. Her offspring? [*Amulius falls back and dies*]
NUM. He's dead! The secret now is torn from us,
    And irretrievably!
ROM. Bear the corse away—[*The soldiers take off the body of Amulius*]
FAUS. [*Coming forward*] Oh, blessed hour! Oh, joy unspeakable!
    That it has fallen to my lot to hear
    This tale of darkness!
ROM. Yours? What mean you. Speak.
FAUS. Most willingly, for I can fill your hearts
    With ecstasy. Bear with me. My old eyes [*Weeping*]
    Are weak, my sons, and my voice trembles, too,
    With this unlooked for, unaccustomed rapture.
    Attend. 'Tis now some nineteen years, since I,
    Returning homeward by Mount Palatine,
    Heard quarrelling voices and the angry clash
    Of weapons. They ceased suddenly; and then
    I ventured near and saw two men escaping
    And on the earth another man. At first
    I thought him dead; but when I felt his heart,
    It beat, though feebly, and I took him home.
    He was bewildered by remorse. He told me
    A bundle had been given him to cast
    Into the Tiber. When he reached its banks,
    The stream had risen o'er them. His deposit,
    Caught in the gathering flood, sailed down the current.
    As he returned, the strangers crossed his path;
    Demanded if he had discharged his orders;
    And being answered that he had, struck at him;
    And my approach hastened their flight before
    They could assure themselves that he was dead.
ROM. And the commission which he bore?
FAUS. Be patient.
    I thought no more of that, believing,
    As he himself did to the last, for he
    Died the next day, the flood had swallowed it.
    But after I had buried him, I passed

Near to a spot we call Germanum, where
Stands a wild fig tree. The retiring flood
Had left it bare, and as I gazed, my eye
Beheld a little woodpecker, that circled
Around one point, watching; and whenever
It seemed unnoticed, diving to the ground
And presently returning to its watch.
I found it lighted near a wolf. I raised
My bow to shoot the animal, when cries
As of an infant caught my wondering ear.
I followed them and saw beneath the wolf
Two little babes. The savage creature seemed
Delighted with my coming, licked my hand,
And when I took the children in my arms,
Followed me, pleased to see them well protected,
And played about me like a household dog.

SIL.   And died the murderer without affording
    A clue to who they were and whence they came?

FAUS.   No. But he bound me by an oath to secrecy,
    For he believed he should recover, and
    He dreaded still Amulius; so did I
    For the poor children's sake; for 'twas Amulius
    That thus to their destruction sent these children,
    Who, through the constancy of Numitorius,
    Can now, in Silius, claim a father's blessing!

SIL.   My sons, my Ilia's sons! Look from the skies,
    Thou blessed spirit, glory in these sons!
    For, oh, the consciousness of sons like these,
    Which makes this earth to me a Heaven, might make
    Even Heaven itself more happy to their mother!

NUM. [Looking upward]   Daughter, thy sons shall be repaid for all
    Their sufferings! Romulus, the crown of Alba
    To me descended, from thy brow shall gain
    A grandeur greater than it can bestow.
    Hail to the King of Alba: Romulus!

ALL.   Hail, Romulus! The King of Alba, hail!

ROM.   No, Numitorius. Retain the crown,
    And be the ally of your daughter's son,
    His friend, his counsellor. On me devolves
    Another duty. I must make a country,

Create my greatness, not inherit it,
And be a benefactor to my race!
That's my ambition and for that I live.
But what's become of Fabius? Where's Valerius?

SIL.   On our way hither Fabius we o'ertook.
He joined us, shared in our disguise. We scarce
Had passed the subterranean way and entered
A street whose tenants had forsaken it
To gaze on the approaching danger from
The heights and ramparts, when we chanced to meet
The guard with Diope. We overpowered them.
Fabius, attended by a trusty band,
Took Diope through the secret way beyond
The city walls.

FAUS.   That was the party, then,
I saw attacked by Albans as the messenger
Guided me near the gate. Oh, how my arms
Longed to assist this Fabius, as he sunk
O'erpowered by numbers and to save that lady!

ROM.   What! Did both fall?

FAUS.   No! For just then a stranger
Rushed with a troop of horse to their relief.
The Albans fled.

ROM.   How did they call the stranger?

FAUS.   I cannot tell, but think 'twas the Valerius
I heard you name; for such a name was shouted,
And I saw Fabius clasp him to his breast,
And both rode off full gallop with the lady.

ROM.   Propitious stars be praised! Now, then, my friends,
Back to the hills again! My brother, come!
My father, and my mother's father, too,
And thou, the guardian of my infancy,
Can I believe the eyes which show you all
Gathered around me? King of Alba, now
We must awhile be parted.

NUM.   No, not yet.
I shall attend you to your honored hills!
Pride of the wilderness, my Ilia's son!

> Behold, the King of Alba pays his homage
> To shepherd Romulus, by Heaven ordained
> To reign o'er millions, to be King of Kings! [*Exeunt*]

SCENE 4: *A rural spot near Mount Palatine. Enter Fabius, Valerius, Septimia, and Diope.*

VAL. [*To Fabius*]   'Twas wisely, kindly thought.
SEPT.   It nobly suits
     A day like this.
DIO.   And if it should result
     As we all wish, 'twould make me happier far
     Than Romulus himself, in at last founding
     The city of his so long cherished dreams.
FAB.   Aye, since the moment that, from broken phrases,
     I guessed his secret, and drew from Valerius
     Who was the object of the hidden passion
     I was resolved that they should meet.
DIO.   The cause
     Of so much bliss to others, claims that others
     Should think of him.
FAB.   And my plot having prospered
     Thus far—
SEPT.   No more—Hersilia and her uncle. [*Enter Polymnius, with Hersilia*]
POLY. [*To Valerius*]   By Jupiter, Valerius, I am glad
     You and Hersilia's newly rescued friend
     Succeeded in persuading her to witness
     The ceremony that you speak of—this
     Founding a city 'mongst these hills—Ha! Ha!
     A pretty city!—palaces of logs!—
     No matter—for Hersilia and myself
     Both owe our thanks to Romulus; and the occasion
     Is opportune—
HER.   Yes, since our citizens
     With churlish prejudice omit the thanks
     Due to this shepherd's generosity
     'Tis right that I, who owe to him my safety,
     Nay, more—such miracles achieved to bless
     Many, most dear, and one [*Looking at Diope*] more dear than all,
     Should make atonement for ingratitude

By saying that to him which should have come
From all Antemnae, not from my weak tongue.

POLY. Now own, Hersilia, there's a stronger reason.

VAL. What's that?

POLY. A woman's curiosity
To see the shepherd who could do such wonders.

DIO. [*Smiling low to Hersilia*] He has not hit so very wide on the mark.

HER. I own, since your Valerius assured me
How very much this Romulus resembles
Our generous unknown, I've more than ever
Desired to see the shepherd to whose fame
Even kings may veil their diadems. [*Distant march*]

FAB. They come!
Both the twin brothers (from Mount Palatine
The one; the other from Mount Aventine)
Return from gathering omens to direct
The spot in which their city must begin:
And now together they proceed, to place
Its first foundations.

VAL. Let us stand aside
Till the train passes. Come with me, Hersilia,
And I will place you where you can observe.

FAB. Yonder, among the trees, there is an eminence,
The only one uncrowded. We can see them
There, as they pass. Quick, or we lose it! Quick! [*Exeunt omnes.*
*The music of the march has gradually drawn nearer since it was first heard
in the distance. Soldiers of Romulus, headed by Manipuli, as in the earlier
part of the play, and plainly attired, open the procession. They are followed
by Alban soldiers in gorgeous dresses and with splendid banners. After them
appear some of the veterans of Romulus; then a carved representation of the
wolf suckling the twins. After this Romulus and Remus appear, on one side
of them Silius, and on the other Numitorius. Silius and Numitorius are
splendidly dressed. Romulus wears a magnificent helmet, a tunic of purple,
and a mantle of white, with a broad border of purple. In one hand he bears
the <fasces>. The dress of Remus is also elegant, though plain. Behind them
follows Faustulus and then a second image of the wolf and twins. The procession closes with officers of Romulus and Numitorius and the troops of
each, as at the opening, but inverted in their order.*

*When Romulus and those nearest him reach the center of the stage, the pro-
cession halts, and Romulus, Remus, Numitorius, and Silius come forward*]

Rom. [*To Remus*] Oh, brother, think not that my heart beats high
        With exultation thus, because to you
        Six vultures only rose on Aventine,
        While twelve on Palatine appeared to me.
        No! 'tis because, like Hercules, I feel
        That such an omen, given by such birds,
        Is earnest of the greatness of the city
        Of which Heaven thus instructs us where to lay
        The first foundation.
Rem.   Romulus, it glads me,
        By Jupiter it does, that not to me,
        But him whose daring genius first conceived
        The thought of such a city, the just gods
        Have thus assigned the choosing of its site.
Num.   My Ilia's sons, in counselling you to leave
        The choice to augury, 'twas not because
        I deemed that either could his brother envy
        But to prevent the lying tongue of slander
        From charging either with usurping rank
        Above his brother. Now, the gods have spoken!
Rom.   We'll laugh at slander. We'll be brothers, Remus,
        In spite of all the lying may invent.
Sil.   On then. The vultures, dear to Hercules,
        The vulture that ne'er robs the fields, nor spoils
        Its kind, nor preys upon the living; that
        Seldom is seen, and when it is, comes only
        From distant regions, as the harbinger
        Of glorious fortunes, has in throngs appeared
        To guide us to our purpose. The brazen
        Ploughshare stands ready to mark out our limits,
        And everyone from every quarter, destined
        To be a citizen, is now prepared
        To fling a portion of his native soil
        Within the circle and thus wed himself
        To the new country.
Rom.   Welcome, doubly welcome
        The hour which sees the wilderness receive
        The blessing of wise laws!

NUM.　The blessing, son, is not
　　　In the wise laws, so much as in the rendering
　　　A people wise enough to heed their laws.
　　　The most enslaved of nations, whether ruled
　　　By one or many despots, has wise laws;
　　　And whether broken by one man or many,
　　　The land where laws don't govern is not free.
　　　Create a people capable of laws
　　　Who'll not distort them for a selfish end
　　　Nor slight them when they thwart a prejudice, ·
　　　Then you create a people free and safe;
　　　But till then, never.

ROM.　Give me then, just gods,
　　　The power to build up such a people, and
　　　On me inflict what scourge you will, I'll bear it
　　　And bless your bounty. To Mount Palatine! [*The march is resumed
and the procession goes out. The moment it is gone, Fabius, Valerius, Sep-
timia, and Diope reappear, with Polymnius and Hersilia*]

DIO.　Hersilia, well?

HER.　The likeness startled me.
　　　Although, his face being turned the other way,
　　　My view was an imperfect one.

DIO.　The voice?

HER.　At such a distance 'twas but now and then
　　　I caught a sound.

POLY.　Good truth! If these old eyes
　　　See not as falsely as they dimly see,
　　　And these old ears don't tell their master lies,
　　　I could almost be sworn your Romulus
　　　Was the unknown who visited Antemnae.

HER.　The color of the hair, the gait, the manner
　　　Of resting on the staff, seem all the same;
　　　But this one's taller; this one in his bearing
　　　Is more majestic. Uncle, I'm not well:
　　　This bustle overpowers me. Let's return.

POLY.　Return without our thanks to Romulus!
　　　Why, child, who knows but if you now go back,
　　　You'll lose the husband promised by the oracle?

HER.　Uncle, pray, pray desist. My resolution—

POLY.   Pshaw! The unknown's not destined by the gods
    To rule Antemnae, not Hersilia destined
    To live unwedded. What replies your heart?
HER. My heart will cease to speak at last—or—break!
POLY. My darling child, I honor resolution
    Even in a woman; and I'll not pretend
    To be unconscious of the cause of yours.
    But, cheerly, cheerly. You'll forget the stranger.
HER. I do not wish, dear uncle, to forget
    Him who possessed the godlike power to sacrifice
    His feelings to his duty. Come, if so we must.
    Let us go on. [*The other characters, who have retired a little and*
conversed among themselves during these last speeches, now advance, and
Diope speaks]

DIO. We wait for you, Hersilia. [*They all depart together, in the direction*
taken by the procession]

SCENE 5: *An open area, at the back of which and somewhat elevated, appears*
the large square summit of Mount Palatine, its center a little loftier than the
rest. The sun appears with remarkable splendor.

 A march is heard. The brazen ploughshare, with a white bull and white
cow harnessed to it, is partly seen as it stops at the side wing, surrounded by
the heads of the procession. Romulus, Numitorius, Silius, Remus, and Faustu-
lus advance from the procession to the center of the stage. Remus approaches
Romulus.

REM. The bounds are here complete. The mundus circle,
    In which the first spade pierced between the second
    And the third hour of sunlight, has received
    First fruits of all the realm we claim affords
    For human sustenance. Each citizen
    Has o'er them thrown a portion of the earth
    From his own birthplace. I myself have watched
    The brazen ploughshare's course, and not a clod
    Of all it raised fell outwards from the city.
    Where'er a gate is meant, your own eyes saw
    The ploughshare lifted and the space left smooth.
    Thus the foundations of the sacred wall
    Are ready, Romulus, and now begins
    A mighty nation. [*Remus and the rest recede, leaving Romulus in*
front]

ROM. Now my dream is out!
      Now, then, I have a country, and 'tis here!
      Here, where my earliest breath was drawn; yes, here
      Where my eyes opened to the smile Heaven gave
      In lieu of that withheld by my own kind!
      How the unconscious dangers of the babe,
      The infant's difficult struggle up to youth,
      The youth's vexed course to manhood, now revive,
      Not with the frown of harshness which they wore
      While they controlled me, but with charms endearing
      As the sweet memories of favored love!
      No, there's not one discomfort I have suffered
      Amid these wild and broken solitudes
      That don't now make them dearer to me than
      The noblest city with its proudest honors!
      Scenes of my birth! whose every object tells
      Some touching story of the past, inwoven
      Even with my heartstrings, oh, ye checkered scenes
      Of thwarted efforts, of unlooked-for triumphs,
      Of baffled longings, strange escapes from evil,
      Intents misconstrued, crowned with the desire
      To make ye scenes of happiness and glory
      For all the universe; scenes of my birth,
      Oh, may my name from ye be ne'er divorced!
      Rise but with ye, or be with ye forgotten!

SIL. [*Advancing*] My son, the secret name by which we all
      In solemn council have agreed to mark
      The dawning city, has, in characters
      Known to the priests alone, been cut in marble
      And now awaits your orders.

ROM. All who know it
      Must be prepared to give the awful oath
      Ne'er to divulge it. Thus, our enemies
      Shall want the charm by which protecting gods
      Are sometimes lured to quit the walls they guarded.
      What name our city with the world shall bear
      The gods hereafter will instruct us; but
      With Numitorius and Remus, now,

Let us determine where this carved memento
Of its most hallowed and mysterious title
Can most securely be deposited. [*Silius makes a sign to Numitorius
and Remus, who come forward and with Romulus and Silius descend to a
front corner of the stage and confer. As they move thither, Polymnius appears
at the upper part of the stage, urged in by Fabius and followed by Valerius,
Diope, Septimia, and Hersilia*]

FAB. [*To Polymnius*]   A Sabine Prince, and yet be overwhelm'd
    In presence of a shepherd?

POLY.   But a moment
    Ago, I had my speech all formed and ready;
    Yet I no sooner look upon him, than 'tis all
    Confused. I can't recall a word on't.
    Hersilia, she's the one that's most obliged.
    Hermes has gifted her, and she must speak.
    Come, girl! Don't falter! Come and I'll stand by you!
    Tell him how kind he was in not resenting
    Our Sabine inroad on his flocks, when he
    Only retook the flocks and let our people
    Unscourged return; how still more kind he was
    In letting off your escort to the cave;
    And how more kind than all he was, to give
    That unknown youth the means of shelt'ring you
    From Dorax and at last restoring you
    Safe to Antemnae. Tell him all this, girl,
    In your own music. Courage! Courage! Courage! [*Polymnius urges
forward Hersilia. The conference of Romulus ends. He is approaching the
center of the stage, not perceiving Hersilia. He stops short a moment, buried
in thought, as if some sudden recollection had come upon him concerning the
subject of the conference, to which he seems intending to return, when Hersilia comes to a line somewhat behind him; and speaks, without seeing his
face. At her voice Romulus starts listening as if transfixed*]

HER.   My lord, our city's idle prejudice
    Preventing those from being just to you
    Who should declare their gratitude; on me
    And my inadequate power to thank you—[*Falls*]

ROM. [*Unable longer to restrain himself, turns, suddenly, and exclaims*]
Hersilia!

HER. [*Starts, gives a shriek*]   Gods! 'Tis he! [*She faints and Romulus
catches her*]

POLY. It is! It is! It is!
    By all the gods and goddesses and demi-gods
    The dreams I thought fantastic prophesied
    And the unknown is Romulus.

ROM. Revive!
    Revive, Hersilia! Thy presence only
    Was wanting to complete the ecstasy
    Of such an hour, and the good gods have given it! [*She recovers*]

POLY. Girl, look you there! My prayers, your wishes, yes,
    Deny them as you may, the oracle, too,
    For our Antemnae and all Latium will
    Be ruled by Romulus. 'Tis in the stars!
    "A foreign prince with power to take you with him
    And make you queen of a most mighty nation."
    All, all at once accomplished! Shepherd, yes,
    Devour that hand, however much it struggle,
    With kisses at your will, for it is yours,
    The fates, by miracle, have made it yours!

FAB. Speak, speak, Hersilia! I crown you with success
    The stratagem by which, unknown to Romulus,
    We sought to make him happy.

ROM. Oh, whatever
    Chance may have blest me with this moment, do not,
    Do not, Hersilia, let me lose the hope
    It kindles in this bosom.

DIO. Grant to us,
    Of proving we are grateful, by returning
    Each bliss to him as he for us has gained.

HER. [*Faltering but smiling*] What the oracle, my uncle, and our friends,
    All bid me do, 'twould not become Hersilia
    To withhold longer—Romulus, take my hand,
    My heart! And yet I know not how you are
    To reconcile Antemnae to this gift.
    Our Sabine women, for themselves and me,
    Are friends to you and yours, but all our men
    Are strangely angered against you and yours.

ROM. [*Smiling*] Perhaps, love, we may sometime find a way
    To make your women reconcile the men:

Your sex are matchless mediators. [*Looking out*] Hold!
Who have we here? My counsellor, my friend! [*Iulus enters and Romulus runs to him and falls upon his knee before him*]
    Honored Iulus, kneeling thus I thank thee
    For so complying with my wish. Your pupil
    Is not a wanderer now, without a country.
IUL. No, nor without a country to outrival
    In future fame, the land of great Aeneas
    From whom he sprang. Now, Romulus, attend!
    Prepare for mighty omens! Listen all!
    When great Aeneas brought the sacred relics
    Hither from Troy, the fire and the palladium,
    Which were to shield whatever realm they dwelt in,
    He prophesied that at some future time
    A city would arise to rule the world
    And in that city must these relics dwell.
    Alba was built and thither were they taken;
    But the gods frowned and they returned from Alba.
    Last night, a tempest swept the sacred grove,
    O'erthrew the temple where they were enshrined,
    Cast down our dwellings! As I gazed, a child
    Touched by an impulse from above, exclaimed,
    "The gods have left this grove!" And at the moment
    Two strangers passing, one cried to the other,
    "To Rome! To Rome! The gods are building Rome!"
ROM. Rome?
IUL. Aye, from Romulus.
VUL. A fitting name.
NUM. Hail to the new-named Rome! The gods have named it!
ROM. Proceed, proceed.
IUL. Scarce had the stranger spoken
    When heavily burst the thunder and the oracle
    Answered me, "Bear the sacred relics hence
    To Rome," and hither, Romulus, they come!
    The cavalcade will presently be here.
    And, oh! the gods of Troy will make of Rome
    A greater Troy, to more than compensate
    The race of Priam, for the first Troy's fall.

Rom. Hail to the fated pledge of Rome's dominion!
      Let it be placed on Palatine: beneath it,
      Deeply in earth, the sacred name be hidden
      Of the new Rome it hallows! Oh, my friend,
      Thou from whom first I heard the wisdom which
      Enlarged my views and changed their character,
      Thou, who now bring'st me such a gift as man
      Never before had power to offer man,
      How can I thank you? Yet there is one gift
      I still can offer you; and to a parent
      Surely there cannot be a gift more precious
      Than a lost child, reclaimed from the pursuit
      Of wild ambitions, to domestic love
      Among his native scenes and earliest friends.
      Behold, I give your lost Valerius back
      And he himself will tell you all the rest. [*He passes Valerius to*
Iulus. They embrace]

Iul. I have no words to utter what I feel,
      But you will own that I have not been less
      Active for you. 'Tis long, King Numitorius,
      Since last I met or you, or Silius, you
      Whom I remember well in days long past.
      I would have both of you draw near and listen. [*They advance*]
      Your daughter, Numitorius, it seems
      Was wedded ere she died.

Num.   Oh, from the skies
          Let her look down and bless this hour of joy!

Sil. While you receive our blessings, for the tomb
      Raised to her memory.

Iul. Her memory ever
      Will be adored by all who honor virtue
      Though hers was slandered. But she did not die
      So early as was said.

Rom. Great Jupiter!
      Our mother living when we might have known her!

Iul. The vestals dwelt within the sacred grove
      Which treasured the palladium, where I
      Ruled as the sovereign pontiff. 'Twas to me
      Your mother was consigned when screened, through Antho,
      From the King's malice. Antho being dead,

The twins, when born, had none with power to shield them.
Your mother's life was menaced; and to guard her,
The body of a female, newly dead,
Who much resembled Ilia, took her place,
And those who came to slay her found the corpse.

NUM.   When did my daughter die, then?

IUL.   Patience, King.
There is one person who can tell you all:
One person who has long, by all unseen,
Dwelt in these solitudes.

ROM.   That person is?

IUL.   Some call her prophetess. The awe which shrouds
Carmenta's name has sheltered her lone grot
From all intrusion. But that hallowed form
Which, for so many years, has been unseen
By all the world, shall now be seen by you
And satisfy your doubts. Come forth! Appear! [*The Unknown Female appears in the center of the stage, at the upper part. The characters range themselves on each side, leaving the center open*]

SIL.   Am I awake?

NUM.   Has age falsified
My vision? Made my brain dote? If I am
Yet Numitorius, this was once my Ilia!

IUL.   This, this is she I rescued from Amulius.
[*To Silius*] Your wife. [*To Numitorius*] Your daughter! [*To Romulus and Remus*] Kneel, twin sons, kneel, kneel
And take a mother's blessing. [*Appropriate groups are formed around Ilia*]

ROM. [*Rising*]   If there be
A stretch of agony too mighty for
The feeble human frame, why, so there is
Of rapture! Stop this flood of exultation,
Or the wild torrent of unlooked-for joy
Will drown my reason. Ha, ha! Is this earth
Or Heaven? Hurt me! Else I must go mad! [*Bursts into a passion of tears*]
Oh, friendly gush, stream on! At other times
I would have scorned you as unmanly. Now

'Tis you alone restore me to myself!
Mother, thy woes are past! Thou art a queen!
The son protected by thee in the storm
Now founds a nation! Thou shalt be its queen!

ILIA. Repress this ecstasy. What I have suffered
Is but small payment for an hour like this,
Restoring me my husband and my father,
Restoring two such sons! [*Distant march*] And lo! where come
The treasures greater than all earth can give,
By which the guardian gods of Troy transfer
Their aegis and Troy's glory to the city
Built by the sons of Silius and Ilia! [*A strange darkness comes over
the scene. An eclipse of the sun begins. The march draws nearer*]

FAB. [*Agitated*] Stop yon procession and suspend the rites;
For lo! the god of day averts his face!
Strange darkness shadowing the startled earth
With omens it were madness to defy
Forbids the ceremony. Let it stop.

ILIA. Let it go on! [*The eclipse becomes total, and all objects are in deep
obscurity. During the earlier part of the following speech the music of the
march continues, but not strongly enough to embarrass the speaker. The pal-
ladium and the tomb of Aeneas both, surmounted with their marble statues,
are drawn on platforms with wheels across the stage, attended by a proces-
sion*] Welcome, extinguishing cloud,
Betokening that all the powers that now
Prevail on earth lose their supremacy
And a new reign begins! Pass, mystic relics;
Mount the palladium, mount the square hill destined
To bear the mightiest kings were ever crowned!
From thee, throughout the universal world,
Shall every princely habitation,
Oh, blessed hill, blest beyond all the seven!
Hereafter be named palace; and from thee
Shall spring a city that a time to come
Shall worship as a god! They mount the hill! [*The tomb and the
palladium appear on the top of the hill; and a red light cast upon them, ap-
parently from the vestal fire on the palladium, makes them very conspicuous*]

Behold! Aeneas's ashes, Troy's palladium
Planted in Rome! Old things are passed away,
And a new age begins; for, look! look! look! [*The eclipse begins to pass; light streams over the scene, which, at the end of the speech, becomes complete and brilliant*]
The god of day bursts forth again and sends
A smile of glory o'er the universe,
Proving what I predict!

Rom.   Let Rome arise!
Her reed-roofed cabins grow to columned halls
Of marble. Let her people earn a name
Which of itself can conquer; let them joy
More in bestowing than acquiring empires;
And may their venerated giant realm,
When time shall claim his rights o'er all that's human,
And cast it into desolation, awe
Beholders with the grandeur of its corpse.
Let Rome arise! And tell the universe
What fortitude and valor can achieve
When nursed by temperance and led by glory.
Let Rome arise! And show the world a model
Which shall, like Troy's palladium given to Rome
Transfer to other times the power to rear
A greater Rome in regions yet unborn. [*The various characters assume the attitude of invoking a benediction*]

CURTAIN

THE BLACK MAN;
Or, THE SPLEEN

THE BLACK MAN;
Or, THE SPLEEN

THE manuscript of *The Black Man; or, The Spleen,* in Payne's own hand, is in the Luquer collection.

It seems impossible to decide the date of composition of the unacted domestic play, *The Black Man;* for although the source is known, it had been available to Payne for many years. Payne's work is based ultimately on Gernevalde's *L'Homme Noir, ou Le Spleen,* performed first on February 20, 1778, at the Théâtre de la Haye, and printed in Paris the same year. Its direct source, however, appears to be Maillé de Marencour's adaptation of Gernevalde's play which was published in 1783 under the same title but with two or three slight abridgments and an altered ending.

The central situation of Gernevalde's play is a domestic problem of considerable interest: the difficult readjustment faced by a wife after her husband develops melancholia, which at the close gives promise of becoming so acute as to be incurable. De Marencour, however, adds a sentimental turn to the dénouement, picturing unconvincingly the husband's sudden recovery and his reunion with his wife; and it is the sentimental ending that Payne chooses for his play.

[CHARACTERS

JOHNSON, *the Black Man*

CHEVILLARD

GUICHARD

WAITERS

MRS. JOHNSON

BETTY, *her Maid*

MADAME GUICHARD

THE ACTION TAKES PLACE IN FRANCE]

ACT I.

SCENE: *Inside of an inn. Enter Guichard and Madame Guichard, Mrs. John-son and Betty; and a waiter bearing a travelling bag and portmanteau.*

GUI. [*To waiter*] Show the ladies to No. 2 on the first floor. Light the fires. Ah, ladies, you're in luck! Though I say it, my house is one of the best in France.

BET. Wait a minute, landlord. I've a word for your ear, when I've shown up missis.

GUI. You'll not be the first pretty girl I've waited for. [*Exeunt Betty and Mrs. Johnson with waiter. Madame Guichard follows them with her eyes, with curiosity*]

MME. GUI. Two such spruce looking women travelling all alone so late in the year! What does it mean, husband? What does it mean?

GUI. What does it mean? It means you're always meddling with things that don't concern you. You're <much> too impertinent, wife, really you're too impertinent! There never drops in a traveller but you must know what he is, what he is not, where he comes from, and where he's going to. You'd make an admirable custom house officer! I tell you again all you have to do is to find out whether people have plenty of cash, that they may be treated and made to pay accordingly.

MME. GUI. These women don't seem to lack. Do you think they're French?

<GUI. What's that to> you? French or not, it's all <one, if they pay> well.

<MME. GUI. Why, only> that if they're foreigners they can't <object!> Stop—I forgot—the Black Man has <given> notice that he's going tonight.

<GUI.> Oh! So much the better. I wish the Poet would follow him. I'm tired of giving that fellow credit.

MME. GUI. I went up to dun him this morning; but he stopped my mouth with a bundle of little verses, where he calls me Iris, as thick as my arm.

GUI. I wish he and his little verses were far enough. That coin don't pass in trade. I can't afford to keep a poet to make little verses in praise of you.

MME. GUI. Hey dey! Don't throw your poet in my teeth! Is it my fault that the man's got no money?

GUI. Oh! You women can be made to do anything with a little flummery.

Mme. Gui.   He gives me his little verses, and better them than nothing.

Gui.   Better than nothing,—perhaps not,—for time's only thrown away in reading 'em. But come. Get me the account book, that I may make out the Black Man's bill.

Mme. Gui.   Take care not to leave out anything.

Gui.   Trust me for that. It's all down.

Mme. Gui.   Charge a little over. We are always forced to take off enough; so there's no harm.

Gui.   You don't think to teach me my business, do you? Let me alone. He shall pay for the frights he's given us. Go you and look to the supper.

Mme. Gui.   Don't leave out the bleeding.

Gui.   I shall take care of the bleeding, don't alarm yourself. And if he don't *bleed freely* 'twont be my fault. [*Enter Betty*]

Gui.   Well, my pretty lass, what's your pleasure?

Bet.   Landlord, have you many people here just now?

Gui.   Scarcely a soul. This is the dead time of year with us, you know. It must be something mighty pressing to make people travel this weather; I don't mean that for you, no, no. We've nobody to keep us, just now, but your party, a poet that don't count because I have to keep him, and a Black Man who's been here it will be a fortnight day after tomorrow.

Bet.   A Black Man!

Gui.   Aye, aye; that's a nickname we've given him, because he's all in black, from his shoes to his wig.

Bet.   To his wig! Do you know his name?

Gui.   Neither his name, nor his nation.

Bet.   Now if it should <by> chance to be him!

Gui.   Him! So you're looking to find somebody? He only looks to keep out of the way of everybody. I've scarcely seen his face myself since he's been here. When we take the things up to him, he don't even give us a glance. Whatever we give him, good or bad, cold or hot, little or much, he says not a word. In short, he's such an odd being, that I keep my young folks in order by threatening 'em with the Black Man.

Bet.   I could almost protest from the portrait 'twas my missis's husband!

Gui.   Pshaw! You're quizzing. Your mistress must have had a great passion for matrimony, to take such a man for a husband.

Bet.   What can a woman do, good Mr. Landlord! When she can't pick out a man, and gets tired of living single, she mustn't be over nice; she's in luck to get a man at all in these old bachelor days. One must put up with a bear, so one gets a husband.

GUI. Then I think this very likely to be your man; for he's as much like a bear as—

BET. Is he young?

GUI. Between the two.

BET. So far so good. Tall?

GUI. Middling.

BET. Nearer and nearer! Fat?

GUI. Not over and above.

BET. Better still. Large eyes?

GUI. Aye, aye; for they frightened me out of the room the only time he ever looked at me.

BET. The very man. Thick eyebrows?

GUI. Very, and as black as his coat.

BET. Feature for feature, the identical man we've been running after for these two months.

GUI. Is it the fashion in your country for women to run after their husbands?

BET. The Black Man you speak of, is named Johnson. After he had been two years married, he became taciturn, melancholy, brutal; got out of humor with everybody, even his child, who was then only six months old. Next by degrees, he grew tired of his wife and would pass months without seeing her; yes, Mr. Landlord, without showing her the least civility. That was very hard, wasn't it, for a young woman like my mistress?

GUI. Is there no remedy for that in your country?

BET. There was none found but to expatriate Mr. Johnson, and give him a change of air. It's now two years since he left England, to come to France. Since then we've heard not a breath of news from or about him. In short, Mrs. Johnson, tired of being a widow, and not able to take a second husband without being sure of the death of the first, determined to come over herself, and find out the truth.

GUI. Ah! I see! You come to France to seek out the certificate of his death?

BET. Pretty nearly, Mr. Landlord; but when we got to Paris, we heard he was not dead then, but left the night before. Though they say the air of that city has not cured him, we're not easy yet. Do people live long in your country with that disease?

GUI. I can't say. We never had it in our family. [*Enter waiter, with a letter*]

WAIT. Your mistress is ringing for you.

BET. I'm going. [*To Guichard*] Landlord, contrive to get us a peep at that man.

GUI. That won't be a very easy matter for he's mighty close. Stay! You can do one thing: wait upon him yourself at supper. But perhaps the sight of a petticoat will make him savage. How can we manage?

BET. Turn it over in your mind. I'll go and see what missis wants and come again presently.

GUI. Make haste, for 'twill soon be his supper hour, and I like to be to the minute with him for fear—[*Exit Betty*]

GUI. What have you got there?

WAIT. A letter the Black Man gave me to put in the post.

GUI. A letter? Hand it here. [*Reads the address*] London—[*Aside, surprised*] Ah! Ah! This agrees—Go to the kitchen; I'll put the letter in myself. [*Exit waiter. Enter Madame Guichard precipitately, with the account book, which she claps down on the table. The dialogue is very rapid*]

MME. GUI. Husband, I know all. She told me everything. She's English, got a husband, don't know what's become of him, left after two years. Husband had a malady—stop—what do they call it? Plin—Pl—Ah! Splin—such a droll malady that they that have it at last kill themselves as quietly as I should drink off a glass of water—

GUI. So, you've been pumping, as usual—

MME. GUI. Don't repeat what I've told you; I don't think they want it known.

GUI. It's in good hands, then.

MME. GUI. There's your account book. Take good care now. Don't be afraid of charging twice over. I'm going to the lady, and I shall make her chat so as to bring you more news presently. Mind the bill. [*Exit Madame Guichard*]

GUI. [*Mimicking*] Tattle, tatta, tattee. That's a downright woman. Prying, tattling, and meddling are her qualities. Let's see if the letter'll give us any clue. The superscription's not to a woman at any rate. [*Reads*] "To Mr. Murray." That's most likely one of his friends—I've a furious itching to unseal it—Aye, but if it shouldn't happen—No matter, here it goes, faint heart never won fair lady—[*Breaks the seal*] Well! This is agreeable. My curiosity's well paid. The letter's in his own country language and I can't make out a word of it. [*Enter Chevillard*]

CHEV. Ah, you're busy, I see; I'll come again. [*Goes out*]

GUI. Zounds, that's the *very* thing. The poet may <make it out for> me. Mr. Chevillard!

<CHEV.> [*Running back*] What, my dear sir!

<GUI.> As you know everything, do you know how to read English?

CHEV. Know how to read it? I know more, sir, I know how to translate it.

GUI. Look here, then. Tell me what this is about.

CHEV. [*Taking the letter*] There's not an author in the language that I haven't treated.

GUI. [*Aside*] So much the worse for them! They must have had a starving time with you.

CHEV. I've caught the true spirit of Pope; I've given new lustre to Shakespeare; I have borne Newton to the third Heaven.

GUI. 'Tis a great pity you couldn't bear yourself as high as the first, for you're cast mighty low on this earth, unfortunately, Mr. Chevillard—

CHEV. What can one expect? The muses wage eternal war with fortune.

GUI. Make peace with her as soon as you can, Mr. Chevillard, pray do, and never mind what the muses say.

CHEV. I'm about it, Mr. Guichard. I am about to bring out a work, which promises to produce me equal profit and renown. 'Tis a *melodrame*. Never was so black a piece seen. I've even engaged the manuscript to the London managers, and it will strike two nations with terror on the same night. The scene is laid among the dead.

GUI. Take care the *melodrame* don't get laid there too. But we're straying from the point. Pray tell me what the letter says.

CHEV. Your interest touches me as if it were my own. [*Puts on his spectacles and as he is going to begin reading, suddenly takes them off and turns to Guichard*] By the bye, did your wife show you the little verses I made on her this morning?

GUI. Aye, aye; but, no offense to your little verses, I'd rather she'd have shown me some of your money.

CHEV. Those verses are more precious than gold.

GUI. Very likely; but, as I'm no judge, I should like the gold better. Come now—the letter.

CHEV. Your curiosity shall be satisfied instantly. [*Resumes his spectacles and then takes them off again*] But a thought strikes me.

GUI. Tell it some other time then. Come, the letter, the letter, pray.

CHEV. What a fortunate circumstance that you happened to have me in your house. You never could have managed this if it hadn't been for me.

GUI. True—true—but make haste—I'm wanted.

CHEV. Then the business now is to tell you what the letter says, hey? [*Resumes the spectacles and pretends to read*] Br—br—br—Ah! Ah!

GUI. Well!

CHEV. Br—br—the devil!

GUI. What? What is it?

CHEV. Br—br—Twenty thousand pounds sterling!

GUI. Hey?

CHEV. Why, this is good news for you, Mr. Guichard, wonderful news, Mr. Guichard.

GUI. What news do you mean?

CHEV. [*Returning the letter*] Your friend in England tells you that one of your relations, being dead, has left you heir to twenty thousand pounds, that's all.

GUI. They tell me that?

CHEV. Yes.

GUI. Me?

CHEV. Yes, you.

GUI. My friends in England?

CHEV. Yes, in England.

GUI. [*Bursting into a loud laugh*] Ha! Ha! Ha!

CHEV. That's right. You may well laugh, Guichard. Ha! Ha! Ha! Let them laugh that win! I congratulate you heartily; and I'll instantly celebrate your good fortune in some verses to Madame Guichard.

GUI. Why you're mad, Mr. Poet. I've no friends in England; and what's more, the letter didn't come from England, but is going there.

CHEV. Why didn't you tell me that before?

GUI. If you didn't treat your authors any better than you've treated this letter, they haven't much reason to be obliged to you, Mr. Chevillard.

CHEV. They never complained. But I came to ask—

GUI. Umph! You're always asking. Well, what now?

CHEV. I hope there's no harm in my asking what ladies those are that are just come?

GUI. They are English. What do you want of 'em?

CHEV. I only saw one of 'em and she's beautiful as love. Do you think she'd refuse some little verses with which her charms inspired me?

GUI. They've other fish to fry, than to waste time with your little verses. They're in pursuit of a lost husband. Have you found one?

CHEV. I should be a little afraid to take him home if I had. The return of such lost goods is not always so very welcome.

GUI. Hold! Here they come. Don't seem to know anything about 'em. [*Enter Mrs. Johnson and Betty*]

BET. [*To Mrs. Johnson*] Yes ma'am, his portrait to the life. If 'tisn't he, 'tis somebody exactly like him, and I should doubt there being two such in the world.

MRS. JOHN. Can chance have so befriended us?

BET. Chance does very odd things, sometimes. Be it as it may, here's the landlord and he'll tell you more than I can about it.

GUI. Aye, and more than even I myself expected, too. I've just got hold of a letter that the Black Man gave one of the waiters for the post. See if you know the handwriting.

MRS. JOHN. 'Tis his! [*Agitated*]

GUI. She seems ill. [*Aside*] Is it joy, or vexation at finding him alive? [*Puts a chair*] Sit down, ma'am, sit down. [*Apart*] It's better never to mind a husband, for it always makes a sort of commotion when—[*During this speech Mrs. Johnson reads the letter, shrieks, and faints*]

BET. Help, landlord, help!

GUI. What's the matter? What's the matter? People don't make such a fuss in this country about losing and finding husbands! [*Madame Guichard running in*]

MME. GUI. Somebody cried out.

GUI. Where's your smelling bottle? The lady's ill.

MME. GUI. [*With great fuss*] Dear me! Here! Quick—yes, quick. [*She feels about in one pocket*] Hold—look—I haven't it about me—husband—run—seek—stop! [*Feeling in the other pocket*] Perhaps—no—in the closet—you'll find—Oh! Here 'tis.

GUI. I hope you've kept me long enough on the trot.

MME. GUI. [*To Betty*] Let her smell it—on her pocket handkerchief—

BET. There's nothing in it.

MME. GUI. Nothing? How's that? [*Shakes it*] 'Twas full two days ago.

GUI. Why, wife, you're mad! That's the brandy flagon!

MME. GUI. Bless my soul, so 'tis! Stay till I fetch—[*Runs out distractedly*]

GUI. My wife's like the doctors. The patients die while they're setting about how to keep 'em alive. [*Enter Madame Guichard running with a phial, of which she makes Mrs. Johnson smell. Guichard picks up the letter Mrs. Johnson has dropped. Gives it to Betty*]

GUI. See, Betty, see what there is in the letter so frightful. Does her husband threaten to go home to England to her? [*To Mrs. Johnson while Betty reads*] Well, ma'am, do you find yourself any better, ma'am?

BET. Bless my soul! If he doesn't advise her to get another husband!

GUI. I don't see anything so very terrible in that.

BET. [*Shrieking*] Oh!

Gui. Hey dey! Are you going to faint away, too?

Bet. Run, landlord, run, or he is dead.

Gui. Who's dead?

Bet. Mr. Johnson.

Gui. How?

Bet. This night—

Gui. Well—this night?

Bet. He blows out his brains!

Gui. Blows out his brains? What! Does he want to ruin my house? Let him blow out his brains, if he likes it, but not in my house; every man to his taste, but not in my house!

Bet. Fly—run to his room—

Gui. Faith, I don't like the job. He might blow out my brains, by mistake. What do you say, Mr. Poet?

Chev. Say? Why I say 'twould supply matter for the stage, and I'll profit by the catastrophe. No bad subject for some little verses to the lady, likewise, by way of monody.

Gui. We consult how to prevent a man's killing himself, and you prate about your trash. A poet's a useless piece of furniture in a house! [*Enter waiter*]

Wait. Master, the Black Man wants you.

Gui. [*Trembling*] Hey? Wh—wh—what does he want of me?

Wait. I can't tell. All I know is, he's nothing like so black as usual; he called me his friend.

Gui. The devil take his friendship!

Mrs. John. [*Having recovered*] Lead me, in mercy, to his room. Perhaps the presence of his wife may bring him back to reason.

Gui. [*Aside*] That has a different effect on different people.

Mrs. John. But if he persist in his fatal resolution, he shall take my life ere I will see him part with his.

Chev. [*Apart*] Good! That'll do for the dénouement—last scene—

Gui. It strikes me the shortest way would be to rouse the police.

Chev. [*Apart*] Bravo! La! Guards! No bailiffs—no, no, they're not dramatic.

Mrs. John. No! Let us not make a public exposure of what may more easily be prevented by milder means.

Mme. Gui. Husband, the lady's right.

Chev. Attend. My brain teems with a project which may prove most particularly important in the existing posture of affairs.

Gui. Let's have it.

CHEV. You'll find that a poet's not such a useless piece of furniture as you would make him out.

GUI. So much the better. Come! Out with the project.

CHEV. Contrive to get me to supper with the Black Man.

GUI. If that's all your grand—

CHEV. Patience, I say. I will show him at table, what one don't see every day.

GUI. Very like. But surely you won't dare to sit at table with such a man?

CHEV. I could sup with the devil himself. Ladies, you must be concealed at hand. [*To Guichard*] Where can you hide the ladies?

GUI. In the bedchamber.

CHEV. Good! You will appear at the first signal. [*To Mrs. Johnson*] From you, madam, I must beg, if you please, some further information which may be necessary for my purpose.

MRS. JOHN. Anything that may save his life.

CHEV. There's no time to be lost. In these cases, dispatch is half the battle.

ACT II.

[SCENE]: *Johnson's sitting room. At the right the door of the chamber. At the left, that of the cabinet. In the center of stage, a table laid for supper. In the flat, a closet. Johnson is discovered writing.*

JOHN. [*Alone, speaking and writing at the same time*] I return to thee, O skies! the charge with which I have been entrusted. Take it back. I return it. I've had enough of it. [*Enter Guichard with two waiters to whom he makes signs to tread softly*]

GUI. [*Low, as he comes in*] He's writing.

JOHN. [*Still writing*] Earth, open thy bosom, and give my body its last asylum. You can't refuse it. I am one of thy vassals who would go home to my own domain.

GUI. No doubt that's his will.

JOHN. For thee, my dear child, if Heaven has prolonged thy life, I ask pardon for having given thee existence; 'tis an unlucky present I've made thee; but I am about to teach thee how to get rid of it. As for you, my wife, I dispense with your shedding tears upon my grave. With regard to mourning, every widow ought to wear it. 'Tis an advertisement to the public that she's to <be> disposed of. Let no one tease himself to discover my reason for renouncing life. I have none but the impossibility of enduring it. I bequeath to the landlord of this house—

GUI. [*Low*] He means me—

JOHN. All my old clothes, and I go back as I came. I thank him—

GUI. [*Low*] What for?

JOHN. For having endeavored to poison me with bad victuals—

GUI. [*Low*] I was mistaken. He can't mean me—

JOHN. And though he was unsuccessful, yet as the will is quite as good as the deed yet <I give> him a thousand crowns—

GUI. [*Low*] I really think he does mean me, after all.

JOHN. By way of recompense Alexander caused the works of Homer to be enshrined in gold. I desire that the same homage should be paid to Young's *Night Thoughts*; for never was there a work, to my taste, better calculated to inspire a disgust for life. Such are the last desires of Ichabod Wilkins Johnson. Now all my affairs are in order. I can take leave of the world, without fear of any impertinent opposition.

GUI. [*In a frightened, half-surprised tone*] Nevertheless I *must* speak.

JOHN. [*Surprised at hearing a voice, calls*] Who's there? [*The waiters escape into the cabinet*]

GUI. [*Timidly*] Sir, 'tis your humble servant, sir.

JOHN. Ah, you, hey? Have you been here long?

GUI. No, sir. Oh, no, only this instant, sir.

JOHN. Take a chair. Sit down, and let us have a chat.

GUI. Thank you, sir—very much obliged to you, sir—very—but—

JOHN. Landlord—

GUI. Sir.

JOHN. I'm going tonight.

GUI. [*Aside*] Going, indeed!

JOHN. Is my bill made out?

GUI. Yes, sir.

JOHN. Let me have it.

GUI. [*Reaching it out to him at arm's length*] Here it is, sir.

JOHN. Now, have you forgotten anything?

GUI. Forgetfulness isn't my failing, sir.

JOHN. So much the better. Everything is charged fairly, I hope.

GUI. Conscientiously. I can't take off a sou, on the word of an honest man, I can't.

JOHN. Don't alarm yourself. I don't want to beat you down.

GUI. Oh, I'm sure of that, sir.

JOHN. The whole amount is—

Gui. Fifty crowns, and what you please for the waiters.

John. Oh! I wish to put everybody in good humor with me today. Guichard?

Gui. Sir.

John. Are you clever?

Gui. Why, sir, I do my best to satisfy my customers; but one don't succeed always.

John. If you are clever, catch. [Throws a purse to him]

Gui. Oh, in such a case, I'm as clever as the best of 'em. How much change am I to return, sir?

John. Change. Why! What should I do with change? I shall find pasturage gratis on the road I'm going. Keep it all. *My* change will be of a different sort.

Gui. [*Pocketing it*] As you insist, sir, I can't refuse. [*Aside*] He's as free with his money as his life. Sir, I have yet a little favor to ask—if I may be so bold—

John. Out with it.

Gui. 'Tis about a poor devil that I have lodged and boarded for the last twelvemonth. I don't know whether 'tis misery, or what, but there are moments when his mind wanders to such a degree, that I fear some of these days he'll take a notion of walking into the other world, without giving anybody notice beforehand, and even without paying his bill, which is worse yet.

John. Who or what is he?

Gui. He's a sort of a poet. He has asked me frequently to mention him to you, but I never could get a chance.

John. Show him in.

Gui. He's worth seeing. He'll make a man laugh in spite of his teeth.

John. I've no desire to laugh.

Gui. Tell him, pray, that 'tisn't honest for anybody to kill himself without paying his debts. That's the main point.

John. Does he owe you much?

Gui. Oh! No great thing. The living of a poet—

John. [*Throws another purse*] Hold. Pay yourself, and don't let the man be annoyed.

Gui. [*Aside*] It's plain this is his last day. He don't care what becomes of his money. [*To Johnson*] Sir, I shall take what is my due, and give him the balance as a mark of your bounty.

John. No. Keep it all. For him I reserve something better.

Gui. [*Aside*] Zounds! If there should happen only a man a year to kill himself in my house, I should soon make a fortune!

John. Send him hither. Invite him from me to supper.

Gui. [*Aside*] The very thing. [*Aloud*] I'll fetch the poet instantly, sir.

John. The sooner, the better. [*Going, Guichard makes a sign to the waiters to watch over Johnson. During the following soliloquy, Betty, Mrs. Johnson, and Madame Guichard enter softly and hide in the bedroom*]

John. [*Alone*] At last the long procrastinated day is come! Soon shall I enjoy a tranquillity nowhere to be found except among the dead. Prejudices of the world, which forbid man to end the sufferings of which you are often the cause, which would keep a poor wretch in the midst of you as devils do for the pleasure of tormenting him, now, now, I soar above ye! The veil is rent. I now see your futility; ignorance in which you bury mortals, the bondage in which you hold the free born soul, and I tear off your yoke. Everything tells me that I ought to get out of the world. The earth is weary of sustaining me; the light seems to regret being obliged to shine upon me; night brings nothing but horrid phantoms to my pillow; and even sleep denies me its gentle consolation. I am friendless and without kindred; I have broken every tie that bound me to those that have unluckily been linked to me by an accident equally unfortunate on both sides. I am now parted from everything but my body and in a few moments I shall bid good night to that. [*Enter Guichard, followed by Chevillard*]

Gui. Come in, Mr. Chevillard, come in! [*To Johnson*] Sir, this is the person—you know—and here's another plate and knife and fork.

John. Go.

Gui. Don't you want a waiter to attend the supper table?

John. No. We can wait upon ourselves.

Gui. [*Low to Chevillard*] We shall be close by—don't be afraid.

Chev. Not I. [*Exit Guichard into the cabinet*] Now to begin my part.

John. [*Believing the landlord gone, rises and double locks the door. Chevillard strides to and fro <across> the stage and heaves every now and then a deep sigh. Johnson observes him. Goes to a closet, takes a covered plate and puts it on the table and says to Chevillard*] Mr. Poet, I mean to treat you to a dish of my sort.

Chev. [*Aside*] You'll have one of mine, in return. [*After a moment's silence, regarding Johnson's covered plate*] Some English dish I suppose, sir? [*Despairingly*] Oh my ungrateful country!

John. What has your country done to you to make you exclaim in such a way against it?

CHEV. What has she done? What has she not done! What has she done! Alas! She has forced me to endure the fate of those great men, that Rome exiled from her bosom for having rendered her services invaluable.

JOHN. [*Aside*] The landlord was in the right. If this man goes on, he'll make me laugh. So be it. I shall die the more merrily.

CHEV. I have sought—I have sought to reform my native land, and my native land has—reformed me.

JOHN. How so?

CHEV. The most marked ingratitude—the most crying injustice—the most infamous conspiracy—with your leave, we'll sit down to supper, for I begin to feel rather hungry.

JOHN. With pleasure; but on condition that you fare freely just as I do.

CHEV. I'll not let a dish escape; the middle one above all shall be my mark. Your English dainties are more solid than ours; and I augur well of that. [*They sit down to table, facing each other. Chevillard eats voraciously and quickly. Johnson eyes him intently*]

JOHN. [*Apart*] The landlord was mistaken. This man has no desire to die.

CHEV. They've of course told you, sir, that to the talent for making little verses, I join that of making *melodrames?*

JOHN. They seldom keep one from starvation.

CHEV. Starvation is my pride, sir, the disgrace of my persecutors—an excellent dish, on my word.

JOHN. Are these all the services you have done your country?

CHEV. They are greater than they appear, sir; and presently you'll own it. Let's take a glass, if you please; drinking creates an appetite. [*Drinks*] You know from the earliest times the ridiculous levity of the French has been a subject of reproach; but nothing has ever been yet proposed which went to the root of the evil. There was wanting striking pictures, there was wanting images—in short there was wanting *melodrames.* I came, I saw, I conquered. Thanks to my labors, the nation is no longer the same. They have taken a dislike to cheerfulness; it is an insult to try to make anybody laugh. France is restored to what it was in the time of the Emperor Julian, when Paris was celebrated for its gravity. Fire, steel, poison are become its recreations; it forsakes paths strewn with roses for those that are embellished with bones, skulls, and corpses. I had only to complete my work with a <finished> melodramatic specimen to teach my own countrymen how to kill themselves as composedly as yours do [*Johnson stares*], and this I have just accomplished. Such, sir, are the services I have done my native land; and [*looking at his <clothes>*] such my recompense! Pray pass that plate, if you please. Since my exile from the capital, I have found no kind bosom to be the depositary of my afflictions; and it was reserved for you to come from a foreign country to console me in my disgrace, to comfort me in my destitution, to—

John. To give you a supper; for it seems as if you stood in need of one.

Chev. As a patron of the muses, may I beg to offer you the homage of the *melodrame* I speak of, and which is coming out immediately.

John. Thank you, thank you.

Chev. 'Tis my *ne plus ultra*—my greatest work of all. Shall I read it to you after supper? The subject is English.

John. You call it—

Chev. *The Black Man.*

John. [*Sneeringly*] A promising title.

Chev. The hero is a victim of the spleen, who deserts his own country and forsakes wife, children, and friends to come and kill himself comfortably in ours. [*Johnson appears surprised*] His wife pursues him, chances to drop into the same inn, and on the very day chosen by him for the catastrophe.

John. Let us hear your *melodrame*. You excite my curiosity.

Chev. No doubt I do. Hadn't we better first attack that dish in the middle?

John. Take off the cover. [*Chevillard takes up the plate and uncovers it, sees two pistols, drops it, and runs in consternation to a corner of the stage*] What! Terror struck? A maker of *melodrames* should be at home among such objects.

Chev. I don't mind horror in the way of business; but this dish, I'm afraid, would be hard of digestion.

John. Recollect your promise.

Chev. Really, I've eaten more than usual, and I've no appetite left. But pray tell me, what in the world do you mean to do with those instruments?

John. They were both meant for myself; but as you happen to be here, you shall have one.

Chev. You are too civil by half. You must either have powerful reasons for what you propose, or else none at all.

John. Mr. Poet, a man like me would not die without reflection. Draw the account with the world—on one side put the strength of man, on the other his miseries, and see if they are proportioned. I have dragged along under the burthen of life for nearly forty years. Is it not time I should have some repose?

Chev. That's dying methodically at any rate.

JOHN. Yes, Poet, when the clock strikes twelve, I bid adieu to the earth, and, if you'll take my advice, you will do the same; for what part are you playing on it?

CHEV. No very important one, I grant; but I'm not ambitious.

JOHN. Weigh well the horror of your situation. The great despise your misery, and the little make their jest of it; even Death has deemed you as beneath his notice, or you would have starved long ago—take courage, and revenge the indignity.

CHEV. [*Aside*] I must pretend to give way. [*Aloud*] You open my eyes. I see that Death has treated me with marked disrespect. One must be beforehand with him and then he can't be impertinent.

JOHN. Now, Poet, you talk rationally. You see you wanted a friend like me.

CHEV. [*Passing his hand over his stomach*] I did indeed.

JOHN. [*Gaily*] Your hand, Poet. We've triumphed! Bravo, fellow traveller. Huzza!

CHEV. [*In the same tone*] Huzza! What a pity we've no fiddlers. 'Twould be jolly to die to music!

JOHN. The hour of liberty approaches. To pass away the time, let's hear a little of your *melodrame.*

CHEV. Willingly. I'll give you the head of it. [*Reads*] *"The Black Man, a melodrame* in three acts—characters, Johnson,—"

JOHN. [*Surprised*] Hey?

CHEV. That's the name I've given to the Black Man. You'll see it's all English, even to the names—"Mrs. Johnson—"

JOHN. [*Gradually more and more surprised*] Mrs. Johnson?

CHEV. Yes, that's the Black Man's wife. [*Reads*] "Betty—" that's their chambermaid—"Charles—"

JOHN. What can this mean!

CHEV. Charles is a child of about three years old, Mrs. Johnson's last expedient for trying to bring the Black Man to his senses. This scene is very pathetic.

JOHN. [*Agitated, aside*] Is this chance or does he know me?

CHEV. [*Reads*] "Act the first. Scene: a well known inn—" I told you that before. "Enter Mrs. Johnson and Betty."—Pray attend now. You'll see if I haven't hit 'em off to the life. [*Reads*] "Betty—'Take my advice, madam: go back to England; your tears,'" for she comes in crying, "'—your tears only sully the brightness of your beautiful blue eyes.'" I've made her a pretty woman, to give more interest.

JOHN. [*Aside, astonished*] Blue eyes—

CHEV. " 'Your husband has forgotten you; return the compliment.' " That's like chambermaid's advice, isn't it? I've drawn that character very well—" 'Return the compliment; call to mind his perpetual ill treatment—' "

JOHN. [*Aside*] Ill treatment! I'm known.

CHEV. " 'And you will endure his absence with less repining.' " So you see, from only one little speech, the audience knows that my Black Man is married, has absconded from his wife; everybody's interested to find out the reason; and the author won't leave 'em long in suspense. "—Mrs. Johnson— 'Betty, my husband's unkindness, though not deserved, cannot efface him from my memory. Can I believe that could he witness the woe he has caused, spite of the ruggedness of his heart—' " *ferocity* would have been more to the purpose; but a well bred woman, when her husband's the subject, is naturally guarded in her expressions—" 'Spite of the ruggedness of his heart, can I believe that he could remain unmoved and not listen to the cries of his child and fly to clasp him!' " Betty replies—" 'During the whole two years that he has been absent from London—' "

JOHN. [*Violently*]—Two years—London—'Tis too much—[*Furiously to Chevillard*] Whoever you be, evil genius, devil, or conjurer, how came you to know me? Who told you my name? My child's? My servant's?

CHEV. W—w—w—

JOHN. Speak—I charge you, speak!

CHEV. Don't be in a rage. I'll show you my authority. [*Rises and runs toward the door*]

JOHN. [*Collars him*] Hold! You stir not! Knowing my secret, you are coward enough to expose it; but I will prevent your treason, by anticipating my purpose. [*Seizing a pistol*]

CHEV. Help! Help! [*All the characters rush in. Mrs. Johnson and Betty tremble. Madame Guichard is in a great bustle. Johnson starts and drops his pistol on seeing his wife*]

JOHN. The devil! My wife! What brought you here?

MRS. JOHN. To save you from yourself.

JOHN. By what means can you have been apprised?

GUI. The letter you wrote to England fell into my hands and I gave it to the lady, who had just chanced to arrive.

JOHN. Then I am ruined.

GUI. Do you call it ruining you to save your life?

JOHN. Yes, I detest my life; and your exertions to save it render you far more odious to me than if you yourselves had taken it away.

MME. GUI. There's gratitude. That's what one gets by kindness. If I'd been your wife, I know what I'd have done. Fie! Man, fie! To turn the house topsy turvy—desert your wife—forget your child, as if you were not the father, and then try to kill yourself? And all for a freak? A whim? A notion? A nothing? Poor little woman! Only to have one husband, and he of no use to her!

GUI. Hold your tongue, I say.

MME. GUI. But we women are all alike, and always make fools of ourselves for those that don't care a straw for us.

GUI. If you don't hold your tongue, wife, your clack will do the work of the pistols.

BET. Landlord, your wife is in the right. It's a very hard thing, so it is, that any woman should be kept two years in suspense.

CHEV. Sir, do not let all our exertions be in vain. Do not reject the affection which comes to restore you to yourself. You may fancy it bravery to dare death; but in my opinion the true courage consists in enduring life patiently, and not skulking from the miseries of existence into the grave. He who stands the tug of battle is the man of valor, but he who runs away from it is a coward.

JOHN. I begin to feel that I've made a fool of myself. If a man like you, Poet, can stand living, I think it really would not be over valorous in me to give up. Wife, pardon me; I'll be a good husband hereafter; and as I meant this for my last hour, I'll make it the first of a new life.

MRS. JOHN. My sufferings are more than overpaid. There's no joy like that of an estranged heart returning to its long forsaken home.

MME. GUI. Now you show you've sense, Black Man. I didn't mean to be rude to you just now; but as your wife wouldn't speak and you deserved a scolding, I thought you'd better have it from me than not at all.

JOHN. Thank ye, hostess. Women are always careful, I know, to prevent our sex from being deprived of that attention. Poet, as I was anxious for your company to the other world, I'll stand by you in this; and you shall feel that I am not ungrateful for being redeemed from death and given back to nature and to love.

CURTAIN

America's Lost Plays